CHARLES IVES

ROUTLEDGE MUSIC BIBLIOGRAPHIES
Brad Eden, *Series Editor*

COMPOSERS

ISAAC ALBÉNIZ (1998) by Walter A. Clark
C. P. E. BACH (2002) by Doris Powers
SAMUEL BARBER (2001) by Wayne C. Wentzel
BÉLA BARTÓK, 2ND EDITION (1997) by Elliott Antokoletz
VINCENZO BELLINI (2002) by Stephen A. Willier
ALBAN BERG (1996) by Bryan R. Simms
LEONARD BERNSTEIN (2001) by Paul F. Laird
BENJAMIN BRITTEN (1996) by Peter J. Hodgson
ELLIOTT CARTER (2000) by John Link
CARLOS CHÁVEZ (1998) by Robert Parker
FRÉDÉRIC CHOPIN (1999) by William Smialek
AARON COPLAND (2001) by Marta Robertson and Robin Armstrong
GAETANO DOINZETTI (2000) by James P. Cassaro
EDWARD ELGAR (1993) by Christopher Kent
GABRIEL FAURÉ (1999) by Edward R. Phillips
CHARLES IVES (2002) by Gayle Sherwood
SCOTT JOPLIN (1998) by Nancy R. Ping-Robbins
ZOLTÁN KODÁLY (1998) by Mícheál Houlahan and Philip Tacka
GUILLAUME DE MACHAUT (1995) by Lawrence Earp
FELIX MENDELSSOHN BARTHOLDY (2001) by John Michael Cooper
GIOVANNI BATTISTA PERGOLESI (2001) by Clara Marvin
GIACOMO PUCCINI (1999) by Linda B. Fairtile
ALESSANDRO AND DOMENICO SCARLATTI (1993) by Carole F. Vidali
JEAN SIBELIUS (1998) by Glenda D. Goss
GIUSEPPE VERDI (1998) by Gregory Harwood
TOMÁS LUIS DE VICTORIA (1998) by Eugene Casjen Cramer
RICHARD WAGNER (2002) by Michael Saffle

GENRES

CENTRAL EUROPEAN FOLK MUSIC (1996) by Philip V. Bohlman
CHAMBER MUSIC, 2ND EDITION (2002) by John H. Baron
CHORAL MUSIC (2001) by Avery Sharp and James Michael Floyd
JAZZ RESEARCH AND PERFORMANCE MATERIALS, 2ND EDITION (1995) by Eddie
  S. Meadows
MUSIC IN CANADA (1997) by Carl Morey
NORTH AMERICAN INDIAN MUSIC (1997) by Richard Keeling
OPERA, 2ND EDITION (2001) by Guy Marco
SERIAL MUSIC AND SERIALISM (2001) by John D. VanderWeg

Charles Ives
A Guide to Research

Gayle Sherwood

Routledge Music Bibliographies
Routledge
New York and London

Published in 2002 by
Routledge
29 West 35th Street
New York, NY 10001

Published in Great Britain by
Routledge
11 New Fetter Lane
London EC4P 4EE

Routledge is an imprint of the Taylor & Francis Group.
Copyright © 2002 by Gayle Sherwood

Printed in the United States of America on acid-free paper.

10 9 8 7 6 5 4 3 2 1

Cataloging-in-Publication Data is available from the Library of Congress

ISBN 0-8153-3821-X

Contents

Preface

A SHORT HISTORY OF IVES STUDIES

The history of scholarship on Charles Ives (1874–1954) has followed an unusual trajectory due to the unique circumstances and lifestyle of the composer. (For a more thorough review of the literature to 1996, see items 64 and 97.) In the 1920s, nearing the age of fifty, Ives began publishing his own compositions including the *Concord Sonata* (1920) and the collection *114 Songs* (1922). Gradually Ives found a group of modernist composers, performers, and scholars who championed his music and fought for his recognition. Among these champions were Henry Bellamann, Henry Cowell, John Kirkpatrick, and Nicolas Slonimsky. All heralded the arrival of "America's musical prophet," "the most potent and original figure" in contemporary music who wrote "the most complex music in existence" (items 132, 297, 298).

By 1939 Ives had achieved a modest level of national fame; in 1947 he was awarded the Pulitzer Prize for his *Symphony No. 3*. Ives's belated recognition was such that on his seventy-fifth birthday *Life* magazine identified him as possibly "America's greatest composer" (item 224). His compositions became known over several decades, primarily after he had finished composing and in many cases posthumously. This mountainous backlog of works continues to be premiered and published even into the present. While most mature-period works–symphonies, string quartets, and sonatas–were available by the mid '60s, many earlier experimental and conservative compositions emerged only during the late 1960s and 1970s. Consequently, scholars have grappled with monumental revelations and surprising contradictions with each new turn in the road.

After a few early notices in local newspapers (items 675, 681, 736), Ives scholarship began in the early 1920s. Bukoff (item 95) details the early stages of published criticism (primarily performance reviews in newspapers and periodicals) from 1920 to 1939. Throughout the 1920s, reviewers such as Bellamann and Downes emphasized Ives's experimental style and his isolation from European contemporaries (e.g., items 83, 150, and 539). During the 1930s, writers such as Cowell and Seeger also stressed Ives's American identity and emphasized his precedence over European contemporaries including Debussy, Stravinsky, and Schoenberg (e.g., items 131, 132, 288).

Ives's election to the National Institute of Arts and Letters in 1945 and the awarding of the Pulitzer Prize in 1947 resulted in a deluge of popular and scholarly writings. These writings tended to stress Ives's significance as a distinctively American composer, as well as his neglect by the musical establishment and vindication through recognition (e.g., items 240, 299, 312).

In 1955, Henry and Sidney Cowell's authoritative biography *Charles Ives and His Music* (item 37) appeared. Drawing heavily on Ives's autobiography, it formed the main scholarly source for over two decades until Kirkpatrick's edition of the *Memos* (item 20) was published. For many non-English publications, it remained highly influential into the 1980s. Two other scholarly milestones from this period are Howard Boatwright's edition of Ives's writings including the *Essays Before a Sonata* (item 21), and John Kirkpatrick's 1960 catalogue (item 5). Kirkpatrick's volume contained datings, compositional history, and memo transcriptions of Ives's manuscripts. It formed a crucial source for the majority of publications until 1999, when it was superseded only by Sinclair's excellent catalogue (item 7).

New editions, recordings (detailed in Warren, item 18), and the much-publicized premiere of the Fourth Symphony in 1965 followed. Descriptions of Ives's life and music reached a mass audience through the popular media, from *Newsweek* to a series of articles in the *New York Times* by Harold C. Schonberg (items 676, 685, 712–715, 759, 760, 767, 774). All discussed the half-century delay between the work's composition and its premiere, and the challenges of editing and performing the work. A surge of interest followed, resulting in numerous recordings, performances, and writings. Ives's sudden popularity caused one writer to label him an "'In' Composer" along with Mahler, Nielsen, and Sibelius; another writer compared Ives's popularity to that of the Beatles (items 434 and 423).

The high profile of this premiere was equaled only by the mass coverage and far-reaching impact of Ives's centennial celebrations in 1974. The centennial and the surrounding years saw a wealth of scholarly and popular writings appear, along with symposia, concert series, and conventions (e.g., items 50, 836, 839, 841, 856, 858). The release of the *Memos* in 1972 and two major volumes from this period helped to redefine Ives's social context and environments in strikingly different ways. Perlis's *Charles Ives Remembered* (item 62) remains an invaluable resource for its published transcriptions of interviews with Ives's family, friends, early supporters, and associates. Rossiter's *Charles Ives and His America* (item 67), the first full-length biography since the Cowell's, analyzed Ives as a product of his society and thus disproved his cultural isolation.

Rossiter's groundbreaking work reflected the growing influence of cultural studies, and also represented an emerging trend of challenging the so-called "Ives legend." Several studies since the mid 1970s have challenged and revised the main themes of Ives's life and career as presented by the composer himself and the first generation of scholars. Morgan (item 451) suggested new connections between Ives and European traditions. Numerous studies by Burkholder (e.g., items 34, 35) reexamined questions of both isolation and Americanism by documenting Ives's stylistic and aesthetic relationship to European models. This trend culminated in a collection of essays connecting Ives to European and European-trained American precursors and contemporaries (item 33). Recent studies of Ives's social context have continued to explore the influence of his environment on both his political thought (items 91, 317) and engendered language (item 318).

Other approaches have questioned the motives and purposes of the Ives legend, as promulgated in the *Memos*. Solomon challenged the "Ives legend" of early innovation and experimentation (item 404), which resulted in several reconsiderations of the chronology of Ives's works (items 395, 397, 401, 402). Solomon's psychoanalytical approach is paralleled and expanded by Feder's studies, culminating in his double biography of Ives and his father, *Charles Ives: "My Father's Song"* (item 42). In this volume, Feder reconsidered Ives's idealized relationship with his father—reported in countless biographies—and posited a much more realistic and complex connection. And, along with Burkholder and others, Feder suggested that Ives owed much in terms of compositional technique to his professor at Yale University, Horatio Parker, rather than to his father.

Almost fifty years after Ives's death, interest in his music continues to flourish. A sampling of recent performance and recording reviews (items 674–835) reveals a knowledge and appreciation of Ives in every region of the United States and around the world. The past decade alone has seen at least four festivals and conferences dedicated to aspects of his life (items 840, 849, 850, 851). Ives's music and image have inspired original creative works from modern dance (e.g., items 875–879, 881–884) and poetry (e.g., items 339, 874, 892) to film (items 904 and 893), visual arts (item 899), and fiction (items 900 and 903). Web sites devoted to the composer ensure even greater public access to his biography, recordings, audio samples, and personal opinions on his work (items 906–918). And despite monumental changes in the scholarly field, Ives has retained his place in American music history texts, from his first inclusion in Howard's 1931 study to a full chapter in Crawford's authoritative study seven decades later (items 657 and 647).

Scholarship continues to adopt new approaches and unearth new findings. A recent biography by Swafford (item 70) revealed much of Ives's private life through his courtship correspondence with his wife Harmony. The influence of Transcendentalism on Ives's musical thought seems to be endlessly fascinating (items 35, 347–370), as is his use of quotation or borrowing (see Burkholder's authoritative study, item 34, and items 371–394). And, as Lambert, Starr, and others have shown, Ives's music is remarkably adaptable to a dizzying array of analytical techniques (e.g., items 54, 69).

As Ives's music enters a new millenium, one can only hope that the current wave of interest continues to produce such varied and exciting scholarship. In any case, Ives's place in musical, cultural, and intellectual history is assured.

PURPOSE AND SCOPE OF THIS VOLUME

In keeping with the intentions of the Routledge Music Bibliographies series, this volume contains the resources necessary to acquaint the nonspecialist or beginning researcher with the core publications in the field. As a result, this collection does not include every published writing on Ives, nor is it meant to be a comprehensive listing of all scholarly writings. Instead, it presents the most significant sources published or forthcoming between 1921 and June 1, 2001. All of these sources are available in the libraries of Indiana University Bloomington, the University of Michigan Ann Arbor, and through the interlibrary loan and database system OhioLINK. The majority of entries are in English, with representative sources in German, Italian, Dutch, Russian, Serbian, Polish, Spanish, and Japanese.

Given this scope, there is some overlap with Block's authoritative bibliography (item 1) in listing the most important sources before 1987. Scholars pursuing intensive study should consult Block's excellent study in addition to the listings contained here for more thorough listings up to 1987. As an alternative, this volume offers supplemental listings to those in Block whenever possible. Some of these publications, such as performance and recording reviews, textbook accounts, conferences, and creative works related to Ives, may prove of value even to the experienced scholar as reception history documents.

Criteria

Entries were limited according to the following criteria:

1. Publications not included in Block's bibliography, primarily those dating from late 1987 and after.

2. Entire books dedicated to Ives's life and works in the form of monographs and essay collections.

3. Articles in musicological and other scholarly journals.

4. Complete chapters within books or essay collections.

5. Many Ph.D. dissertations from North American universities available through Dissertation Abstracts Database.

6. Several master's theses and D.M.A. documents in English that are of interest due to high quality, unique content, and/or early date.

7. Significant discussions of Ives within books, chapters, articles, and dissertations on other topics.

8. Selected English-language music history textbooks that include extensive, early, or otherwise significant discussion of Ives.

9. Representative articles and reviews from popular American journals and newspapers, particularly in conjunction with major events (the premiere of the Fourth Symphony, the Ives centennial, etc.).

10. Selective reviews of premieres. For more thorough listings, see Block (item 1, 11–56) and Sinclair (item 7).

11. Reviews of books, monographs, and dissertations, particularly those in scholarly journals. These are listed either under the main entry or as a separate cross-referenced entry when the review represents a significant contribution to the literature.

12. Selective reviews of recordings and published editions.

13. Translations of significant sources, listed under the main entry.

14. Conferences and festivals devoted to Ives.

15. Original creative works (dance, poetry, theater, etc.) inspired by or dedicated to Ives.

16. Web sites devoted to Ives.

17. Additional publications of value listed in the following databases, as accessed through the OhioLINK, University of Michigan, and Indiana University Library systems: Art Full Text/Art Index Retrospective; Arts and Humanities Citation Index; Book Review Digest; Dissertation Abstracts; ERIC; Education Abstracts; Lexis-Nexus; RILM; and WorldCat.

Annotation Content

Annotations contain a general overview of the work's content with attention to keywords and musical works discussed. Additional information can include format and organization, comparisons with related sources, and discussion of methodology or resources. Significant published reviews are cross-referenced or listed at the end of the entry along with translations. For multiple editions, the annotation is based on the latest edition unless otherwise specified.

In most cases I have not attempted a critical appraisal of the value of the work. Such evaluation could bias the user unnecessarily against the source. Instead, curious researchers are advised to come to their own conclusions. The only exceptions to this rule occur when the literature is of a sufficiently high or low quality to merit distinction.

Works

For a list of complete and nearly complete works, see the Appendix (pp. 193–208), based on Burkholder's Ives article in the *New Grove Dictionary* (item 645); for a list of all compositions and fragments, see Sinclair's catalogue (item 7). Annotations use abbreviated titles (e.g., Concord Sonata), which are cross-referenced with the full titles in the Keyword Index.

ACKNOWLEDGMENTS

I wish to thank the library staff at the following institutions for their assistance: William and Gayle Cook Music Library at Indiana University, Bloomington; the Harlan Hatcher Graduate Library, Fine Arts Library, Media Union Library, Music Library, and Shapiro Undergraduate Library at the University of Michigan, Ann Arbor; and the Carlson Library Circulation and Microfilm Departments at the University of Toledo.

Sincere thanks are due to my own bibliography instructor, Frederic A. Hall of McMaster University, Hamilton, in whose class this project had its humble beginnings. His patience as a teacher and intellectual rigor as a scholar remain inspiring. This project was completed only with the support of my family and friends, all of whom encouraged its progress with sympathetic prodding: Laura Gray, Lee Heritage, Jacqueline Layng, Melinda Reichelt, and the Sherwoods. I am particularly grateful to Jeffrey Magee for his editorial, intellectual, and moral support. Special thanks to the graduate students in my bibliography class at the University of Toledo between 1997 and 2000. Their energy and inquisitiveness in pursuing their own bibliographic assignments encouraged me to investigate all available avenues while completing this project.

Ives Timeline

This timeline emphasizes biographical milestones, supplemented with select publications and independently documented performances before 1920. For more detailed chronologies that include Ives's recollections of specific compositions and performances, and more post-1920 performances and publications, see Ives 1972 (item 20), 325–37; and Sinclair 1999 (item 7), 664–83. Dates for compositions are included in the Appendix (193–208).

1845	2 August	George Edward Ives born, father of Charles Edward Ives (CEI)
1849	2 January	Mary Elizabeth ("Mollie") Parmelee born, mother of CEI
1863	16 June	George Ives sworn in to Union Army as Bandmaster of First Connecticut Volunteer Heavy Artillery
1874	1 January	George Ives marries Mollie Parmalee
1874	20 October	CEI born, Danbury, CT
1876	5 February	Joseph Moss Ives born, Danbury, brother of CEI
	4 June	Harmony Twichell born, Hartford, CT, future wife of CEI
1881	12 April	CEI attends New Street School and later Danbury High, Danbury
1888	16 January	*Holiday Quickstep* premieres in concert conducted by George Ives, Danbury
1889	10 February	CEI organist at 2nd Congregational Church, Danbury until 20 October
	21 May	CEI begins organ lessons with J.R. Hall, Danbury
	20 October	CEI organist at Baptist Church, Danbury until 30 April 1893
	22 October	CEI begins organ lessons with Alexander Gibson, Danbury
1891	September	CEI attends Danbury Academy, Danbury

1892	17 February	CEI performs and possibly premieres *Variations on "America"* in Brewster, NY
1893	7 May	CEI organist at St. Thomas Church, New Haven, CT until 29 April 1894
1893	late August–early September	CEI visits Columbian Exposition in Chicago with his uncle Lyman Brewster
1894	30 September	CEI organist at Center Church on the Green, New Haven until 1898 (possibly 19 June)
	3 October	CEI enters Yale, graduates in June 1898 with a "gentleman's C" average
	4 November	George Edward Ives dies from stroke, Danbury, CT
1896		*For You and Me* published by Geo. Molineaux, New York
		William Will published by Willis Woodward and Co., New York
	December	*A Scotch Lullaby* published in *Yale Courant*, New Haven, CT
1897	late February	*A Song of Mory's* published in *Yale Courant*, New Haven, CT
1898	summer	CEI moves to Manhattan and begins working at Mutual Life Insurance
	summer	CEI organist and choir director at Bloomfield Presbyterian Church, Bloomfield, NJ, until April 1900: position may have begun on 26 June
	September	CEI moves in with other recent Yale graduates, form communal housing nicknamed "Poverty Flat"
1899	spring	CEI transferred to Raymond and Company, meets Julian ("Mike") Myrick, future business partner
1900	April	CEI organist and choir director at Central Presbyterian Church, Manhattan until 1 June 1902
1902	18 April	Ives conducts the premiere of *The Celestial Country* at Central Presbyterian Church, Manhattan
	1 June	Ives plays his last service at Central Presbyterian Church, Manhattan and resigns as a church musician
1903		*Bells of Yale* published by Thomas G. Shepard, New York
1905	1–8 September	CEI spends week with roommate David Twichell and his sister Harmony, Ives's future wife
1906	December	CEI vacations at Old Point Comfort, VA with Myrick on advice of Mutual doctor
1907	1 January	CEI forms business with Myrick, "Ives & Co." which ceases operation in the fall of 1908

	22 October	CEI proposes to Harmony Twichell, Farmington, CT
1908	9 June	CEI and Harmony Twichell marry, Hartford, CT
	21 December	CEI forms new business venture with Myrick, "Ives & Myrick"
1909	20 April	Harmony Twichell Ives suffers a miscarriage
1910	19 March	Walter Damrosch and New York Symphony read through second, third and fourth movements of Symphony No. 1
1913	2 August	Iveses move into summer house in West Redding, CT
1914	4 October	Franz Milcke attempts Sonata No. 1 for Violin and Piano
1915	7 May	Lusitania sinks, inspiring the third movement of *Orchestral Set No. 2*
	August	Iveses care for 15-month-old baby Edith Osborne, legally adopt her 16 October 1916
1917	April	"In Flanders Fields" premieres at Waldorf-Astoria Hotel, Manhattan, possibly on 15 April
	22 April	*Sonata No. 3 for Violin and Piano* premieres at Carnegie Chamber Music Hall, Manhattan
1918	1 October	CEI suffers debilitating breakdown, precipitating publications of early 1920s
1919	January	Iveses vacation in Asheville, NC through March
1921	18 January	Printing of *Sonata No. 2 for Piano: Concord, Mass.* completed, CEI begins distribution
1922	August	Printing of *114 Songs* completed, CEI begins distribution
1924	18 March	*Sonata No. 2 for Violin and Piano* premieres at Aeolian Hall, Manhattan
	August–September	Iveses take a cruise to England
1925	8 and 14 February	*Three Quarter-Tone Pieces* premieres at Chickering Hall and Aeolian Hall, Manhattan
1927	29 January	Symphony No. 4, first and second movements, premiere at Town Hall, Manhattan
1928	27 November	Sonata No. 1 for Violin and Piano premieres at Rudolph Schaeffer Studios, San Francisco
1929	January	Symphony No. 4, second movement, published in *New Music*
	25 January	Mollie Parmelee Ives dies, Danbury, CT
	15 March	"Serenity" and "The Things Our Fathers Loved" premiere at Carnegie Chamber Music Hall, Manhattan

1930	1 January	CEI retires from Ives & Myrick
	21 April	*Set No. 8* premieres at Carnegie Chamber Music Hall, Manhattan
1931	10 January	*Orchestral Set No. 1* premieres at Town Hall, Manhattan
	6 June	*Orchestral Set No. 1* performed in Paris as part of Slonimsky's Pan-American concerts
	August	CEI begins writing *Memos* as response to negative reviews
1932	January	"The Fourth of July" published in *New Music*
	16 February	*Set for Theatre Orchestra* premieres at St. Thomas College Auditorium, St. Paul, MN
	21 February	"The Fourth of July" premieres at Salle Pleyel, Paris
	May	Iveses leave for Europe and England, remain abroad until July 1933
	1 May	"Evening," "The Indians," "Maple Leaves," "The See'r," and "Walking" premiere at Yaddo Festival, Saratoga Springs, NY
1933	25 October	*Thirty-Four Songs* published in *New Music*
1934	August-October	Iveses in England
1935	29 March	*Orchestral Set No. 1* published by C.C. Birchard, Boston
	25 October	*Eighteen Songs* published in *New Music*, contains 19 songs
1936	5 March	"The Innate," "Majority," "Paracelsus," "Requiem," and "Resolution" premiere at Salle des Concerts de la Schola Cantorum, Paris
1937	17 February	"Washington's Birthday" published in *New Music*
1938	May-July	Iveses in Scotland and England
	28 November	*Sonata No. 2 for Piano: Concord, Mass.* premieres at The Old House, Cos Cob
1939	24 February	"Autumn," "Berceuse," "Down East," "The Side Show," and "Two Little Flowers" premiere at Town Hall, Manhattan
	7 April	Joseph Moss Ives dies, Danbury, CT
	29 July	Edith Ives marries George Grayson Tyler, West Redding, CT
1940	14 January	Sonata No. 4 for Violin and Piano premieres, Museum of Modern Art, Manhattan
1945	27 December	National Institute of Arts and Letters admits CEI
1946	5 April	Symphony No. 3 premieres, Carnegie Hall, Manhattan

	11 May	String Quartet No. 2, *Central Park in the Dark* and *The Unanswered Question* premiere, Columbia University, Manhattan
	29 June	Charles Ives Tyler born, Manhattan, grandson of CEI
1947	27 March	Symphony No. 3 published by Arrow Music Press, New York
	5 May	CEI receives Pulitzer Prize for Symphony No. 3
	7 October	Second edition of *Sonata No. 2 for Piano: Concord, Mass.* published by Arrow Music Press, New York
1948	3 March	*Three Harvest Home Chorales* premieres at Carnegie Hall, Manhattan
	24 May	*Trio* premieres at the Baldwin-Wallace Conservatory of Music, Berea, OH
1949	17 February	Sonata No. 1 for Piano premieres, Kauffman Hall, Manhattan
	25 April	*Three-Page Sonata* premieres, Museum of Modern Art, Manhattan
1951	22 February	Symphony No. 2 premieres, Carnegie Hall, Manhattan
	11 May	Sonata No. 2 for Violin and Piano published by G. Schirmer, New York
	15 August	Sonata No. 3 for Violin and Piano published by Merion Music, Bryn Mawr
1953	23 April	Sonata No. 1 for Violin and Piano published by Peer International, New York
	26 April	Symphony No. 1 premieres, National Gallery of Art, Washington, D.C.
1954	9 April	*A Symphony: New England Holidays* premieres, Northrop Memorial Auditorium, Minneapolis
	19 May	CEI dies from stroke after hernia surgery, Manhattan
1956		Edith Ives Tyler dies
	14 October	*Robert Browning Overture* premieres at Carnegie Hall, Manhattan
1957	24 April	String Quartet No. 1 premieres at Museum of Modern Art, Manhattan
1962	6 December	*Set No. 3* premieres at Carnegie Recital Hall, Manhattan
1965	26 April	Symphony No. 4 premieres at Carnegie Hall, Manhattan
1966	25 March	*Processional: Let There Be Light* and *They are There!* premiere at Berkshire Auditorium, Danbury, CT

1968	23 March	Study No. 2, 5, 6, 7, 15, 20 and 22 and the *Set of Five Take-Offs* premiere at Town Hall, Manhattan
1969	4 April	Harmony Twichell Ives dies, Manhattan
1974	3 March	*Set No. 2* and *Overture and March "1776"* premiere in Sprague Memorial Hall, New Haven, CT
	18 October	*Crossing the Bar* premieres at Hunter College Playhouse, Manhattan
1991	19 April	Study No. 16 premieres at Wesleyan University, Middleton, CT
1993	29 October	Porter edition of parts of the *Universe Symphony* premieres at Monfort Concert Hall, Greeley, CO
1994	28 January	Austin realization of the *Universe Symphony* premieres at College-Conservatory of Music, Cincinnati, OH
1996	6 June	Reinhard realization of the *Universe Symphony* premieres at the American Festival of Microtonal Music, Manhattan
1998	1 October	*Emerson Overture* premieres at Severance Hall, Cleveland, OH

1

Primary Reference Materials

BIBLIOGRAPHIES

See also item 64 for a prose survey of the literature.

1. Block, Geoffrey. *Charles Ives: A Bio-Bibliography*. Bio-Biobliographies in Music, No. 14. Westport, CT: Greenwood Press, 1988. ISBN 0313254044. ML 134 .I9 B6 1988.

   Block's extensive bibliography remains an excellent reference source for publications prior to 1988. It includes a brief biography of Ives; a list of works and premieres, selected performances, and publication facts; a discography of recordings commercially available in 1987; and the main bibliography itself, which divides its 817 entries by topic. Block's annotations are thorough and knowledgeable. He includes every major Ives publication in the English language, plus several foreign-language sources. As stated in the introduction, the bibliography tends to include more works published between 1974 and 1987, and fewer pre-1974 sources.

   Reviews: Thomas D. Winters, *Notes* 49/1 (September 1992): 133–134.

2. Gleason, Harold, and Warren Becker. "Charles Ives." In *20th-Century American Composers*. Music Literature Outlines, Series IV. 2nd edition. Bloomington, IN: Frangipani Press, 1980, pp. 105–28. ISBN 0899172660. ML 161 .G52 1980 ser. 4.

   Idiosyncratic but excellent bibliographic source. Lists 416 books, articles, and dissertations with specific citations, plus innumerable general textbooks, music histories, newspaper, and magazine references to Ives. Also includes a very helpful bibliography of publication and performance reviews of major works listed by title. With a biographical outline, select list of compositions with publisher, and somewhat ineffectual description of style. This source is particularly useful for pre-1975 publications, as well as nonmusical periodicals.

3. Henck, Herbert. "Literatur zu Charles Ives." *Neuland* 1 (1980): 25–27, 46, and 52; 2 (1981–82): 208 and 268–69; 3 (1983–84): 243–46.

Original article (1980) and two later supplements offer an excellent general bibliography of almost 300 items to the early 1980s. Particularly thorough listing of German books, articles, dissertations, and publication reviews, although American, British, and other European sources are well represented.

CATALOGUES

4. De Lerma, Dominique-René. *Charles Ives, 1874–1954: A Bibliography of His Music.* Kent, OH: Kent State University Press, 1970. ISBN 0 87338 057 6. ML 134 .I9 D4.

Preliminary source listing Ives's compositions, their performance medium, text source, date, number identification, alternate title(s), approximate duration, contents, published scores, recordings, and cross-references based on Kirkpatrick's catalogue (item 5). Although superceded by Sinclair (item 7) and Warren (item 18), De Lerma's volume offers an early condensation, clarification, and extension of Kirkpatrick's catalogue. Indexed by publishers, medium, chronology, arrangers, poets, librettists, record label, and performer.

Reviews: Dale Higbee, *American Recorder* 11/4 (Fall 1970): 147; John Kirkpatrick, *Notes* 27/2 (September–December 1970): 260–62.

5. Kirkpatrick, John. *A Temporary Mimeographed Catalogue of the Music Manuscripts and Related Materials of Charles Edward Ives 1874–1954.* New Haven, CT: Library of the Yale School of Music, 1960; reprint 1973. ML 134 .I9 K6 1973.

Original catalogue of the Ives music manuscripts. Despite its title, Kirkpatrick's volume was the standard reference in the field until Sinclair's catalogue (item 7). Includes detailed listings for every composition's manuscript content and order, chronology, music paper type, and negative numbers, as well as transcriptions of Ives's manuscript memos and other commentary. Invaluable for its insight and comprehensiveness.

6. Perlis, Vivian, compiler. *Charles Ives Papers, Yale University Music Library Archival Collection Mss. 14.* Unpublished: compiled at the Yale Music Library, 1983. ML 134 .I9 P47 1983.

Detailed listing of the Charles Ives Collection at the Yale Music Library. Organized in ten sections: I. Music Manuscripts; II. Literary Writings; III. Correspondence; IV. Scrapbooks; V. Diaries; VI. Photographs; VII. Programs; VIII. Writings About Ives; IX. Ives's Collection of Music by Others; X. Miscellaneous (including Ives's jottings on folders and envelopes, materials relating to the Ives Oral History Project, library correspondence, etc.). Perlis's listing of the correspondence is particularly useful, because it catalogues each letter to and from Ives and his family alphabetically by sender or recipient.

7. Sinclair, James. *A Descriptive Catalogue of the Music of Charles Ives.* New Haven, CT: Yale University Press, 1999. ISBN 0300076010. ML 134 .I9 .S56 1999.

The successor to Kirkpatrick's catalogue (item 5), which collates intervening research into a comprehensive listing of Ives's compositions. Numbered sequentially, each of the 728 entries details not only extant manuscript order and contents, cross-references, memo transcripts, and dates, but also incipit, publication history, premieres, first recording, models, borrowing, significant literature, and citations in published discographies. Several appendices and indices aid in correlating entries with Kirkpatrick (item 5) as well as the microfilms of the Ives manuscripts.

Reviews: R. Hartsock, *Choice* 37/6 (February 2000): 1080; Timothy J. McGee, *Library Journal* 125/1 (January 2000): 90; David Nicholls, *Notes* 57/1 (September 2000): 114–15; Arnold Whittall, *Music and Letters* 81/4 (November 2000): 647–48; anonymous, *American Music Teacher* 49/4 (February/March 2000): 94.

COLLECTIONS

8. New Haven. Ives Collection. Yale Music Library, New Haven, CT.

The largest collection of Ives's autograph music and prose manuscripts. Almost all of Ives's autographs are preserved in this archive, along with his correspondence, diaries, scrapbooks, family documents, and published scores in his possession.

9. New Haven. John Kirkpatrick Collection. Yale Music Library, New Haven, CT.

Archives of one of the earliest significant Ives scholars contains extensive correspondence, editions, transcriptions, and reconstructions.

10. New York. Music Division. The New York Public Library at Lincoln Center. New York, NY.

   Primarily photostats of music manuscripts found in the Yale archive. This incomplete collection includes copies of several chamber works.

11. Washington, DC. The Music Division of the Library of Congress. Washington, DC.

   Includes numerous photostats of sources from the Yale archive, as well as a few fragmentary autographs, copyist scores, and reconstructions.

DISCOGRAPHIES

12. Block, Geoffrey. "Discography." In *Charles Ives: A Bio-Bibliography* (item 1), 57–69.

   Lists sixty-seven commercial recordings available in 1987 divided by genre.

13. Cohn, Arthur. "Charles Ives." In *Recorded Classical Music: A Critical Guide to Compositions and Performances.* New York: Schirmer Books, 1981, pp. 902–27. ISBN 0 02 870640 4. ML 156.9. C63.

   Highly selective annotated listing that lists one recording for each major work categorically (Orchestra; String Orchestra; Band; Instrumental; Chamber Music; Vocal Choral; and Cantata and Oratorio) and alphabetically by title of composition. Cohn's extensive annotations often include critical evaluation of other significant recordings, as well as commentary on the compositions and the composer.

14. Hall, David. "Charles Ives: A Discography. Parts I, II and III." *HiFi/Stereo Review* 13/4 (October 1964): 142–44, 146; 13/5 (November 1964): 102, 104, 106; 13/6 (December 1964): 92, 94, 96.

   Annotated listing of recordings by title of each work, ordered chronologically following Kirkpatrick (item 5). Part I lists works dating between 1889 and 1907; Part II, from 1907 to 1914; and Part III, from 1914 to 1921. Multiple recordings for each work are listed when available, up to 1964. Commentary includes compositional history and style in addition to critical evaluations. See also item 177 for a history of Ives recordings.

15. Morgan, Robert P. "The Recordings of Charles Ives's Music." *High Fidelity* 24/10 (October 1974): 70–76.

   Following a general description of Ives's output, Morgan presents a listing of contemporarily available recordings by genre. Includes a paragraph-long synopsis of the major works, plus commentary on the strengths and weaknesses of significant recordings.

16. Myers, Kurtz. *Index to Record Reviews*. Boston: G. K. Hall, 1978, Vol. 2, pp. 74–78, and Vol. 5, pp. 130–31. ISBN 081610087X. ML 156.9 .M88.

Later supplements include idem, *Index to Record Reviews 1978–1983*. Boston: G. K. Hall and Co., 1985, pp. 165. ISBN 0 8161 0435 2. ML 156.9 .M89 1985; and idem, *Index to Record Reviews 1984–1987*. Boston: G.K. Hall and Co., 1989, pp. 98. ISBN 0-8161-0482-4. ML 156.9 .M89 1989.

Includes thorough index of published reviews of Ives recordings. Myers 1978 indexes reviews of recordings between 1949 and 1977 in 50 periodicals ranging from standard sources (*HiFi/Stereo Review*) to general interest periodicals (*Atlantic Monthly*, *The New York Times*). Later supplements from 1985–1989 index fewer periodicals (19 and 21 respectively) for the specified time span. Unfortunately, Myers lists entire recordings only once, both alphabetically and categorically by "major work," without cross-references or individual title listings. Helpful for locating reviews, if somewhat challenging in its layout.

17. Oja, Carol J., ed. "Charles Ives." In *American Music Recordings: A Discography of 20th-Century U.S. Composers*. Institute for Studies in American Music. Brooklyn: Brooklyn College of the City University of New York, 1982, pp. 171–80. ISBN 0914678191. ML 156.4 N3 U52.

Supplements Warren (item 18) by listing recordings released between 1971 and June 1980. Unannotated, ordered alphabetically by title of work, includes performers, label numbers, and availability as of June 1980. Individual recordings are given multiple entries under each individual work.

18. Warren, Richard. *Charles E. Ives: Discography*. Historical Sound Recordings Publication Series No. 1. New Haven, CT: Historical Sound Recordings, Yale University Library, 1972. ML 156.5 I95 W29.

Comprehensive unannotated list of over 600 commercially issued recording to 1970: Some recordings from 1971 are included, but many others are listed in Oja 1982 (item 17). Includes performers, label numbers and recording dates when available. Ordered alphabetically by title of composition, and chronologically by recorded performances. In addition to music recordings, Warren lists 54 recorded interviews with Ives's friends, associates and family (later preserved in the Ives Oral History Project at Yale University); and six audio and film documentaries in the Ives Collection produced and/or broadcast between 1965 and 1970.

Reviews: Dominique-René DeLerma, *American reference books annual* (1974): 400; Michael H.Gray, *Notes* 31/1 (September 1974): 63–66; Max Harrison, *Composer* 62 (Winter 1977–78): 48–50; Everett Helm, *Music*

Review 34/2 (May 1973): 175–76; Nors S. Josephson, *Die Musikforschung* 27/2 (1974): 236.

CORRESPONDENCE AND IVES'S OWN WRITINGS

19. Garland, Peter, ed. "Charles Ives: Notes for Lou Harrison (1947)." In *A Lou Harrison Reader*. Santa Fe, NM: Soundings Press, 1987, 20–28. ISBN 9991983236. ML 55 .H27 1987.

    Facsimiles and transcriptions of Ives's drafts of six notes to Harrison concerning the *Third Symphony* score. Includes many editorial details, plus a letter draft to Harrison concerning the Pulitzer Prize.

20. Ives, Charles E. *Memos*, edited by John Kirkpatrick. New York: W. W. Norton, 1972; reprint, 1991. ISBN 0393307565. ML 410 .I94 A3.

    One of the most important resources in the field. Edited and notated by Kirkpatrick, the main body is Ives's autobiography that he wrote between 1931 and around 1934. Part 1, "Pretext," contains Ives's reactions to criticisms of his music by the French critic Prunières, and the New York critics Philip Hale and William Henderson. Part 2, "Scrapbook," is full of compositional anecdotes, while Part 3, "Memories," documents Ives's musical influences and opinions. Kirkpatrick fastidiously documents, clarifies, and expands Ives's references, supplementing the volume with 21 appendices. These include collated chronological lists, transcriptions of some of Ives's other unpublished writings on insurance, and memos from musical manuscripts, as well as biographical sketches of the major figures in Ives's life including his father and wife.

    Reviews: Peter Dickinson, *Musical Times* 115 (November 1974): 947–48; Max Harrison, *Composer* 55 (Summer 1975): 37–38; Alan Mandel, *Notes* 29/4 (June 1973): 716–19; Bayan Northcott, *BBC Music Magazine* 4/5 (January 1996): 21; Frederik Prausnitz, *Tempo* 114 (September 1975): 28–30; Frank Rossiter, *Yearbook for Inter-American Music Research* 9 (1973): 182–85; Elie Siegmeister, *High Fidelity/Musical America* 23/3 (March 1973): MA 29–31; Christopher Small, *Music in Education* 37/362 (1973): 187–88; Michael Tilmouth, *Music and Letters* 55/1 (1974): 112–13; Gianfranco Vinay, *Nuova rivista italiana di musicologica* 11/2 (April–June 1977): 270–74; Laurence Wallach, *Musical Quarterly* 60/2 (April 1974): 284–90.

21. Ives, Charles E. *Essays Before a Sonata, The Majority and Other Writings*, edited by Howard Boatwright. New York: W. W. Norton, 1961; reprinted without alteration, 1962.

    Important early edition of Ives's most important writings, including the independent volume *Essays Before a Sonata*, and the shorter writings "The Majority," "Some Quarter-Tone Impressions," "Postface to *114 Songs*,"

"Stand By the President and the People," "Concerning a 20th Amendment," "A Peoples' World Nation," "The Amount to Carry," and a small portion of Ives's correspondence. Although somewhat helpful, Boatwright's notes contain errors, and his editing decisions have been questioned.

For the *Essays*, see also item 25. *Essays* and "Some Quarter-Tone Impressions" are available in a Polish translation as "Eseje przed sonata. 'Cwierctonowe' impresje." *Res Facta* 5 (1971): 52–103. For a Spanish translation of the *Essays*, see item 22. "Prologue" reprinted in Kostelanetz, Richard and Joseph Darby, eds. *Classic Essays on 20th-Century Music: A Continuing Symposium.* New York: Schirmer, 1996.

Reviews: Henry Leland Clarke, *Musical Quarterly* 50/1 (January 1964): 101–03; Everett Helm, *Musical America* 83/2 (February 1963): 52; Wilfrid Mellers, *Musical Times* 110 (July 1969): 744–45; Johannes Riedel, *Journal of Research in Music Education* 13/1 (1965): 61–63; Christopher Small, *Music in Education* 37/362 (1973): 187–88; Tim Souster, *Tempo* 89 (Summer 1969): 34–35; Ronald Woodham, *Music and Letters* 50/4 (1969); 526–27; Victor Fell Yellin (item 28).

22. Ives, Charles. *Ensayos ante una sonata.* Translated and with an introduction and notes by Jorge Velazco. Instituto de investigaciones esteticas, cuadernos de música 3. México: Universidad Nacional Autónoma de México, 1974. 2nd ed. México: Universidad Nacional Autónoma de México, 1982. ISBN 9685803110. ML 410 .I94.

    Spanish translation of the *Essays* contains an introductory essay plus a list of significant works, select discography, and a large collection of photographs.

23. Ives, Charles. " 'Children's Day at the Camp Meeting' by Charles Ives." *Modern Music* 19/2 (January–February 1942): pages not available; reprinted in item 221, 48–51.

    Detailed notes on the program of the Fourth Violin Sonata, much of which is reprinted in *Memos* (item 20). According to Lederman, Ives compiled the notes "from remarks written on the back of some old music manuscripts."

24. Ives, Charles E. "Music and Its Future." In *American Composers on American Music*, edited by Henry Cowell. Stanford, CA: Stanford University Press, 1933. Reprinted with a new introduction. New York: Frederick Ungar Publishing, 1962, 191–98. Reprinted in Kostelanetz, Richard, and Joseph Darby, eds. *Classic Essays on 20th-Century Music.* New York: Schirmer, 1996, 129–33. ISBN 0028645812. ML 55 .C6 1996.

Primarily a discussion of the uses and effects of spatial organization in music, including numerous reminiscences and examples. Also includes a brief overview of progressive music in America, and a statement on the role of the listener in new music.

German translation by Felix Meyer available in *Amerikanische Musik seit Charles Ives: Interpretation, Quellentexte, Komponistenmonographien* (item 38).

25. Ives, Charles E. *Essays Before a Sonata.* New York: Knickerbocker Press, 1920; reprinted in *Three Classics in the Aesthetic of Music.* New York: Dover, 1962, 103–185. ML 3845 .T497 1962.

    Unedited and unannotated version of the *Essays* from the original Knickerbocker source. See also item 21 for an annotated version.

26. Owens, Tom, ed. "Selected Correspondence 1881–1954." In *Charles Ives and His World* (item 36), 199–270.

    The only extensive published collection of correspondence includes transcriptions of letters between Ives, his family, friends, copyists, and musical contacts. Of particular interest are the eleven courtship letters of Ives and his future wife Harmony, and the numerous letters from the 1930s to 1950s between Ives and his supporters, who included Nicolas Slonimsky, Henry Cowell, Aaron Copland, John Becker, Lou Harrison, John Cage, and Leonard Bernstein. Owens's helpful comments introduce each section and effectively contextualize the letters within Ives's life and career.

27. Porter, David G. "Definitely Maybe." *Musical Times* 138/1853 (July 1997): 11–17.

    Comparison and critique of editorial revisions, interpretations, and omissions in published versions of the *Memos* as found in Cowell's biography (item 37) and Kirkpatrick's edition (item 20). With excerpts from various versions of Ives's original text.

28. Yellin, Victor Fell. Review of *Essays Before a Sonata, The Majority and Other Writings* by Charles Ives. *Journal of the American Musicological Society* 17/2 (Summer 1964): 229–31.

    In his positive review of the volume, Yellin comments on the relationship between Ives's compositions and writings, suggesting that the music and words "are simply two aspects of one idea; that the *Concord Sonata* together with the *Essays* forms a kind of cantata."

2

Book-Length Studies

Includes published single-author biographies and genre studies, and edited essay collections (individual essays are listed under specific headings by topic). Most reviews of these volumes are listed under the annotation, although a few select reviews are itemized separately. Dissertations, theses, and other unpublished documents and portions of larger volumes are listed under individual topics.

29. Alexander, Michael J. *The Evolving Keyboard Style of Charles Ives.* Outstanding Dissertations in Music From British Universities. New York: Garland, 1989. ISBN 0824001850. ML 410 .I95 A4.

    Wide-ranging survey of the diverse educational, philosophical, creative, and cultural influences on Ives's keyboard music. With chapters on pianistic traditions, ragtime, New England hymnody, and other vocal traditions, temporal and structural experiments, and the compositional and performing diversity of the take-offs and studies. Based on Alexander's 1984 dissertation from the University of Keele.

    Reviews: Geoffrey Block, *American Music* 10 (Spring 1992): 98–100; David Nicholls, *Music and letters* 72/3 (August 1991): 494.

30. Barker, John W. "Who Owns Charles Ives?" *Reviews in American History* 4/3 (September 1976): 442–450.

    In his review of Rossiter's book (item 67), Barker describes Ives's music and places him within the context of American intellectual and social history.

31. Bernlef, J., and Reinbert de Leeuw. *Charles Ives.* Amsterdam: DeBezige Bij, 1969. ML 410 .I95 B5. Pages 133–209 published in an English translation by Bertus Polman, "Charles Ives—Zijn Muziek: Inleiding, Ives' Gebruik van Muzikaal Materiaal [Charles Ives—His Music: Introduction,

Ives' use of musical material]." *Student Musicologists at Minnesota* 6 (1975–76): 128–91.

The most significant Dutch survey of Ives's life and works. Biography, based primarily on the first edition of Cowell (item 37), is written by Bernlef with analyses of Concord Sonata and Universe Symphony and translations from Ives's own writings (*Essays Before a Sonata,* "Postface" from *114 Songs,* and "Music and Its Future"). De Leeuw's section discusses Ives's musical style with emphasis on his uses of borrowing as melodic and structural elements; experimental rhythmic and harmonic structures; simultaneity of hetergeneous elements; multidimensional style; and unique notation, orchestration, and instrumentation. The book also includes several song texts and their translations, comments on Ives by Stravinsky, Schoenberg, and Cage, and a list of works following Kirkpatrick (item 5).

32. Block, Geoffrey. *Ives: Concord Sonata.* Cambridge Music Handbooks. Cambridge: Cambridge University Press, 1996. ISBN 052149656X. ML 410 .I94 B56 1996.

Block's examination of the Concord Sonata is thorough, concise, and readable. This volume investigates every significant aspect of the work in great detail, tracing its reception, genesis, form and design, musical borrowings, and program. Also includes a detailed motivic analysis. An invaluable source for this composition.

33. Block, Geoffrey, and J. Peter Burkholder, eds. *Charles Ives and the Classical Tradition.* New Haven, CT: Yale University Press, 1996. ISBN 0300061773. ML 410 .I94 C35 1996.

A collection of essays that examines Ives's connection to the European classical tradition through comparisons to his precursors and contemporaries. See also individual listings (items 411, 415, 416, 442, 451, 469, 472).

Reviews: Kathryn Bumpass, *Notes* 54 (March 1998): 677–80; J. Fisk, *Hudson Review* 50/1 (Spring 1997): 129–136; Larry Lipkis, *Library Journal* 121 (August 1996): 74; Sabine Meine, *Neue Zeitschrift fur Musik* 158/2 (July–August 1997): 75; David Nicholls, *Times Literary Supplement* 4881 (18 October 1996): 18; R. Stahura, *Choice* 34 (November 1996): 469.

34. Burkholder, J. Peter. *All Made of Tunes.* New Haven, CT: Yale University Press, 1995. ISBN 0300056427. ML 410 .I94 B87 1995.

Exhaustive study of Ives's uses of existing music. In this comprehensive volume, Burkholder thoroughly examines every major work, and numerous smaller compositions, according to their utilization of borrowed material.

Each chapter explores how Ives employed borrowing throughout his career by first examining individual works in detail and then placing them within the context of his compositional career. Additionally, Burkholder convincingly ties specific compositional techniques to the musical traditions that Ives knew, demonstrating how Ives extended and eventually surpassed these inherited devices in the mature works. This approach works especially well in the chapters on modeling, paraphrase, and cumulative setting where the first three symphonies are analyzed. An excellent source for discussions of specific compositions as well as general musical styles, with ample musical excerpts and supporting material.

Reviews: Liz Bird, *Brio* 33/1 (Spring–Summer 1996): 74; Peter Dickinson, *Music and Letters* 80/3 (August 1999): 479–82; Josiah Fisk, *Hudson Review* 50/1 (Spring 1997): 129–136; Clayton Henderson, *Choice* 33/8 (April 1996): 1320; Alan Hirsch, *Booklist* 92 (15 December 1995): 678; Sabine Meine, *Neue Zeitschrift für Musik* 158/2 (July–August 1997): 74–75; David Nicholls, *BBC Music Magazine* 4/8 (April 1996): 24, and *Times Literary Supplement* 4881 (18 October 1996): 18–19; Burton W.Peretti, *American Studies* 38/1 (spring 1997): 139–149; Ron Wiecki, *Journal of Musicological Research* 16/4 (1997): 305–321.

35. Burkholder, J. Peter. *Charles Ives, The Ideas Behind the Music*. New Haven, CT: Yale University Press, 1985. ISBN 0300032617. ML 410 .I94 B48 1995.

Study of Ives's aesthetics, compositional development, and influences, framed by his relationship with Transcendentalism as expressed and interpreted through the *Essays* and later writings. Burkholder refines the labeling of Ives as a Transcendentalist composer by illustrating that many of Ives's ideas did not derive from either the literary or the philosophical tradition. This book offers original insights on Ives's musical and intellectual environment, with equal coverage of his early and later works.

Japanese translation available as *Charuzu Aibuzu: Ongaku ni hisomu amerika shiso [Charles Ives: American ideas behind the music.]* Trans. Kazuhiko Kimura. Tokyo: Oushi, 1993.

Reviews: Michael Alexander, *Tempo* 157 (June 1986): 35–37; Andreas Ballstaedt, *Neue Zeitschrift fur Musik* 151/6 (June 1990): 52–53; Geoffrey Block, *Journal of Musicology* 5/2 (Spring 1987): 308–11; J. Bunker Clark, *American Studies* 28 (Fall 87): 58–59; Paul Echols, *Newsletter of the Institute for Studies in American Music* 15/1 (November 1985): 5; Michael Hall, *Journal of American Studies* 21 (April 1987): 117–118; Dietrich Kamper, *Musiktheorie* 6/1 (1991): 93–94; Philippa Kiraly, *Library Journal* 111 (January 1986):

71; Wilfrid Mellers, *Times Literary Supplement* (7 February 1986): 143; Frank Rossiter, *American Historical Review* 91/4 (October 1986): 1007; Nachum Schoffman, *Tempo* 175 (December 1990): 31–32; Giselher Schubert, *Neue Zeitschrift für Musik* 148/1 (January 1987): 63; R. Stahura, *Choice* 23 (February 1986): 876; Anne Swartz, *American Music* 5/2 (Summer 1987): 222–23.

36. Burkholder, J. Peter, ed. *Charles Ives and His World*. Princeton, NJ: Princeton University Press, 1996. ISBN 069101163X. ML 410 .I94 C33 1996.

Volume commissioned by the Bard Music Festival (item 849). Includes five critical essays (items 91, 98, 322, 413, and 555) that redefine Ives's musical inheritance from the European classical tradition, and the contemporary influences of American culture. Especially valuable are the selected correspondence (item 26), the reprints of reviews from 1888 to 1951 (item 762), and the eleven profiles by contemporary critics and composers published between 1932 and 1955 (including items 114, 132, 223, 240, 274, 285, 297, 312, 489, and 691).

Reviews: A. Blake, *History* 83/272 (1998): 686; Josiah Fisk, *Hudson Review* 50/1 (Spring 1997): 129–136; Arnold Whittall, *Music and Letters* 78 (May 1997): 301–3.

37. Cowell, Henry, and Sidney Cowell. *Charles Ives and His Music*. New York: Oxford University Press, 1955. Rev., 2nd ed. New York: Oxford University Press, 1969: reprint, New York: DaCapo Press, 1983. ISBN 0306761254. ML 410 .I94 C6 1983.

The first book-length biography of Ives, enormously influential for decades. Part 1, "Life," traces Ives's life from childhood to 1954 based on the *Memos* (item 20), with the most extensive coverage dealing with Ives's activities after 1920. Part 2, "Music," discusses Ives's use of polyphony, harmony, melody, rhythm, form, instrumentation, and voice writing, and analyzes three works: "Paracelsus"; Concord Sonata; and the Universe Symphony. Of particular interest are Henry Cowell's personal memories of Ives in the 1930s. For information on the writing of the volume, see item 133.

Polish translation of the 1969 edition available as *Ives*. Monografie popularne. Krakow: Wyd. Muz., 1982. ISBN 8322402112.

Reviews of the first edition: Arthur Berger, *New York Times Book Review*, 9 January 1955, section 7, 3; Richard Goldman, *Notes* 12/2 (March 1955): 217–18; Edward Lockspeiser, *Musical Times* 96 (October 1955): 532–33; Wilfrid Mellers, *Music and Letters* 36/4 (October 1955): 400; C.W. Orr, *Music Review* 17/2 (May 1956): 169–70; Harold C. Schonberg, *Musical*

Courier 151/4 (15 February 1955): 45, reprinted in *Tempo* 36 (Summer 1955): 31–32.

Reviews of the second edition: Wilfrid Mellers, *Musical Times* 110/1521 (November 1969): 1144; Ernst Vermeulen, *Melos* 37/9 (October 1970): 347.

38. Danuser, Hermann, Dietrick Kämper, and Paul Terse, eds. *Amerikanische Musik seit Charles Ives: Interpretation, Quellentexte, Komponistenmonographien.* Laaber: Laaber-Verlag, 1987, 201–205. ISBN 3890071171. ML 200.5 .H4 A55.

Contains four relevant essays on Ives (items 141, 186, 201, and 616).

Reviews: Christian Baier, *Österreichische Musikzeitschrift* 43/9 (September 1988): 511–12; Peter Gradenwitz, *Die Musikforschung* 42/1 (1989): 81–82; Bernd Leukert, *MusikTexte* 23 (1988): 57; Hans Oesch, *Literature, Music, Fine Arts* 22/1 (1989): 70–71; Heinrich W. Schwab, *Musik und Bildung* 20/4 (April 1988): 364–65; Peter Niklas Wilson, *Musica* 42/2 (1988): 205–7.

39. Elkus, Jonathan. *Charles Ives and the American Band Tradition: A Centennial Tribute.* American Arts Pamphlet 4. Exeter: University of Exeter, 1974. ML 410 .I94 E4.

Brief but perceptive study of Ives's relationship to American band music of the late nineteenth century. Includes a condensed history of band instrumentation, form, and repertoire to the late 1890s, with additional commentary on Ives's use of specific playing techniques and band quotations in his later works.

Reviews: Peter Dickinson, *Musical Times* 117 (November 1976): 910–11; Max Harrison, *Composer* 62 (Winter 1977–78): 48–50; Joseph A. Mussulman, *Journal of Popular Culture* 9 (Fall 1975): 345–346; Charles Kaufman, *Notes* 34/2 (1975): 273–75; Frederik Prausnitz, *Tempo* 114 (September 1975): 28–30.

40. Emerson, Gordon. "Looking at Ives—Warts and All. [Review of *From the Steeples and the Mountains* by David Wooldridge.]" *New Haven Register*, 26 May 1974, 1, 4.

Review of item 73 includes an extended interview with the author in which he discusses his research methods and sources.

41. Feder, Stuart. *The Life of Charles Ives.* Musical Lives Series. Cambridge: Cambridge University Press, 1999. ISBN 0521590728. ML 410 .I94 F42 1999.

Condensed biographical study aimed at the general reader. Draws heavily on item 42 with minimal musical detail and numerous photos.

Reviews: D. Burrell, *Musical Times* 140/1869 (1999): 75–76; H. Wood, *TLS: The Times Literary Supplement*, 5045 (10 December 1999): 32.

42. ———. *Charles Ives: "My Father's Song."* New Haven, CT: Yale University Press, 1992. ISBN 0300054815. ML 410 .I94 F4 1992.

First extensive biography since Rossiter's *Charles Ives and His America* (item 67). This volume is a double biography of Ives and his father George Ives that is well written and often persuasive. Feder uniquely integrates biography and psychoanalysis with musical interpretation by using *114 Songs* as a framework for exploring Ives's relationship with his father. The biographical portraits are thoroughly researched and documented, and Feder's psychological insights are provocative and perceptive. Occasionally his speculations on George Ives's posthumous influence over his son produce strained conclusions and less-than-convincing musical analyses. Overall, a valuable contribution to the literature.

Reviews: Carol Baron, *Musical Quarterly* 78/2 (Summer 1994): 206–219; Kathleen M. Dalton, *American Historical Review* 98 (June 1993): 960; H. Wiley Hitchcock, *Journal of the American Musicological Society* 46/2 (Summer 1993): 319–329; Alan Mandel, *American Music* 12/3 (Fall 1994): 320–322; Wilfrid Mellers, item 57; David Nicholls, *Music and Letters* 75/2 (May 1994): 246–252; David Schiff, *Atlantic Monthly* 273/1 (January 1994): 106; R. Stahura, *Choice* 30 (November 1992): 476; Judith Tick, *New England Quarterly* 67/3 (September 1994): 520; Barbara L. Tischler, *Journal of American History* 80/2 (September 1993): 711; anonymous, *American Journal of Psychiatry* 149/12 (December 1992): 1741–1742.

43. Fisk, Josiah. "Discovering Ives, Once Again. [Review of *All Made of Tunes* by J. Peter Burkholder and *Charles Ives: A Life With Music* by Jan Swafford.]" *Hudson Review* 50 (Spring 1997): 129–36.

Review of Burkholder (item 34) and Swafford (item 70) gives an overview of new trends in Ives research, including comparisons with the European tradition and cultural studies.

44. Frankenstein, Alfred. Review of *Charles Ives and His Music* by Henry and Sidney Cowell. *Musical Quarterly* 41 (1955): 253–256.

Presents a summary of the book's contents along with comments concerning the current state and future expectations of Ives scholarship, and the role of Henry Cowell in promoting Ives's music.

45. Giebisch, Thomas. *"Take-Off" als Kompositionsprinzip bei Charles Ives.* Vol. 181 of *Kölner Beiträge zur Musikforschung*, Klaus Wolfgang Niemöller, ed. Kassel: Gustav Bosse Verlag, 1993. ISBN 3764926120. ML 410 .I95 G5.

Thorough study of Ives's "take-offs" as well as related works including *Yale-Princeton Football Game, All the Way Around and Back, "Gyp the Blood," Skit for Danbury Fair*, etc. Investigates the musical representation of humor, sports, and reality in these works, as well as their origin and meaning to Ives, and their general musical character and structure. Concludes with specific analyses of each work and several transcriptions. Published version of the author's 1993 dissertation from the University of Koln.

46. Gilmore Bob. "Reinventing Ives. [Review of *The Music of Charles Ives* by Philip Lambert, *Ives: Concord Sonata* by Geoffrey Block, and *Ives Essays*, edited by Philip Lambert.]" *Music Analysis* 19/1 (March 2000): 101–123.

Substantive review of books by Lambert and Block (items 54 and 32) as well as the *Ives Essays* (item 55) includes commentary on editorial and analytic challenges. Also considers recent challenges to received scholarship on all fronts.

47. Henderson, Clayton W. *The Charles Ives Tunebook.* Bibliographies in American Music Number 14. Warren, MI: Harmonie Park Press, 1990. ISBN 089990050X. ML 134.I9A2 1990.

Useful index of Ives's borrowed tunes. Although the volume is not comprehensive, Henderson identifies and reprints 191 known sources for Ives's borrowings, divided by genre into hymns, patriotic songs and military music, popular songs, college music, popular instrumental tunes, and "classical music." Each source tune is followed by a list of the compositions in which it appears.

Reviews: Geoffrey Block, *Notes* 49 (September 1992): 134; Peter Dickinson, *Music and Letters* 74/1 (February 1993): 116–117; Harald Manfred Krebs, *Die Musikforschung* 45/4 (1992): 435–436; G. A. Marco, *Choice* 28 (April 1991): 1290.

48. Hentoff, Nat. Review of *Charles Ives Remembered: An Oral History* by Vivian Perlis. *New York Times Book Review*, 20 October 1974, 3, 20.

Extensive commentary on the volume with excerpts, photographs, and background on the oral history project.

49. Hitchcock, H. Wiley. *Ives: A Survey of the Music.* I.S.A.M. Monographs, No. 19. Brooklyn: Institute for Studies in American Music, 1977; and London:

Oxford University Press, 1977; reprinted with corrections, 1983. ISBN 0914678213. ML 410 .I94 H62.

Concise but insightful survey of the structure, form, texts, and experimental techniques in Ives's works. Organized by genre as follows: Songs, Choral Music, Keyboard Music, Chamber Music, and Orchestral Music. Works in each genre are generally summarized in chronological order, followed by more detailed analyses of large compositions.

Reviews: Stephen Banfield, *Music and Letters* 59/3 (July 1978): 346–47; Peter Dickinson, *Musical Times* 119 (March 1978): 239; Max Harrison, *Composer* 62 (Winter 1977–78): 48–50; David Keane, *Queen's Quarterly* 86/1 (Spring 1979): 169–70.

50. Hitchcock, H. Wiley, and Vivian Perlis, eds. *An Ives Celebration: Papers and Panels of the Charles Ives Centennial Festival-Conference.* Urbana: University of Illinois Press, 1977. ISBN 0252006194. ML 410 .I94 C4.

Papers, transcriptions of panel discussions, and brief commentaries from the Charles Ives Centennial Festival-Conference of 1974 (item 841), the first international conference devoted to Ives. Divided into five topics: I. Ives and American Culture; II. Ives Viewed from Abroad; III. On Editing Ives; IV. On Conducting and Performing Ives; and V. Ives and Present-Day Musical Thought. Appendices include more statements from foreign participants (supplementing II), the complete concert programs of the festival-conference; and brief descriptions of the participants and contributors.

For individual entries, see items 89, 90, 137, 165, 187, 188, 230, 242, 275, 414, 527, 634, and 636.

Reviews: Michael J. Alexander, *Journal of American Studies* 13 (August 79): 282–283; Stephen Banfield, *Music and Letters* 60/2 (April 1979): 216–17; Simon Emmerson, *Music and Musicians* 27 (June 1979): 44; Everett Helm, *Fontis Artis Musicae* 25/3 (1978): 278–79; Jean-Remy Julien, *Revue de musicologie* 67/1 (1981): 118–19; Jannelle Warren-Findley, *American Studies* 19 (Fall 1978): 85–87.

51. Ivashkin, Aleksandr. *Charl'z Aivz i muzyka XX veka.* Moskva, Russia: Sovetskij Kompozitor, 1991. ISBN 5852851337. ML 410 .I94 I93.

Life and works survey with emphasis on experimentation and "open process" in musical works, as well as the influence of Transcendentalism. Ivaskin also considers the impact of Ives's business activities on his compositions and aesthetics. Based on the author's Ph.D. dissertation, the title translates as *Charles Ives and 20th-Century Music* and appears in different sources as *Carl'z Aijz i muzyka XX veka* and *Charl'z Aivz i muzyka dvadt-satogo veka.*

Reviewed in *Muzykal'naja akademija* 1 (1994): 50–52.

52. Kirkpatrick, John. "Review of *From the Steeples and the Mountains* by David Wooldridge." *High Fidelity/Musical America* 24/9 (September 1974): 33–36.

Scathing review of item 73. Kirkpatrick's criticisms range from correcting documented inaccuracies to fervent disagreements over Wooldridge's conjectures and musical analysis. For Wooldridge's rebuttal, and a further statement by Kirkpatrick, see item 53.

53. Kirkpatrick, John and David Wooldridge. "The New Ives Biography: A Disagreement." *High Fidelity/Musical America* 24/12 (December 1974): 18–20.

Strong rebuttal by Wooldridge to Kirkpatrick's earlier review (item 52), in which he maintains that the majority of criticisms are "a tissue of misreadings, false assumptions, and wilful misrepresentations." In his equally strong response, Kirkpatrick maintains that Wooldridge's conjectures are misleading and that his scholarship is faulty.

54. Lambert, Philip. *The Music of Charles Ives.* Composers of the 20th Century. New Haven, CT: Yale University Press, 1997. ISBN 0300065221. ML 410 .I94 L36 1997.

Thorough examination of Ives's experimental language and its employment in various compositions throughout his career. Lambert's analyses employ the sophisticated methodologies and apparatus of posttonal theory, including set theory and modified Schenkerian graphing, particularly in his discussions of Ives's cyclic compositions. Although a wide range of compositions are discussed, Lambert devotes full chapters to *Tone Roads No. 1*, *Study No. 5*, "The Cage," and the *Universe Symphony*.

Reviews: J. P. Ambrose, *Choice* 35/5 (January 1998): 831; and David Matthews, *The Times Literary Supplement* 4939 (28 November 1997): 12.

55. Lambert, Philip, ed. *Ives Studies.* Cambridge: Cambridge University Press, 1997. ISBN 0521582776. ML 410 .I94 I98 1998.

Collection of ten disparate essays addressing Ives's connection to the European tradition, revision in the *Concord Sonata*, editing practices, chronology, use of "potentiality," political beliefs, influence of Thoreau, performances and artistic context of the *Universe Symphony*; and current views on Ives. See items 97, 262, 317, 357, 401, 476, 497, 542, 618, and 633.

Reviews: Harry White, *Journal of American Studies* 33/3 (December 1999): 578–81; Arnold Whittall, *Music and Letters* 79/3 (August 1998): 441–44.

56. Maske, Ulrich. *Charles Ives in seiner Kammermusik für drei bis sechs Instrumente.* Kölner Beitrage zur Musikforschung 64. Regensburg: Bosse, 1971. ISBN 3764920688. ML 55.K6.

    Addresses the style of Ives's chamber music, with individual chapters on melody, harmony, meter, rhythm, dynamics, form, programs, and musical conception. Includes observations on the significance of the chamber music for representing Ives's philosophy.

    Reviews: Horst Leuchtmann, *Neue Musikzeitung* 24/4 (1975): 15; Nors S. Josephson, *Die Musikforschung* 27/4 (1974): 490–91; Wulf Konold, *Musica* 28/1 (1974): 59.

57. Mellers, Wilfrid. "Ta-Tas and Toodle-Doodles. [Review of *Charles Ives: "My Father's Song"* by Stuart Feder.]" *Times Literary Supplement* 4661 (31 July 1992): 17.

    Informed review recounts the major findings of Feder's volume (item 42) and comments on his interpretation of the *114 Songs* as a musical autobiography.

58. Metcalf, Steve. "A Cause for Celebrity: Demystifying Charles Ives, an Often-Overlooked Native Son." *Hartford Courant,* 30 September 1996, E1.

    Profile of Ives discussing the release of Swafford's book (item 70) includes an interview with the author and a detailed biography. Considers Ives's reputation within Connecticut and his legacy for future composers.

59. Meyer, Felix. *"The Art of Speaking Extravagantly": Eine vergleichende Studie der Concord Sonata und der Essays before a Sonata von Charles Ives.* Publikationen der Schweizerischen Musikforschenden Gesellschaft, Series II, Vol. 34. Bern, Stuttgart: Haupt, 1991. ISBN 3258043590. ML 410.I94 M5 1991.

    Comparative study of the *Concord Sonata* with the *Essays,* in which Meyer asserts that the two works are analogous. Meyer compares and contrasts Ives's uses of rhetorical devices, including quotation, in both. With ample musical illustrations, particularly of the sonata's main themes, and a thorough bibliography, especially of German sources on Ives.

Reviews: Geoffrey Block, *Notes* 48/4 (June 1992): 1297–1299; and anonymous, *Neue Zeitschrift für Musik* 153/2 (February 1992): 48–49.

60. Pavlyshyn [Pavlisin], Stepanikila Stefanivna [Stefanija]. *Charlz Aivz [Charles Ives].* Moscow: Vsesoyuznoe izdatel'stvo "Sovetskii Kompozitor," 1979. ISBN 9010525448679. ML 410 .I95 P38.

Rare life and works survey in Russian. Overview of works includes sections on the symphonies and chamber music, and a discussion of Ives's overall musical style emphasizes experimentation. Alternate transliterations of the author's name and the book title appear in different sources. Published by the "All-Union Publishers 'Soviet Composer.'" Copies available in the United States in the Library of Congress and Indiana University Library.

61. Peretti, Burton W. *"All Made of Tunes*: Composers, Music and American Culture. [Review of *All Made of Tunes* by J. Peter Burkholder.]" *American Studies* 38/1 (1997): 139–149.

Review of item 34 alongside studies of American popular song. Peretti considers the means by which nineteenth- and twentieth-century composers "mediated between popular tastes and artistic achievement."

62. Perlis, Vivian. *Charles Ives Remembered: An Oral History.* New Haven, CT: Yale University Press, 1974; reprint, New York: Da Capo Press, 1994. ISBN 0306805766. ML 410 .I94 P5 1976.

Unique volume containing transcriptions of interviews with Ives's family, friends, peers, business associates, musical collaborators, and supporters. Still relevant for the portraits of Ives and his community that emerge.

Reviews: Peter Dickinson, *Musical Times* 117 (November 1976): 910–11; Max Harrison, *Composer* 55 (Summer 1975): 37–38; Charles Kaufman, *Notes* 34/2 (1975): 273–75; Wilfrid Mellers, *Times Literary Supplement* (24 January 1975): 81; Frederik Prausnitz, *Tempo* 114 (September 1975): 28–30; Michael Tilmouth, *Music and Letters* 56/2 (1975): 214–15; Neal Zaslaw, *Notes* 32/2 (December 1975): 273–75. See also item 48.

63. Perry, Rosalie Sandra. *Charles Ives and the American Mind.* Kent, OH: Kent State University Press, 1974. ISBN 0073381521. ML 410 .I94 P54.

Compares Ives's aesthetics and compositional techniques with five intellectual trends in late nineteenth- and early twentieth-century America: innovation; Transcendentalism; stream-of-consciousness techniques; realism; and pragmatism. Although sometimes lacking in focus, Perry's comparison of

American cultural values with Ives's musical thought is often insightful, and prefigures later discussions of the impact of his social and political environment on his compositional style. Revision of the author's 1971 Ph.D. dissertation, "Charles Ives and American Culture."

Reviews: Paul R. Baker, *Journal of American History* 62 (March 1976): 1031; John Braeman, *American Studies* 16 (Fall 1975): 92; Wilfrid Mellers, *Times Literary Supplement* (24 January 1975): 81; Joseph A. Mussulman, *Journal of Popular Culture* 9 (Fall 1975): 345–346; David Robinson, *American Literature* 47 (November 1975): 458–460.

64. Rathert, Wolfgang. *Charles Ives.* Ertrage der Forschung no. 267. 2nd ed. Darmstadt, Germany: Wissenschaftliche Buchgesellschaft, 1996. ISBN 3534032497. ML 410 .I9 R35 1996.

Prose survey of published literature on Ives first published in 1989, rather than an original study. Divided into three sections: Biography and Cultural History; On Aesthetics, including a section on Transcendentalism; and The Musical Compositions, with subsections devoted to (among others) philology and editorial problems, and the use of quotations. Also considers current trends in Ives scholarship. Substantial bibliography, excellent for non-English sources.

65. Rathert, Wolfgang. *"The seen and unseen": Studien zum Werk von Charles Ives.* Berliner musikwissenschaftliche Arbeiten no. 38. Munich: Musikverlag Emil Katzbichler, 1991. ISBN 3873970783. ML 410.I94 R37 1991.

Examines Ives's aesthetics from two perspectives: in comparison with Coleridge's theory of art, and the Transcendentalism of Emerson, Thoreau, and Hawthorne; and through detailed structural, harmonic, rhythmic, and programmatic analyses of the *Second String Quartet,* the *Concord Sonata,* and the *Fourth Symphony.* Concludes with a study of the significance of the fragment in Ives's music. Extensive bibliography, particularly useful for German sources. Published version of the author's 1987 Ph.D. dissertation from Freie University, Berlin.

Reviews: Dietrich Kämper, *Die Musikforschung* 45/4 (1992): 436–437.

66. Riedel, Johannes, and Robert Oudal. *A Charles Ives Primer.* Minneapolis: University of Minnesota, 1969. MT 92 .I55 R5.

A unique volume, subtitled "A tentative introduction to music idioms as found in Charles Ives' music" that collates excerpts to illustrate: rhythmic superimposition and displacement; notated meters; melodic outlines, including recitative, octave displacements and tonally static melodies;

quarter-tone and tone clusters; triadic, quartal, and tritone harmonies; diverging and converging harmonic directions; polytonality, extended chord clusters, and pedal points; various types of cadential motion; and melodic quotations.

67. Rossiter, Frank. *Charles Ives and His America.* New York: Liveright, 1975. ISBN 0871406101. ML 410 .I94 R68.

Important consideration of Ives's relationship to contemporary American culture. Rossiter questions Ives's "isolation" by presenting thorough and original research about his childhood in Danbury and education at Yale. He further argues that both Ives's actions—including his business career and political thinking—and compositions betray the strong influence of his surroundings. Also includes an early consideration of Ives's gender issues.

Reviews: John Adams, *New England Quarterly* 49 (June 1976): 313–314; Paul R. Baker, *Journal of American History* 63 (March 1977): 1054–1055; Stephen Blum, *Musical Quarterly* 62/4 (October 1976): 597–603; Gilbert Chase, *High Fidelity/Musical America* 26/7 (July 1976): MA 38–39; Robert Craft, *Sunday Times* (London), 28 November 1976, 40; reprinted as "Ives's World" in *Current Convictions: Views and Reviews.* New York: Alfred A. Knopf, 1977; Peter Dickinson, *Musical Times* 117 (November 1976): 910–11; Simon Emmerson, *Music and Musicians* 25 (January 1977): 28; Donal Henahan, *New York Times Book Review*, 30 November 1975, section 7, 41–42; Robert Morgan, *Yearbook for Inter-American Musical Research* 11 (1975): 225–28; Albert Stoutamire, *American Historical Review* 81 (December 1976): 1264; Jannelle Warren-Findley, *American Studies* 19 (Fall 1978): 85–87.

68. Sive, Helen R. *Music's Connecticut Yankee.* New York: Atheneum, 1977. ISBN 0689305613. ML 3930 .I94 S6.

Extremely general life and works aimed at the younger reader without citations or other scholarly apparatus. While somewhat simplistic, Sive's account does include a balanced description of Ives's later efforts to promote his music and the reception of his work through the 1940s. Contains several photos.

69. Starr, Larry. *A Union of Diversities.* New York: Schirmer Books, 1992. ISBN 0028724658. ML 410 .I94 S7 1992.

Considers stylistic heterogeneity in Ives's works through extensive analyses of his songs "Ann Street," "The Cage," "General William Booth," "The Housatonic at Stockbridge," "Majority," "On the Antipodes," "Serenity," and

"The Things Our Fathers Loved," among others. Starr writes that his book is intentionally accessible to the nonspecialist and is intended to introduce Ives's musical language from a listener's perspective. In addition to the analyses, Starr briefly considers other issues such as influence and quotation.

Reviews: Arved Ashby, *American Record Guide* 56/2 (March 1993): 214; Carol Baron, *Notes* 50/1 (September 1993): 167–168; William Brooks, *American Music* 11/4 (winter 1993): 488–491; David Nicholls, *Music and letters* 75/2 (May 1994): 246–252.

70. Swafford, Jan. *Charles Ives: A Life with Music.* New York: Norton, 1996. ISBN 0393038939. ML 410 .I94 S93 1996.

Highly readable volume integrates cultural background with accessible musical analysis and biography. Draws on previously unpublished letters between Ives and Harmony in discussing their courtship and later marriage, and reconstructs anecdotal portraits of Ives's daily life in relation to the development of his music. A portion of the first chapter is available online at washingtonpost.com/wp-srv/style/longterm/books/chap1/ives.htm (accessed 14 May 2001).

Reviews: J. P. Ambrose, *Choice* 34 (December 1996): 624; Michael Carlson, *Spectator* 277/8781 (2 November 1996): 44; J. Bunker Clark, *American Studies* 39/3 (1998): 196–197; Robert Crunden, *Modernism-Modernity* 4/3 (1997): 154–159; Josiah Fisk, *Hudson Review* 50/1 (1997): 129–136; Stewart Gordon, *American Music Teacher* 46/6 (June–July 1997): 88–89; Donal Henahan, *The New York Times Book Review*, 4 August 1996, 11; Alan Hirsch, *Booklist* 92 (15 March 1996): 1233; Malcolm Jones, *Newsweek* 128 (9 September 1996): 74; Robert C. Jones, *American Scholar* 67 (Winter 1998): 187–89; Larry A. Lipkis, *Library Journal* 121 (March 15 1996): 74; David Matthews, *Times Literary Supplement* 4939 (28 November 1997): 12; Kenneth Singleton, *Washington Post* 28 July 1996, sec. WBK, 4; S. Frederick Starr, *Wilson Quarterly* 20/2 (Spring 1996): 83–84; Genevieve Stuttaford, *Publishers Weekly* 243/7 (12 February 1996): 68; Judith Tick, *American Music* 17/2 (Summer 1999): 200–5; anonymous, *The Economist* 341 (7 December 1996): 12; anonymous, *New Yorker* 72/30 (7 October 1996): 96.

71. Vinay, Gianfranco. *L'America musicale di Charles Ives.* Turin, Italy: Einaudi, 1974. ML 410 .I94 V6.

Life and works based primarily on Cowell. Emphasis on Transcendentalism, the distinction between "manner" and "substance," quotations, form, and layering.

Reviews: Nors S. Josephson, *Die Musikforschung* 31/3 (1978): 347–49; Giovanni Morelli, *Rivista italian di musicologia* 9 (1974): 316–22; Frederik Prausnitz, *Tempo* 114 (September 1975): 28–30; Tito Tonietti, *Nuova rivista musicale italiana* 9/1 (January–March 1975): 137–40; Michèle Victor, *Musique en Jeu* 17 (January 1975): 120.

72. Wooldridge, David. *Charles Ives: A Portrait*. London: Faber and Faber, 1975. ISBN 0571106870. ML 410 .I94 W7 1975.

Reprint under a new title of item 73.

73. Wooldridge, David. *From the Steeples and Mountains: A Study of Charles Ives*. New York: Alfred A. Knopf, 1974. ISBN 0394481100. ML 410 .I94 W7.

Provocative and highly problematic biography of Ives that includes much original research, extensive primary source quotations (from letters, musical manuscripts, newspaper articles, and reviews), imaginative musical analysis, and fanciful speculations. The volume's greatest weakness is not its creative and confusing writing style, but rather the complete absence of citations, rendering many of Wooldridge's "discoveries" highly suspect.

For review by Kirkpatrick and subsequent responses, see items 52 and 53. Other reviews: Peter Dickinson, *Musical Times* 117 (November 1976): 910–11; Max Harrison, *Composer* 62 (Winter 1977–78): 48–50; Frederik Prausnitz, *Tempo* 114 (September 1975): 28–30; Elie Siegmeister, *Notes* 31/2 (December 1974): 291–93; Michael Tilmouth, *Music and Letters* 57/2 (April 1976): 173–75.

3

General Music Studies

74. Adler, Paula. "El mundo de Charles Ives." *Heterfonia* 12/3 (1979): 25–27.

    Brief life and works summary with general comments on experimentation, quotation, and Transcendentalist influences.

75. Alexander, Shaina. *Charles Ives: His Life and Esthetic Theories.* Morris Moore Series in Musicology, No. 11. Silver Spring, MD: Shazco, 1999. ML 410 .I94 A8 1999.

    Reprint of an early unpublished paper written in 1953 that summarizes Ives's biography and aesthetics, mostly drawing on the *Essays* and *114 Songs*. Includes a brief quotation from a telephone interview with Elliot Carter from 1953, otherwise unpublished.

76. Austin, William. "Ives and Histories." In *Bericht über den internationalen musikwissenschaftlichen Kongress Bonn 1970*, edited by Carl Dahlhaus et al. Kassel: Bärenreiter, 1971, 299–303. ISBN 3761801467. ML 36 .I6277.

    Thoughtful consideration of Ives's changing historical context, including his status as an "outsider," and his relationship to American popular and experimental musics, European traditions, and Beethoven in particular.

77. Bambarger, Bradley. "Classical Music: Jazzical Gas." *Billboard* 111/36 (4 September 1999): 46.

    Invokes Ives's use of ragtime as the starting point for the relationship between classical music and jazz.

78. Baron, Carol K. "George Ives's Essay in Music Theory: An Introduction and Annotated Edition." *American Music* 10/3 (Fall 1992): 239–88.

First complete published edition of an essay on music by Ives's father that survives in both handwritten and typed sources. Unlike Eiseman (item 152), Baron strongly argues that George's theories testify to his experimental views, which in turn influenced his son to create avant-garde compositions. Includes facsimiles and diagrams from the original sources.

79. Baron, Carol. "Meaning in the Music of Charles Ives." In *Metaphor: A Musical Dimension*. Australian studies in the history, philosophy, and social studies of music, 1. Sydney, Australia: Currency, 1991, 37–50. ISBN 0868192775. ML 3797.1 .M469 1991. Reprint, Musicology: A Book Series, 15. Basel: Gordon and Breach, 1994. ISBN 2884491368. ML 3797.1 .M469 1994.

Discusses the means by which Ives "composed analogues for life experiences in his music that frequently shape the formal design and even the language of his music."

80. Battisti, Frank. "The Legacy of Charles Ives." *Instrumentalist* 52/7 (February 1998): 68–74.

Good introduction for music educators to Ives's music with descriptions of his musical borrowings, education, influence of Transcendentalism, musical layering, and imitations of amateur music-making. Recommended band works listed by grade level.

81. Becker, John J. "Charles E. Ives, '. . . a composer with something to say.' " *Etude* 74 (May–June 1956): 11, 20, 49, 57; 74 (July–August 1956): 14, 46.

Detailed biography in part 1, followed by a general outline of experimental procedures and use of quotations in his compositions. With some discussion of the Fourth Symphony, *Universe Symphony* and *Concord Sonata*, and excerpts from the *Essays*.

82. Bellamann, Henry. "Charles Ives: The Man and His Music." *Musical Quarterly* 19/1 (January 1933): 45–58; excerpt reprinted in *Charles Ives and His World* (item 36), 373–75.

Well-considered introduction to Ives through biography and musical analysis. Bellamann draws on his personal acquaintance as well as interviews to sketch Ives's personality, and his ideas about life, business, and music. Analysis focuses primarily on excerpts from *114 Songs* with brief consideration of the *Concord Sonata* and the Fourth Symphony.

83. Bellamann, Henry. "The Music of Charles Ives." *Pro-Musica Quarterly* 5/1 (March–April 1927): 16–22.

Biographical summary mentions George's influence and Ives's training at Yale. Discussion of the *Concord Sonata* mentions its evocation of nineteenth-century Transcendentalism and considers the significance of the *Essays*.

84. Bessom, Malcolm E. "Overtones." *Music Educator's Journal* 61/2 (October 1974): 5.

Introduction to the excellent all-Ives issue of *MEJ* (including items 93, 381, 487, 525, 560, 588, 601, and 808). Bessom recounts the flurry of activities associated with the Ives Centennial and his metamorphosis from "a sort of curiosity" to an established composer in the university and elementary-secondary curriculum. Mentions the Ives centerfold in this issue (pp. 62–63) intended for use in the classroom.

85. Blum, Robert S. "Ives's Position in Social and Musical History." *Musical Quarterly* 63 (1977): 459–82.

Considers Ives's response to his contemporary social and musical world based on three factors: his understanding of the demands of history, as expressed through his use of nostalgia and experiential sound; his use of musical materials to depict and reconcile tonal and social oppositions; and his own identity, as based on his Transcendental beliefs and a rejection of "manner."

86. Boatwright, Howard. "Ives' Quarter-Tone Impressions." *Musical Quarterly* 3/2 (Spring-Summer 1965): 22–31. Reprinted in *Perspectives on American Composers*, edited by Benjamin Boretz and Edward T. Cone. Norton Library, No. 549. New York: W. W. Norton, 1971. ISBN 0393021556. ML 200.1.B67.

Analyzes the article "Some 'Quarter-Tone' Impressions" with commentary on the origin of and influences on the work, and its relationship to Ives's education and later writings. Contains extensive quotations from the original source.

87. Brady, Tim. "Death of the Masterpiece: The Changing Social Context for Creative Music." *Musicworks: The Journal of Sound Exploration* 61 (Spring 1995): 29–33.

Examines "the death of the musical masterpiece," as a result of changing musical values. Brady suggests that Ives's *Essays* prophesied this change in social context from a creative standpoint.

88. Brodhead, Thomas M. "Ives's *Celestial Railroad* and His Fourth Symphony." *American Music* 12/4 (Winter 1994): 389–424.

Detailed comparison of music, programs, and manuscript sources that illuminates the interrelationships between *The Celestial Railroad*, the lost *Hawthorne Piano Concerto*, the "Hawthorne" and "Emerson" movements of the *Second Piano Sonata*, the *Four Transcriptions from Emerson*, the *Emerson Overture*, and the second movement of the Fourth Symphony. Includes numerous excerpts and manuscript facsimiles.

89. Brooks, William. "Ives Today." In *An Ives Celebration: Papers and Panels of the Charles Ives Centennial Festival-Conference* (item 50), 209–23.

   Considers the study of Ives within the context of structuralism and self-referentiality. Contains an extended comparison between Ives and Buckminster Fuller.

90. Brown, Earle and Vivian Perlis, Co-Chairs. "Ives Viewed From Abroad." Panel discussion transcript published in *An Ives Celebration: Papers and Panels of the Charles Ives Centennial Festival-Conference* (item 50), 45–63.

   Panel discussion based on "Essays by Foreign Participants" (item 187) expands on the international reception and promotion of Ives's music. Contains an extended discussion of the perception of specifically American quotations for non-American listeners.

91. Broyles, Michael. "Charles Ives and the American Democratic Tradition." In *Charles Ives and His World* (item 36), 118–160.

   Examines Ives's political views as expressed in the essay "Majority" and in political song texts. Broyles addresses the question of whether Ives was a progressive or a populist, and thoroughly explores the impact of the Armstrong insurance investigation of 1905 on Ives's politics and philosophy.

92. Buechner, Alan Clark. "Die Welt des Charles Ives. Protaganist der amerikanischen Musik." *Österreichische Musikzeitschrift* 34/2 (February 1979): 75–89.

   Condensed biography centered on an examination of the specifically "American" components in Ives's music including: quotations from religious and patriotic sources; geographic associations such as "Putnam's Camp" and "St. Gaudens' in Boston Common"; experimentation and tradition; and the influence of Transcendentalist philosophers. Concludes with thoughts on Ives's legacy and influence on later composers.

93. Buechner, Alan. "Ives in the Classroom: A Teaching Guide to Two Compositions." *Music Educator's Journal* 61/2 (October 1974): 64–70.

Lesson plans for teaching *Variations on "America"* and the finale of the Second Symphony in the general music classroom. With outlines of each work, quotations, photographs of Ives's sports teams, and general background information.

94. Buhles, Günter. "Amerikanische Komponisten: Von Charles Ives und Carl Ruggles bis John Cage und Morton Feldman." *Das Orchester* 48/9 (September 2000): 2–9.

Considers the legendary figure of Ives within a larger consideration of the character and history of American music. Survey of experimental approaches emphasizes collage form, polytonality, and quotations from American popular musics, in comparison with Mahler.

95. Bukoff, Ronald. "Charles Ives, a History and Bibliography of Criticism (1920–1939), and Ives Influence (to 1947) on Bernard Herrmann, Elle Siegmeister, and Robert Palmer." Ph.D. dissertation, Cornell University, 1988.

Illuminating reception history focuses on two aspects of Ives criticism. The first section thoroughly covers published criticism of performances and publications (music and literary) from 1920 to 1939. The second section discusses his influence from 1924 to 1947 on Herrmann, Palmer, and Siegmeister, with lesser discussions of the music of Israel Citkowitz, Lou Harrison, and Jerome Moross. Bukoff concludes that Ives exerted "a tremendous influence upon American music, from 1920 through the end of World War II."

96. Burkholder, J. Peter. "Ives and Yale: The Enduring Influence of a College Experience." *College Music Symposium* 39 (1999): 27–42.

Recounts the impact of Ives's Yale education, with emphasis on his coursework with Parker, the social environment of the university, and critical accounts of Ives's relationship with Parker from the 1930s to the present.

97. Burkholder, J. Peter. "Ives Today." In *Ives Studies* (item 55), 263–90.

In his valuable survey of Ives reception from 1974 to 1996, Burkholder outlines the most significant scholarly topics: Ives's command of musical materials, in his use of stylistic diversity, alternative compositional systems, and musical borrowing; connections to the European tradition, through his inheritance from classical precursors as well as parallels with his European contemporaries; and his training, development, and chronology, primarily in reconsiderations of the influence of Ives's father on his style.

98. Burkholder, J. Peter. "Ives and the Four Musical Traditions." In *Charles Ives and His World* (item 36), 3–34.

In this important stylistic overview, Burkholder outlines four traditions that influenced Ives at different stages in his life: American popular music; Protestant church music; European classical music; and experimental music. Furthermore, Burkholder suggests that Ives synthesizes all four traditions in his mature music, and that the mixing of these four traditions in isolation and in combination account for the unmatched diversity of Ives's output.

99. Burkholder, J. Peter. "Charles Ives the Avant-Gardist, Charles Ives the Traditionalist." In *Bericht über das Internationale Symposion "Charles Ives und die amerikanische Musiktradition bis zur Gegenwart' Köln 1988*, edited by Klaus Wolfgang Niemöller. Kölner Beiträge zur Musikforschung, No. 164. Regensburg: Gustav Bosse Verlag, 1990, 37–51. ISBN 3764924063. ML 200.5 .I58 1990.

Reconciles the image of Ives as a purely experimental composer with his connections to the European Romantic tradition. Includes discussions of Ives's nationalism, his uses of musical borrowing, and resettings of Lieder texts.

100. Burkholder, J. Peter. "The Critique of Tonality in the Early Experimental Music of Charles Ives." *Music Theory Spectrum* 12/2 (Fall 1990): 203–23.

Examines Ives's questioning of diatonic structures in several small works including *Psalm 67, Psalm 100, Psalm 54,* and *Processional: Let There Be Light.* Burkholder concludes that Ives's deployment of nontraditional techniques in the challenging of tonality indicates a position within the European tradition, not outside of it.

101. Burkholder, J. Peter. "The Evolution of Charles Ives's Music: Aesthetics, Quotation, Technique." Ph.D. dissertation, University of Chicago, 1983.

Significant examination of the relationship of Ives's ideas and music to European models, with emphasis on Transcendentalism, quotations, musical forms, and stylistic eclecticism. Although superceded by later publications (items 34 and 35), still a relevant source.

102. Cage, John. "The Future of Music." In *Empty Words*. Middletown, CT: Wesleyan University Press, 1979, 179–80. ISBN 0819550329. ML 60 .C12.

Includes a mention of Ives's belief in the necessity of musical open-mindedness, to which Cage responds that "the fences have come down and the labels are being removed."

103. Cage, John. "Two Statements on Ives." In *A Year from Monday: New Lectures and Writings*. Middletown, CT: Wesleyan University Press, 1967, 36–42.

The first statement includes reprints of Cage's handwritten correspondence from 7 April 1964 in which he reflects on Ives's importance as the beginning of American music history. He criticizes, however, Ives's insurance career, saying that "it made his life too safe economically." The second statement is an essay critiquing Ives's quotations for their nationalist identity, but praising his exploration of spatial relationships and his understanding "of inactivity and silence."

104. Cage, John. "History of Experimental Music in the United States." In *Silence*. Middletown, CT: Wesleyan University Press, 1961, 70. ML 60 .C13.

Includes a brief statement recognizing Ives as a precursor of spatial experimentation and indeterminacy through the introduction of performance variants.

105. Carr, Cassandra I. "Charles Ives's Humor as Reflected in His Songs." *American Music* 7/2 (Summer 1989): 123–39.

Divides Ives's uses of humor in his songs into four categories: parody; whimsical reminiscence; philosophical; and exaggerated insignificance. Carr suggests that Ives's use of humor gradually evolved throughout his life, from the early wit of caustic and whimsical songs through more sophisticated parodies and exaggerations later in life. She also notes that many of Ives's humorous songs address artistic attitudes from the past.

106. Carter, Elliot. *Collected Essays and Lectures, 1937–1995*, edited by Jonathan W. Bernard. Eastman Studies in Music. Rochester, NY: University of Rochester Press, 1997. ISBN 1878822705. ML 197 .C3425 1996.

Includes previously published articles and lectures discussing Ives. See items 107, 108, and 110–15.

107. Carter, Elliot. "Brass Quintet." In *Collected Essays and Lectures, 1937–1995* (item 106), 256–58.

The introduction includes a recollection of Ives's influence on and reactions to Carter's early work, as well as a comparison of their similar goals of "musical expressivity."

108. Carter, Elliot. "Documents of a Friendship with Ives." *Parnassus: Poetry In Review* 3/2 (Spring/Summer 1975): 300–315; reprinted in *Collected Essays and Lectures, 1937–1995* (item 106), 107–18.

Part of the Parnassus collection (item 168). Recollections of Carter's inter-actions with Ives illustrated through extensive correspondence. Carter dis-cusses his somewhat negative review of the *Concord Sonata* in *Modern Music* (item 115), and examines the nature of revision by Ives and Harmony in their correspondence.

109. Carter, Elliot. "Expressionism and American Music." *Perspectives of New Music* 4/1 (Fall–Winter 1965): 1–13. Revised version published in *Perspectives on American Composers*, edited by Benjamin Boretz and Edward T. Cone. New York: W. W. Norton, 1971, 217–29. ISBN 0393021556. ML 200.1.B67.

Comparison of Schoenberg's concept of Expressionism with statements by Ives in the *Essays*. Also considers the "expressionistic intensity" of the song "Walt Whitman," Ives's rhythmic experiments, and Carter's own "emanci-pation of dissonance" and hetergeneity.

110. Carter, Elliot. "Shop Talk by an American Composer." *Musical Quarterly* 46 (1960): 189–201; reprinted in *Collected Essays and Lectures, 1937–1995* (item 106), 214–24.

The final, substantial section (pp. 198–200) answers the question "What do you think of Charles Ives now?" Discusses Carter's admiration for the man, misgivings about the music, and the conflicts between business, public, and art that, Carter argues, affected not only Ives but all American composers since.

111. Carter, Elliot. "The Rhythmic Basis of American Music." *Score and I.M.A. Magazine* 12 (June 1955): 27–32; reprinted in *Collected Essays and Lectures, 1937–1995* (item 106), 57–62.

Includes analyses of Ives's use of rhythmic devices such as distortion or rubato, "artificial divisions," polyrhythms, and multiple rhythmic planes. With examples from the second movement of the Fourth Symphony and *Calcium Light Night* as well as mentions of *The Unanswered Question* and *Central Park in the Dark*.

112. Carter, Elliot. "Genial Sage." In *Paul Rosenfeld: Voyager in the Arts*, Jerome Mellquist and Lucie Wiese, eds. New York: Creative Age Press, 1948, 163–65; reprinted and expanded in Carter, *Collected Essays and Lectures, 1937–1995* (item 106), 306–7.

Brief but intriguing report of a projected collaborative book by Rosenfeld and Carter on Ives "as a touchstone to bring all the problems of the artist and his times into pattern," as well as their changing ideas about Ives and his significance to American music.

113. Carter, Elliot. "An American Destiny." *Listen* 9/1 (November 1946): 4–7; reprinted in *Collected Essays and Lectures, 1937–1995* (item 106), 93–98.

   Profile of Ives's personality and disposition, with secondary coverage of his life and only cursory mention of the music. Includes brief mentions of Ives's Transcendentalist views, his attitudes toward contemporary musicians, his insurance business, and his choice of an "amateur" status.

114. Carter, Elliot. "Ives Today: His Vision and Challenge." *Modern Music* 21 (1943–44): 199–202; reprinted in *Collected Essays and Lectures, 1937–1995* (item 106), 90–93; and in *Charles Ives and His World* (item 36), 390–93.

   Overview of the challenges of performing Ives's music well, including the level of difficulty and the "amount of detail left to the interpreter's discretion."

115. Carter, Elliot. "The Case of Mr. Ives." *Modern Music* 16 (1938–39): 172–76; excerpts reprinted in *Perspectives of New Music* 2/2 (Spring–Summer 1964): 27–29; reprinted in *Collected Essays and Lectures, 1937–1995* (item 106), 87–90; and in *Charles Ives and His World* (item 36), 333–37.

   Review of Kirkpatrick's famous 1939 performances of the *Concord Sonata*, including the reactions of the critics, the history of Ives performances in the late 1920s, and Carter's own reflections on Ives and his music. He concludes that, despite Kirkpatrick's "extraordinary feat of interpretation . . . the sonata is formally weak," lacking in logic and clarity, and "more often original than good."

116. "Charles E. Ives Dies at 79." *New York Herald Tribune*, 20 May 1954, 14.

   Obituary recounting the Pulitzer Prize award, his New England roots, and the "Yankee flavor" of his works. Includes a brief biography and discussion of his "vast musical knowledge and technical skill." Also mentions his insurance career.

117. "Charles Ives, 79, Composer, Is Dead." *New York Times*, 19 May 1954, 31.

   Identifies Ives as a modernist, and recounts his New England youth and insurance career. Emphasizes the Pulitzer Prize awards and states that, in addition to the Third Symphony, his most important works were the Second String Quartet and the *Concord Sonata.*

118. Chase, Gilbert. "Charles Ives and American Culture." *High Fidelity/Musical America* 24/10 (October 1974): MA 17–19.

Insightful commentary on Ives's relationship to trends in American culture, including the "genteel" tradition and the rise of the "highbrow" concept of culture. Chase also relates the growing field of cultural studies to papers presented at the Charles Ives Centennial Festival Conference (see items 50 and 841).

119. Chase, Gilbert. "A Communication. The Music of Charles Ives." *Kenyon Review* 17/3 (Summer 1955): 504–06.

Rebuttal of item 154 that defends Ives's music on the grounds of performances and recordings that were increasingly well-received, as well as the substantial body of literature on Ives.

120. Clark, Robin C. "Plaque Marking Charles Ives' Birthplace Dedicated." *Danbury News-Times*, 28 June 1965, 3.

Dedication of a plaque donated by the Danbury Music Centre reviews Ives's history in Danbury, including an anecdote concerning his generosity. Describes the growing acceptance of Ives's music and expected future recognition.

121. Clarke, Gary E. "Charles Edward Ives." In *Essays on American Music.* Westport, CT: Greenwood Press, 1977, 105–31. ISBN 0837194849. ML 200.1 .C6.

Profile emphasizes Transcendentalism, pragmatism, use of quotations, "substance" and "manner," revision, aspects of choice in performance, and programs. Suggests that Ives's compositional techniques and aesthetics stem from two influences: George Ives and Horatio Parker. With several musical excerpts and manuscript facsimiles.

122. Clements, Andrew. "All about Ives." *Guardian*, 19 January 1996, 210.

Comments on the style and background of Ives's music. Interviews Andrew Davis, the conductor of the BBC Symphony Orchestra on conducting Ives's works.

123. Coakley, John Pius. "The Artistic Process as Religious Enterprise: The Vocal Texts of Charles Ives and the Poetry of E. E. Cummings." Ph.D. dissertation, Brown University, 1982.

Examines Ives's song texts as an expression of his religious values based on his own writings. Coakley suggests that composing was "a revelatory activity which was executed, at least to some degree, through a process of play" that involved an "interwoven dynamics of recreation and struggle."

124. Cole, Hugo. "Music 'Like the Rocks Were Grown.' " *Country Life*, 2 January 1975, 16.

Basic biography with significant discussion of Ives's relationship with his father and Horatio Parker. Briefly compares Ives's attitudes towards popular music with those of Constant Lambert.

125. Conn, Peter J. "Innovation and Nostalgia: Charles Ives." In *The Divided Mind: Ideology and Imagination in America, 1898–1917.* Cambridge: Cambridge University Press, 1983, 230–50. ISBN 0521253926. PS 223 .C66 1983.

Analyzes Ives's rhetoric concerning his father and Parker as shown in passages from *Memos*, and his "idealization of business." Focuses on the importance of nostalgia both musically and ideologically, stating "at the core of Ives's dissonant nostalgia lies his assent to a cluster of reactionary values that virtually prohibited him from directly engaging in music in or for itself."

126. Cooney, Denise Van Glahn. "A Sense of Place: Charles Ives and 'Putnam's Camp, Redding, Connecticut.' " *American Music* 14/3 (Fall 1996): 276–312.

Investigates the relationship between the orchestral movement and the historical and personal significance of the actual Putnam's Camp. Includes original background on Israel Putnam, after whom the camp was named, and Lyman Brewster's involvement in the preservation of the camp. Concludes with an extensive discussion of the program, musical structure, and quotations in Ives's work.

127. Cooney, Denise von Glahn. "Reconciliations: Time, Space and American Place in the Music of Charles Ives." Ph.D. dissertation, University of Washington, 1995.

Study of Ives's "place" pieces, that is, works that referred to, reflected upon, and sonically recreated locations that were significant locally, regionally, and nationally. Cooney proposes that Ives's invocation of place echoes mainstream American culture through quotations, programs, and manipulation of musical space.

128. Cott, Jonathan. "Charles Ives, Musical Inventor." *New York Times*, 20 October 1974, section D, 21, 26.

     Profile of Ives on his centenary stresses experimental techniques that foreshadowed later developments, the influence of his father, and his use of quotations.

129. Covington, Katherine Russell. "A Study of Textural Stratification in 20th-Century Compositions." Ph.D. dissertation, Indiana University, 1982.

     General discussion of the features, forms, and utilization of sound layers, or strata, and how strata are characterized through timbre, register, dynamics, density, and melodic and harmonic forms. Ives's *The Unanswered Question* and *Scherzo: Over the Pavements* are analyzed with emphasis on their timbral and rhythmic strata, along with works by Stravinsky, Messiaen, Schuman, Debussy, Varèse, and Webern.

130. Cowell, Henry. "Charles E. Ives." *American Composers on American Music*, edited by Henry Cowell. Stanford, CA: Stanford University Press, 1933; reprinted with a new introduction by the editor. New York: Frederick Ungar Publishing, 1962, 128–45. ML 200.5 .C87.

     Profile stresses the "universal" aspects of Ives's musical material; availability of choices for performers; and experimental techniques including microtones, piano drumming, tone clusters, polyrhythms, atonality, and polyharmony.

131. Cowell, Henry. "American Composers. IX. Charles Ives." *Modern Music* 10 (1932–33): 24–33.

     Outline of Ives's life, influences, and musical style. Particular emphasis on his American origins and use of "folk" materials, as well as precedence over Schoenberg and Stravinsky. Details his use of unconventional rhythmic structures, polytonality, and atonality.

132. Cowell, Henry. "Charles E. Ives." *Disques* (November 1932): 374–76; reprinted in *Charles Ives and His World* (item 36), 368–72.

     Survey covers his New England upbringing and use of "folk-themes" and "typical American usages" as quotations. Considers the role of the performer in interpreting the works. Suggests that the sudden recognition of Ives as "the most potent and original figure" in American music is due to his European recognition.

133. Cowell, Sidney. "The Cowells and the Written Word." In *A Celebration of American Music: Words and Music in Honor of H. Wiley Hitchcock,*

edited by Richard Crawford, R. Allen Lott, and Carol J. Oja. Ann Arbor: University of Michigan Press, 1990, 79–91. ISBN 0472094009. ML 200 .C44 1989.

Includes a detailed account of the writing of the Cowell's full biography of Ives (item 37), with personal recollections of reactions of the Iveses to the project. Also briefly discusses Henry Cowell's work on the Fourth Symphony.

134. Cowell, Sidney. "Ivesiana: 'More Than Something Just Usual.' " *High Fidelity/Musical America* 24/10 (October 1974): MA 14–16; reprinted as the "New Forward" in Henry and Sidney Cowell. *Charles Ives and His Music*. Reprint edition. New York: DaCapo Press, 1983 (item 37).

Personal recollections of visiting the Iveses at their residence at East 74th Street, and also in West Redding. Includes some details of Henry Cowell's work on behalf of Ives including preparing scores for *New Music* and other publications.

135. Crawford, John C., and Dorothy L. Crawford. "Charles Ives." In *Expressionism in 20th-Century Music*. Bloomington: Indiana University Press, 1993, 204–28. ISBN 0253314739. ML 197 .C8.

General "life and works" overview with emphasis on Ives's philosophical ideas and influences (especially Emerson), as well as his experimentation and use of quotations within the context of early twentieth-century America.

136. Crunden, Robert M. *A Brief History of American Culture*. New York: Paragon, 1994, 213–15 and passim. ISBN 1557787050. E 169.1 .C8358 1994.

Considers Ives and his cultural background within a survey of the arts of various ethnic communities between 1901 and 1941. Describes Ives as "the towering figure" of classical music. Examines his specifically American approach and materials and their roots in his upbringing and education.

137. Crunden, Robert M. "Charles Ives's Place in American Culture." In *An Ives Celebration: Papers and Panels of the Charles Ives Centennial Festival-Conference* (item 50), 4–15.

Discusses Ives as a product of his society through his relationship to progressivism. Crunden examines Ives's political, religious, and social values in comparison with those of other "Progressive Era" figures like John Dewey and Woodrow Wilson. He concludes that Ives's Progressivism is also reflected in his process-oriented compositions.

138. Crutchfield, Will. "Why Our Greatest Composer Needs Serious Attention." *New York Times*, 10 May 1987, section 2, 19, 22.

     Thoughtful assessment of contemporary criticisms of Ives such as his "amateur" status and his use of humor. Crutchfield maintains that a lack of knowledge of Ives's music, and few quality performances, could be responsible for a decline in the composer's reputation. Examines Elliott Carter's ideas about Ives, especially his negative review of the *Concord Sonata* (item 115).

139. "Danbury Fifty Years Ago." *Danbury Evening News*, 9 February 1939, 3.

     Reprints an announcement from 9 February 1889 that "Charles Ives, a young song of George E. Ives, is to take charge of the organ at the West Street Congregational church and will enter upon his duties as organist tomorrow. Charlie has inherited a generous supply of his father's musical talent."

140. Danner, Gregory. "Ives' Harmonic Language." *Journal of Musicological Research* 5/1–2 (1984): 237–49.

     A brief summary of Ives's juxtaposition of diatonic, whole-tone, and atonal structures, using pitch-class set analysis. Includes a consideration of the influence of Transcendentalism on Ives's harmonic language, as well as several short musical excerpts to illustrate commonly found pitch-class sets.

141. Danuser, Hermann. "Auf der Suche nach einer nationalen Musikasthetik." In *Amerikanische Musik seit Charles Ives: Interpretation, Quellentexte, Komponistenmonographien* (item 38), 51–59.

     Translated as "In search of a national music aesthetic," traces the historical development of specifically American music. Danuser divides composers into two somewhat artificial groupings of idealistic nationalism and folk-art synthesis. He places Ives outside of these divisions as part of the modernist group, along with Babbitt, Carter, Cage, and Ruggles.

142. Davenport, Guy. "Ives the Master." *Parnassus: Poetry in Review* 3/2 (Spring/Summer 1975): 374–80. Reprinted in *Words on Music*, edited by Jack Sullivan. Athens: Ohio University Press, 1990, 294–98. ISBN 082140959X. ML 160 .W95 1990.

     Part of "A Garland for Charles Ives" (item 168), this uneven commentary includes a review of Wooldridge's book (item 73) as well as general observations on Ives's biography, the sound of the music, and overall comparisons with T. S. Eliot, Ezra Pound, and James Joyce.

143. Dayton, Daryl D. "Charles Ives in the USIA." *Student Musicologists at Minnesota* 6 (1975–76): 87–94.

Discusses the reception of American music, particularly Ives's, in Europe and speculates on his appeal to foreign listeners. With details on American Music Festivals sponsored by the U.S. Information Agency.

144. Deutsch, Lawrence. "Overstimulation by a Father: An Alternate View of Charles Ives." In *Fathers and Their Families*, edited by Stanley H. Cath, Alan Gurwitt et al. Hillsdale, NJ: Analytic Press, 1989, 327–336. ISBN 0881630527. HQ 756 .F3834 1989.

Psychoanalytic study of Ives's childhood and early life suggests that his withdrawal from music and early retirement were related to overstimulation as a child by his father George.

145. Dickinson, Peter. "A New Perspective for Ives." *Musical Times* 115/1580 (October 1974): 836–38.

Reports on the reception and influence of Ives's works in 1974, including discussions of multiplicity and quotation in works by Berio, Cage, Tippett, Musgrave, Crosee, and Holloway. Concludes with a comparison to James Joyce's literary works primarily through their use of nostalgia, their originality, and their difficulty achieving publication.

146. Donohue, John, and Michael Petersen. "Connecticut's Music Man: Charles Ives." *Hartford Courant Magazine*, 20 October 1974, 2–9.

Biography focuses on Ives's "American heritage," family history, and insurance business. Describes modernist techniques as well as the four symphonies. With numerous photographs of Ives and his family.

147. Downes, Olin. "Ives Memorial: His Scores and Papers Given to Yale." *New York Times*, 5 June 1955, section 2, 9.

Reports the donation of the Ives archives to Yale, along with an overview of efforts by Lou Harrison, Kirkpatrick, Cowell, and Joseph Braunstein to order and integrate the manuscripts. Also recounts his lack of recognition and Harmony's work on behalf of his legacy.

148. Downes, Olin. "Composer's Need: Ives's Career Lacked Audience to Accept or Reject His Creative Experiments." *New York Times*, 6 June 1954, section 2, 7.

Description of Ives's life and music based on a letter to Downes by T. Carl

Whitmer. Details George Ives's influence, Ives's isolation, and the potential impact of his lack of audience. Also briefly describes a private performance of *Concord Sonata.*

149. Downes, Olin. "American Original." *New York Times,* 30 May 1954, section 2, 7; reprinted as "Charles Ives." *American Composers Alliance Bulletin* 4/1 (1954): 17.

Obituary profiling reactions to Ives's work during the late 1920s and early 1930s. Reprints much of Downes's 1927 review of the Pro Musica performance of the Fourth Symphony, first and second movements (item 150).

150. Downes, Olin. "Music: Pro-Musica Society." *New York Times,* 30 January 1927, 28; reprinted in *Charles Ives and His World* (item 36), 293–95.

Review of the Pro Musica premiere of the Fourth Symphony, first and second movements repeatedly refers to the work of "Mr. St. Ives" as "an extraordinary hodgepode [sic], but something that lives and vibrates with conviction." The review is primarily positive, although Downes criticizes the work's ineptitudes and incongruities.

151. Drew, James. "Information, Space and a New Time-Dialectic." *Journal of Music Theory* 12/1 (Spring 1968): 86–103.

Places Ives's spatial experiments within a larger musical tradition of redefining space and time relationships (pp. 95–96). Drew asserts that Ives's "understanding of multiplicity as a frame of reference" was based on a theory that "each spatial dimension is self inclusive and is therefore of an autonomous nature."

152. Eiseman, David. "George Ives as Theorist: Some Unpublished Documents." *Perspectives of New Music* 14/1 (Fall–Winter 1975): 139–47.

Summary and description of an essay on music by Ives's father that survives in both handwritten and typed sources. Unlike Baron (item 78), Eiseman sees the article as essentially traditional and pragmatic, with the exception of George's assertion that consonance and dissonance are based on habits of listening and exposure. See item 78 for the complete text of George Ives's article.

153. Eiseman, David. "Charles Ives and the European Symphonic Tradition: A Historical Reappraisal." Ph.D. dissertation, University of Illinois, 1972.

Insightful reconsideration of Ives and the classical tradition in general, and as reflected in the first two symphonies. Includes summaries of Ives's recital programs through the 1890s, plus programs of the New Haven Symphony Orchestra between 1895 and 1898. Good bibliography to 1972.

154. Evett, Robert. "Music Letter: A Post-Mortem for Mr. Ives." *Kenyon Review* 16 (Autumn 1954): 628–36.

Scathing critique of Ives's music as "incredibly banal," "mindless banging around," and the work of "a talented amateur." Evett argues that Ives did not use polytonality "as a serious technique in the sense that Milhaud later did," and dismisses his music as impractical, stylistically extravagant, standardless, and chauvinistic (in his use of "folk" musics). Includes a negative comparison to Whitman and comments on the music's reception. For a rebuttal, see item 118.

155. Ewen, David. "The Belated Discovery of Charles Ives." *Tomorrow* 9/9 (May 1950): 10–14.

Report on Ives's recent seventy-fifth birthday observes that "the same sublime indifference which over the years he has demonstrated toward his neglect, he now displays toward his acceptance." Describes Ives's unusual career, his isolation, and extreme privacy, and gives an overview of his orchestral works and *Concord.*

156. Fairfield, Patrick Kenneth. "Representations of Gender and Sexuality in the Music and Writings of Charles Ives." Ph.D. dissertation, Brandeis University, 2000.

Examination of misogynist language in Ives's writings including the correspondence and manuscript memos. Specifically, Fairfield traces Ives's concepts of gender and sexuality to the upheaval of gender roles in American culture at the turn of the century. He also discusses the influence of this rhetoric on Ives's music, through engendered texts, marginalia that describe certain passages, and the process of revising, which Ives often described as "weakening" the music. Includes a very useful index of all "gender-based language" in these sources.

157. Feder, Stuart. "This Scherzo is [not] a Joke." In *Humor and Psyche: Psychoanalytic Perspectives*, edited by James W. Barron. Hillsdale, NJ: Analytic Press, 1999, 203–217. ISBN 0881632570. BF175 .H85 1999.

Psychoanalytic analysis of Ives's use of humor—in his music and writings—as a defense mechanism. With discussion of connections to George Ives, and its role in defining Ives's sexual identity.

158. Feder, Stuart. "Charles and George Ives: The Veneration of Boyhood." In *Psychoanalytic Explorations in Music*, edited by Stuart Feder, Richard Karmel and George H. Pollock. Applied Psychoanalysis Series, No. 3. Madison, CT: International Universities Press, 1990, pp. 115–176. ISBN 0823644073. ML 3830 .P89 1990.

Early, abbreviated version of item 42, with more emphasis on psychoanalytical theories of childhood development. Feder surveys Ives's relationship with his father, and suggests how his boyhood shaped the remainder of his life, including his musical compositions and his crisis of 1918. Originally published in *The Annual of Psychoanalysis* IX (1981).

159. Feder, Stuart. "The Nostalgia of Charles Ives: An Essay in Affects and Music." In *Psychoanalytic Explorations in Music*, edited by Stuart Feder, Richard Karmel, and George H. Pollock. Applied Psychoanalysis Series, No. 3. Madison, CT: International Universities Press, 1990, pp. 233–266. ISBN 0823644073. ML 3830 .P89 1990.

Discussion of the general theoretical background for analyzing nostalgia through psychoanalysis, using Ives as a case study. Provides insight into Feder's later work, especially item 42. Originally published in *The Annual of Psychoanalysis* X (1982).

160. Feder, Stuart. " 'Calcium Light Night' and Other Early Memories of Charles Ives." In *Fathers and Their Families*, edited by Stanley H. Cath, Alan Gurwitt, et al. Hillsdale, NJ: Analytic Press, 1989, 307–326. ISBN 0881630527. HQ 756 .F3834 1989.

Examines both the formation of Ives's masculine musical identity through his relationship with his father, and the musical and biographical impact of related memories. Much of this material is incorporated into item 42.

161. Feder, Stuart. " 'Decoration Day': A Boyhood Memory of Charles Ives." *Musical Quarterly* 61/2 (April 1980): 234–61.

Discusses Ives's relationship with his father, and presents an analysis of *Decoration Day* as a biographical idealization of that relationship. Much of this work is expanded in item 42.

162. Feldman, Jay. "Sports Were Music to His Ears." *Sports Illustrated* 75/15 (7 October 1991): 106–108.

Profile of Ives with emphasis on the importance of baseball and other sports in his childhood. Discusses several baseball-themed works including *Some South-Paw Pitching (Study No. 21)* and *Take-Off No. 3: Rube Trying to Walk 2 to 3!!*

163. Fennell, Frederick. "Charles Ives and the Conductor." In *South Florida's Historic Festival* (item 858), 59.

   Brief remarks on the challenges of conducting Ives, with general recommendations and advice.

164. Forte, Allen. "The Diatonic Looking Glass, or An Ivesian Metamorphosis." *Musical Quarterly* 76/3 (Fall 1992): 355–82.

   Pitch-class set analysis of the third movement of the *Second Violin Sonata* with a focus on the first twenty-nine measures. Forte concludes that Ives employs "a comprehensive pitch metamorphosis" that transforms the diatonic hymn tune "Nettleton" into the whole-tone scales and motives that structure the piece.

165. Forte, Allen. "Ives and Atonality." In *An Ives Celebration: Papers and Panels of the Charles Ives Centennial Festival-Conference* (item 50), 159–186.

   Using set theory analysis, Forte examines Ives's various uses of atonal configurations. Includes comparisons of Ives's employment of specific sets, set complexes, and transpositional and inversional processes with works by Schoenberg and Berg.

166. Frank, Alan R. "The Music of Charles Ives: For Presentation in the Listening Program of the Secondary School." Ed.D. dissertation, Columbia University, 1969.

   Includes a brief biography of Ives, profiles of his American contemporaries, and analyses of several works including but not limited to "Washington's Birthday," "Decoration Day," *The Unanswered Question*, *Variations on "America,"* and *Three-Page Sonata*. Focuses on how to present analyses in the secondary classroom.

167. Gardner, Kara Anne. "Living by the Ladies' Smiles: The Feminization of American Music and the Modernist Reaction." Ph.D. dissertation, Stanford University, 1999.

   Valuable consideration of Amy Beach, Edward MacDowell, and Ives within the context of engendered musical roles of the late nineteenth and early twentieth centuries. Discusses how each composer absorbed and reacted against the gender stereotypes of their era. Also suggests the transformation of music from a "feminized" to a "masculine" art with the emergence of modernism.

168. "A Garland for Charles Ives." In *Parnassus: Poetry in Review*   3/2 (Spring/Summer 1975): 294–393.

Unique collections of compositions, original artwork, poetry, articles, and commentary assembled at the end of the Centennial year with contributions by Carter, Copland, Harrison, and others. See items 108, 142, 178, 325, 339, 439, 880, 888, and 905.

169. Gaudet, Michael Ronald. "A study of selected essays and songs of Charles Ives as expressions of progressive idealism." Master's thesis, University of Victoria, 1985.

Places Ives's work within the context of the Progressive reform movement, with emphasis on his writings "Stand by the President and the People" and "The Majority."

170. Geselbracht, Raymond. "Evolution and the New World Vision in the Music of Charles Ives." *Journal of American Studies* 8/2 (1974): 211–27.

Biographical survey with attention to the style of the *114 Songs*. Also discusses reception through the 1950s and 1960s and the growing appreciation of his music.

171. Gingerich, Lora L. "A Technique for Melodic Motivic Analysis in the Music of Charles Ives." *Music Theory Spectrum* 8 (1986): 75–93.

Introduces an analytical system for describing and relating melodic motivic transformation. Gingerich illustrates this system through an analysis of the transformation of five melodic motives in Ives's Fourth Violin Sonata, third movement.

172. Gingerich, Lora L. "Process of Motivic Transformation in the Keyboard and Chamber Music of Charles E. Ives." Ph.D. dissertation, Yale University, 1983.

Detailed analyses of the motivic structure of the Fourth Violin Sonata, the *Three-Page Sonata,* and the First Piano Sonata, movements one, three, and five. Gingerich demonstrates that Ives's alterations of motivic material is sophisticated and thorough.

173. Glarner, Robert Lewis. "An Investigation into the Relationship of Instrumental Density and Dynamics of the Fourth Symphony by Charles Ives." Ph.D. dissertation, University of Arizona, 1993.

Presents a specific analytical method for measuring textures, based on rhythm, instrumental groups, and dynamics, and applies this method to the Fourth Symphony. Glarner summarizes the changing relationship between instrumental groups and "soloistic" instruments through graphs that illustrate both small- and large-scale organizational principles.

174. Goss, Madeleine. "Charles Ives." In *Modern Music-Makers: Contemporary American Composers*. New York: E. P. Dutton, 1952, 14–33. ISBN 0837129575. ML 390.G69.

Substantial biographical account with discussions of early life, education, political views, and reception through the 1940s. Very basic musical discussion covers songs, orchestral works, and chamber works, with Ives's own descriptions of *Concord Sonata*. Concludes with list of works.

175. Green, Judith. "American Ingenuity Appeals to Spano." *Atlanta Journal/Atlanta Constitution*, 13 February 2000, sec. L, 7.

Recounts the near-resignation of Robert Shaw from the Atlanta Symphony Orchestra in 1971 over his decision to program an Ives work in every concert: the board of directors rejected his plan.

176. Grunfeld, Frederic. "Charles Ives: Yankee Rebel." *High Fidelity* 4/9 (November 1954): 34–36, 103, 105, 107–08; reprinted in *American Composer Alliance Bulletin* 4/3 (1955): 2–5.

Standard biography with accounts of a possible encounter with Mahler, the influence of George Ives, interactions with Horatio Parker, and general descriptions of the New England inspirations for Ives's music. Concludes with recommended listening chosen from available recordings.

177. Hall, David. "Charles Ives: An American Original." *HiFi/Stereo Review* 13/3 (September 1964): 42–58.

General biographical study based on Cowell (item 37). The section "Charles Ives—The Essential Recordings" outlines the history of Ives on disc and offers critical opinions on the best recordings. Lavishly illustrated, including rare photos of Ives's study at West Redding.

178. Harrison, Lou. " 'Such Melodies and Clutter': Thoughts Around Ives, 1974." *Parnassus: Poetry In Review* 3/2 (Spring/Summer 1975): 316–317.

Part of the Parnassus collection (item 168). Brief but informative view of Ives's relevance to contemporary "alternate" culture. Harrison identifies Ives as "the Medicine Man of the nation, snake-oil and all," and describes his music, in comparison to Frank Lloyd Wright's architecture, as "Usonian."

179. Harvey, Mark Sumner. "Charles Ives: Prophet of American Civil Religion." *Soundings* 72/2–3 (Summer–Fall 1989): 501–525.

Applies Robert Bellah's theory of civil religion to Ives's life and music, and considers the influence of Transcendentalism. Particular emphasis on his use of quotations to renew traditions and reintegrate community through memory and association. Harvey suggests that the diversity of quotations parallels both the use of source traditions in American civil religion, and the emerging plurality of American society. Based on item 180.

180. Harvey, Mark Sumner. "Charles Ives: Prophet of American Civil Religion." Ph.D. dissertation, Boston University, 1983.

Consideration of the influence of Transcendentalism and civil religion on Ives's life, writings, and music. Suggests that Ives's use of quotations served as a metaphor for the unifying element of civil religion. For a condensed version, see item 179.

181. Helms, Hans G. "Charles Edward Ives. Hommage zum 100. Geburtstag." *Student Musicologists at Minnesota* 6 (1975–76): 95–127.

Two essays on Ives's relationship to the European musical tradition, his influence on later composers including Stockhausen, Cage, and Brown, and his socialist views compared to those of Eisler and Ruskin. The first essay is entitled "Zur physiognomie eines rvolutionären Komponisten und Citoyen [Concerning the physiognomy of a revolutionary composer and citoyen]," the second is "Zur Phänomen der ungleichzeitigkeit kompositorischer Konzeptionen un ihrer technischen Realiserbarkeit! [Concerning the phenomenon of non-simultaneity of compositional conception and the possibility of its realization]."

182. Helms, Hans G. "Der Komponist Charles Ives." *Neue Zeitschrift für Musik* 125/10 (1964): 425–33.

Subtitled "Leben, Werk und Einfluß auf die heutige Generation," this article offers a conventional life and works survey based primarily on Cowell (item 37). Emphasizes George's influence, Ives's insurance activities, experimentation and use of quotations, and his own writings including the *Essays*. Concludes with a discussion of the similarities between Ives's aesthetics, instrumentation, use of spatial organization, proto-serialism, and twelve-tone composition to the music of Cage, Stockhausen, Henry Brant, and Earle Brown.

183. Henahan, Donal. "Maverick Composers Make Their Own Choices." *New York Times*, 14 December 1986, section 2, 25.

Response to an article entitled "Who Owns American Music?" by Andrew

Stiller (*Opus* December 1986), which examines the American compositional fabric as descended from two streams: Ives, the experimenter and out-
sider; and John Knowles Paine, the academician and insider. Henahan
responds by discussing the apparently contradictory placement of Elliot
Carter within both camps.

184. Herchet, Jörg. "Polifonia es tarea." Translated by Rutilo Silva. *Pauta:
Cuadernos de teoria y critica musical* 12/46 (April–June 1993): 62–68.

Translated from the Spanish as "Polyphony is work," this article traces the
use of polyphony, primarily by Bach, Ives, and Messiaen, to create a sense
of space. Not a substantial source, but does include a very brief discussion
of the use of polyphony in *Holidays Symphony* to create spatial relationships.

185. Herrmann, Bernard. "Charles Ives." *Trend* 1/3 (September–November
1932): 99–101. Available online at "The Bernard Herrmann Society:
Charles Ives" [www.uib.no/herrmann/articles/archive/trend/]. Accessed 15
May 2001.

Portrait of Ives as "a fundamental expression of America," specifically New
England. Discusses his modernist techniques in comparison with Milhaud
and others, and briefly describes the *Concord Sonata* and Fourth Symphony.

186. Hitchcock, H. Wiley. "Charles Ives und seine Zeit." In *Amerikanische Musik
seit Charles Ives: Interpretation, Quellentexte, Komponistenmonographien*
(item 38), 21–29.

Outlines Ives's biography and education, and discusses influences from and
contributions to the contemporary "cultivated" and "vernacular" traditions.
Also catalogues the use of experimental procedures including collages,
polytonality, polyrhythms, and microtones.

187. Hitchcock, H. Wiley, and Vivian Perlis, eds. "Appendix 1: Essays by Foreign Participants." In *An Ives Celebration: Papers and Panels of the Charles
Ives Centennial Festival-Conference* (item 50), 227–56.

The basis for the panel discussion (item 90) includes essays by Louis
Andriessen, Guido Baggiani, John Beckwith, J. Bernlef, Martine Cadieu,
Austin Clarkson, Peter Dickinson, Hans G. Helms, Alfred Hoffman, Yannis
Ioannidis, Betsy Jolas, Karl Aage Rasmussen, Andrej Rijavec, and Ilhan
Usmanbas. Topics range from Ives's influence on individual composers to
the introduction and reception of his music in England, Canada, and

throughout Eastern and Western Europe. Includes a poetic tribute to Ives by Bernlef entitled "Wild Gardening" (pp. 233–38).

188. Hitchcock, H. Wiley, and Vivian Perlis, eds. "Five Composers' Views." In *An Ives Celebration: Papers and Panels of the Charles Ives Centennial Festival-Conference* (item 50), 187–208.

Transcription of a multimedia presentation of textual, musical, and visual tributes to Ives by Roger Reynolds, Charles Dodge, Lou Harrison, Salvatore Martirano, and Gordon Mumma. With reactions and discussion between the participants.

189. Holland, Bernard. "How Ives Used Faulty Memory to Good Effect." *New York Times*, 29 September 1996.

Examines the role of memory in Ives's works, from the realistic representations of marching bands to the distortions of nostalgia, loss, and death. Includes brief comparisons with Virgil Thomson and Mahler.

190. Holloway, Robin. " 'Use Your Ears like a Man.' " *Spectator* 276/8740 (20 January 1996): 42.

Discusses the choice of Ives for the BBC annual retrospective, and profiles the reception of his music after the 1920s.

191. Hommel, Friedrich. "Andere funfziger Jahre? Familienbild mit Ives, Cowell, Varèse und Cage." In *Die Musik der funfziger Jahre*, edited by Carl Dahlhaus. Veroffentlichungen des Instituts fur Neue Musik und Musikerziehung Darmstadt, Vol. 26. Mainz: Schott, 1985, 39–47.

Translated as "Another 1950s? Family Portrait with Ives, Cowell, Varèse, and Cage," this essays traces interactions between the four composers, and outlines the reception of their music at the Darmstadt Ferienkurse für neue Musik in the 1950s.

192. Houtchens, Alan and Janis P. Stout. "Intertextuality and Meaning in Charles Ives's *In Flanders Fields*." In *The Maynooth International Musicological Conference 1995, Selected Proceedings: Part Two*. Irish Musical Studies, Vol. 5. Dublin: Four Courts, 1996, 356–63. ISBN 1851822615. ML 287 .M39 1996 pt. 2.

Investigates the historical and political resonance of both the original poem and Ives's setting of it, particularly the third stanza. Analyses of text, melodic line, use of quotations and form, plus consideration of Ives's statements, suggest that Ives was conflicted about America's entry into the war, and that his apprehension and ambivalence are reflected in the song.

193. Howard, John Tasker, and Arthur Mendel. *Our Contemporary Composers: American Music in the 20th Century*. New York: Thomas Y. Crowell, 1941, 243–47.

Significant early summary of life and works emphasizing Ives's father's influence, his early education, experimentation, precedence over Schoenberg, Stravinsky, and Strauss, and isolation. Briefly describes "Washington's Birthday" and the *Concord Sonata*, with an excerpt from Gilman's review of Kirkpatrick's January 1939 Town Hall performance (see item 36, 316–21).

194. Hutchinson, Mary Ann. "Unrelated Simultaneity as an Historical Index to the Music of Charles Ives." Master's dissertation, Florida State University, 1970.

Discusses the employment of multiple, disconnected layers in Ives's music and historical precedents from the medieval period to the early twentieth century. Also compares Ives's music with Schoenberg and Stravinsky, and discusses the relationship of all three to relativity and indeterminacy.

195. Hutton, Edna Rait. "The Legacy of Charles Ives." *Pan Pipes* 55/2 (January 1963): 13–14, 30.

General source with a list of published works organized by performing forces, as well as reprinted comments by Cowell, Downes, Gilman, and Slonimsky.

196. Hutton, Edna Rait. "Years Add Luster to Ives Legacy." *Pan Pipes* 57/3 (March 1965): 35.

Briefly discusses increasing interest in Ives, particularly in the decade since his death. Also cites recent recordings and publications, as well as a series of radio programs on Ives broadcast in New York over WBAI by Paul Dwinell.

197. Isham, Howard. "The Musical Thinking of Charles Ives." *Journal of Aesthetics and Art Criticism* 31/3 (Spring 1973): 395–404.

Following a general biographical summary, Isham examines Ives's ideas about music in relationship to human experiences, and succinctly compares these views to those of Mahler, Stravinsky, Schoenberg, and Boulez. Includes brief discussions of the philosophical and musical significance of

Transcendentalism, substance, and manner, experimental processes and quotation in Ives's works.

198. Ivaskin, Aleksandr. "Das Paradoxon des Traditionellen in der Musik von Charles Ives." *Kunst und Literatur* 35/6 (1987): 822–31.

   Translates as "The paradox of the traditional in the music of Charles Ives," considers the use of traditional musics in Ives, often alongside the innovative techniques for which he is better known. Concludes that Ives is "at once the first representative of 20th-c. music and a classic figure who brought together everything new in his music with the traditions of 19th-c. American culture."

199. "Ives Revived." *Newsweek* 62 (14 October 1963): 65.

   Reports on New York performances of *Robert Browning Overture* and *Concord Sonata*. Also mentions the growing popularity of performances and recordings of Ives, as well as positive audience reactions to the music.

200. Johnson, Russell I. "A View of 20th-Century Expression." *Journal of Aesthetics and Art Criticism* 28/3 (Spring 1970): 361–68.

   Considers Ives's blending and juxtaposition of disparate materials (including program and absolute music), as well as polyharmony and polyrhythm as typical of twentieth-century expressive devices. Discusses the use of quotations that "aid in merging past and present."

201. Kämper, Dietrich. "Wandlungen des Ives-Bildes." In *Amerikanische Musik seit Charles Ives: Interpretation, Quellentexte, Komponistenmonographien* (item 38), 3–14.

   Translated as "Changes in the Ives Image," this article summarizes Ives scholarship through the mid 1980s, including the impact of the Centennial publications and cultural studies such as Perry (item 63) and Rossiter (item 67). Also briefly reconsiders Ives's relationship to European music.

202. Khittl, Christoph. " 'Jenseits im Diesseits': Ubungen zur Rezeptionsasthetik und Rezeptionsdidaktik." *Polyaisthesis* 3 (1995): 98–106.

   Translated as " 'The beyond in this world': Exercises in reception aesthetics and reception didactics," this article refers to both Heimito von Doderer's concept of "a psychic condition comparable to the state described in religious writings as being touched by God," and Robert Musil's psychology of mystical experience outside of religion. Khittl uses these theories, as well as listening exercises, to suggest that aesthetic responses to works such as *The Unanswered Question* can lead to "the beyond in this world."

203. Kirkpatrick, John. "Ives as Prophet." In *South Florida's Historic Festival* (item 858), 61–63.

Discusses Ives's innovative uses of polytonality, polyrhythm, polytexture, and quotation. Considers his advances in insurance and the extraordinary conception of the *Universe Symphony*.

204. Klemm, Eberhardt. "Musikalischer Neuerer und Demokrat: Der Komponist Charles Ives." *Musik und Gesellschaft* 27/12 (1977): 731–35.

Reviews Ives's life and the delayed reception of his works, and speculates on Mahler's endorsement of his work. Also describes the structured experimentation of his works as part of an "American pioneering spirit."

205. Koch, Gerhard R. "Charles Ives. Musik als reale Utopie." *HiFi-Stereophonie* 12/7 (July 1973): 689–98.

Translated as "Charles Ives: Music as Realistic Utopia," this article examines the place of Utopian ideals in Ives's writings and music, through comparisons with Mahler and Cage, as well as: descriptions of his anticipations of avantgarde techniques; the "organized chaos" of his quotation-based collages; the relationship between music, economics and politics; and the Transcendentalist ideals of *Concord Sonata*. Concludes with an overview of Ives's influence on other composers including Cage, Berio, Lutoslawski, and Ligeti. Includes German translations of excerpts from *Essays Before a Sonata*, as well as a rarely published photograph of Ives with his business partner Julian Myrick.

206. Kolodin, Irving. " 'Are My Ears on Wrong?' " *Vogue* (1967): 6–7, 23, 25, from the Ives archives.

Profile with photographs. Overview of significant events from 1924 to 1966 traces significant performances and recordings. Reprint of program notes for the New York Philharmonic (see Block, item 109).

207. Kolter, Horst. "Zur Kompositionstechnik von Charles Edward Ives." *Neue Zeitschrift für Musik* 133/10 (1972): 559–67.

Discusses Ives's use of ostinati to integrate heterogeneous musical elements in the orchestral works, as demonstrated in the Fourth Symphony, second movement, and the *Robert Browning Overture*. Includes a cursory comparison to ostinato structures in the works of Schoenberg, Webern, and Stravinsky, and a consideration of the ostinati technique as applied to quotations.

208. Konold, Wulf. "Neue Music in der Neuen Welt: Der Komponist Charles Ives." *Musica* 26/3 (May–June 1972): 239–44.

Concise life and works summary based on Cowell (item 37) and Ives's own writings. Focuses on experimental techniques, use of quotation, the influence of Transcendentalist philosophy on the *Concord Sonata*, and the significance of "Utopian" imagery in works such as *Universe Symphony*.

209. Kozinn, Allan. "Chinese-Born Composer Wins $225,000 Ives Prize." *New York Times*, 21 December 2000, section E, 11.

Announces the awarding of the second Charles Ives Living to the composer Annou Chen Yi. Includes a description of the establishment of the prize from Ives's royalties by Harmony Ives, its terms and conditions, and the procedures and rationale in its selection.

210. Kozinn, Allan. "Composer Wins Freedom, but It's Temporary." *New York Times*, 15 January 1998.

Report on the first Charles Ives Living award to Martin Bresnick, with a summary of the background and purpose of the award: to "do what Ives could not: give up the day job and concentrate fully on composition." Outlines the history of other awards from the composer's bequest. Includes Bresnick's comments on the influence of Ives's music and writings.

211. Kramer, Lawrence. "Powers of Blackness: Africanist Discourse in Modern Concert Music." *Black Music Research Journal* 16/1 (Spring 1996): 53–70.

Includes an evaluation of Ives's uses of ragtime and Stephen Foster songs in the First Piano Sonata and Second Orchestral Set respectively. Kramer suggests that both works invoke "racialized fantasies" in light of their utilization of "musical Africanisms" through quotational context and structural procedures.

212. Kramer, Lawrence. "Cultural Politics and Musical Form: The Case of Charles Ives." In *Classical Music and Postmodern Knowledge*. Berkeley: University of California Press, 1995, 174–200. ISBN 0520088204. ML 3845 .K813 1995.

Relocates Ives's music within the social fabric of late nineteenth-century America. Kramer suggests that the nonhierarchical structure of the Second String Quartet evokes American democratic social space, while his quotational collages, extensive misogynist writings and, use of domination as an aesthetic component champion privileging by race and gender.

213. Kuhn, Clemens. "Charles Ives: eine Bestandsaufnahme." *Musik und Bildung* 8/2 (February 1976): 61–67.

Survey of Ives's modernist techniques including polytonality, polyrhythms, polymeters, dissonant counterpoint, collage form, quotations, and quarter-tone music. Includes a brief overview of the influence of Ives's quotation- and collage-based works on later composers including Berio and Stockhausen.

214. Lambert, Philip. "Toward a Theory of Chord Structure for the Music of Ives." *Journal of Music Theory* 37/1 (Spring 1993): 55–83.

Lambert outlines an analytic framework for identifying and understanding Ives's unique harmonic vocabulary based on juxtaposed, or "stacked" triads, and chromatically embellished triads, plus their extensions and variations as understood through cyclic analysis. After applying his analytic perspective to several experimental works, Lambert concludes that the future application of "cyclic modeling principles" to Ives's works is promising.

215. Lambert, J. Philip. "Ives and Counterpoint." *American Music* 9/2 (Summer 1991): 119–48.

Complete study of Ives's use of counterpoint throughout his career, including a summary of his early education, and his employment of canons and fugues in some of his most progressive works. Includes numerous musical excerpts and diagrammatic summaries.

216. Lambert, J. Philip. "Interval Cycles as Compositional Resources in the Music of Charles Ives." *Music Theory Spectrum* 12 (1990): 43–82.

Explores Ives's use of interval cycles (or repetitive intervallic structures) in creating a coherent, nondiatonic musical language. Lambert identifies and examines numerous experimental compositions, which include cycles consisting of single interval repetitions (e.g., chromatic or whole-tone scales), and two alternating intervals in combination cycles. Analysis of and excerpts from, among others, *In re con moto et al*, "The Fourth of July," "On the Antipodes," and *Universe Symphony*.

217. Lambert, J. Philip. "Aggregate Structures in Music of Charles Ives." *Journal of Music Theory* 34/1 (Spring 1990): 29–55.

Thorough discussion of Ives's exploration of aggregate structures in his experimental music, with insightful contrasts to Schoenberg's twelve-tone system. Lambert classifies and catalogs various types of aggregate orderings, and identifies their utilization as thematic and formal features. Concludes with a further response to Solomon (item 404) regarding the chronological placement of works using aggregate structures, including *Chromâtimelôdtune.*

218. Lambert, J. Philip. "Ives's 'Piano-Drum' Chords." *Integral* 3 (1989): 1–36.

Dense study of Ives's use of "piano-drum chords," or piano-based structures that simulate drum sounds, in both early and later works. Lambert concludes that Ives used specific pitch-class collections that, while an extension of or counter to standard diatonic usages, nonetheless create logical and coherent structures of increasing subtlety and sophistication.

219. Lambert, J. Philip. "Compositional Procedures in Experimental Works of Charles E. Ives." Ph.D. dissertation, University of Rochester, 1987.

Comprehensive study of Ives's experimental works using a plethora of analytic techniques and numerous excerpts, reductions, charts, and tables. Some topics include contrapuntal techniques, interval cycles, structural models, and pitch-class aggregates. Expanded and revised in item 54.

220. Larson, Gary O. "Charles Ives and American Studies." *Student Musicologists at Minnesota* 6 (1975–76): 237–49.

Compares and contrasts the biographies and philosophies of Ives and Henry Adams. Although fundamentally different in their views of the past, both figures rejected the primary schools of thought of their time and embraced a specifically American multiplicity.

221. Lederman, Minna. *The Life and Death of a Small Magazine (Modern Music, 1924–46)*. I.S.A.M. Monographs, No. 18. Brooklyn: Institute for Studies in American Music, 1983. ISBN 0914678205. ML 200.5 .L4 1983.

Extraordinary book by the editor of the journal *Modern Music* that carried several early notices of Ives's music. Reprints several articles in their entirety or in excerpts including items 23, 270, and 380. Also includes details of Lederman's interactions with Ives and Harmony, and includes a letter from Harmony on Ives's behalf of 27 November 1945 discussing financial support for the magazine.

222. Levine, Lawrence W. *Highbrow/Lowbrow: The Emergence of Cultural Hierarchy in America*. Cambridge, MA: Harvard University Press, 1988, 141, 143 and passim. ISBN 0674390768. E 169.1 L536 1988.

Levine discusses Ives's attitudes toward "highbrow" and "lowbrow" music within the larger context of American culture in the late 19th century. Mentions the influence of George Ives as well as the Second and Fourth Symphonies.

223. Lieberson, Goddard. "An American Innovator, Charles Ives." *Musical America* 59/3 (10 February 1939): 22, 322–23; reprinted in *Charles Ives and His World* (item 36), 377–89.

Biographical summary and general style description focuses on experimentation (particularly polytonality), training with Parker, and intervallic structure in songs with excerpts from "Resolution," "Soliloquy," and "Down East." Concludes with a general description of *Concord Sonata* and orchestral works.

224. "*Life* Congratulates . . . Charles E. Ives." *Life* 27/18 (31 October 1949).

Included among other notable achievers, Ives, who had just celebrated his 75th birthday, is identified as possibly "America's greatest composer." Includes a photograph by *Life* photographer W. Eugene Smith (reprinted in item 62). The caption summarizes Ives's "double life" and mentions the Pulitzer and his delayed recognition.

225. Lindley, Nancy Eagle. "Singer Radiana Pazmor and American Music: The Performer as Advocate." Ph.D. dissertation, University of Maryland, College Park, 1993.

Study of singer Radiana Pazmor (1892–1986), who was an early performer of Ives's songs as well as works by other modernists.

226. "Local Boy Makes Polyrhythms." *Village Voice* 38/34 (24 August 1993): 85.

Describes the Ives Museum in Danbury and gives background on Ives's family history and childhood.

227. Low, Ruth. "Ives Not Appreciated Until End of His Life." *Danbury News-Times*, 15 April 1961, 1.

Biographical profile recounts the steady growth of interest since 1947, despite years of isolation and neglect.

228. Low, Ruth. "Danbury Boyhood Marks Music of Charles Ives." *Danbury News-Times*, 14 April 1961, 8.

Recounts Ives's childhood in Danbury with a thorough profile of George's activities and their memorialization in Ives's later music.

229. Lück, Hartmut. "Provokation und Utopie: ein Porträt des amerikanischen Komponisten Charles Edward Ives." *Neuland* 1 (1980): 3–15.

Considers Ives's political and social beliefs as revealed through his writings and compositions. Includes a discussion of Transcendentalism, specifically Thoreau's political beliefs, and their influence on Ives's *Essays* and the *Concord Sonata*. Concludes with a select annotated discography of German and American recordings.

230. Mauceri, John, moderator. "Conductors' Experiences." Panel discussion transcript in *An Ives Celebration: Papers and Panels of the Charles Ives Centennial Festival-Conference* (item 50), 113–26.

Panel discussion between Mauceri, Nicolas Slonimsky, Lehman Engel, Gregg Smith, Gunther Schuller, Arthur Weisberg, and James Sinclair. Considerable discussion on the topic of conducting Ives's rhythms, as well as his idiosyncratic notation and changing audience reactions to the music.

231. McClure, John. "Charles Ives—Lonely American Giant." *Gramophone* 44/527 (April 1967): 516–17.

Discussion of Ives's isolation, emphasizing his independent experimentation and precedence over Stravinsky and Schoenberg. Also recounts the delayed process of publishing, performing, and recording his music.

232. Mead, Rita H. "The amazing Mr. Cowell." *American Music* 1/4 (Winter 1983): 63–89.

Account of Cowell's efforts to publish and perform Ives's and others' music, mostly through the *New Music* publications and concert series. Some overlap with items 233–35 but noteworthy for excerpts from an original interview with Herman Langinger, the engraver of the *New Music* edition of the second movement of Ives's Fourth Symphony.

233. Mead, Rita H. "Henry Cowell's New Music Society." *Journal of Musicology* 1/4 (October 1982): 449–63.

Detailed account of the founding, financing, and end of this organization that performed new music between 1925 and 1936, including several works by Ives. Most valuable is a listing of the works performed and their dates, in addition to personal recollections of other performers and composers involved with the concerts. See also items 232, 234, 235.

234. Mead, Rita H. *Henry Cowell's "New Music," 1925–36: The Society, the Music Editions and the Recordings.* Studies in Musicology No. 40. Ann Arbor: UMI Research Press, 1981. ISBN 0835711706. ML 200.5 .M35 1981.

Revised version of Mead's 1978 Ph.D. dissertation (City University of New York), the most extensive account of Ives's relationship with Cowell, his financial support of *New Music* projects, and the publications, performances, and recordings of his works. Ample excerpts from the correspondence between Cowell and Ives, as well as details of engraving, distribution, and proceeds from publications, and reviews of performances in the United States and Europe. Excellent source for primary materials on Cowell.

235. Mead, Rita H. "Cowell, Ives, and *New Music*." *Musical Quarterly* 66/4 (October 1980): 538–59.

Derived from item 234, this article traces the relationship between Henry Cowell and Ives, particularly the active financial role Ives played from the late 1920s until his death in the production of the *New Music* published scores and recordings, as well as Cowell's other projects. Documents Ives's attitudes about this patronage, which was considerable. Extensive quotations from their correspondence as well as *New Music* sources. See also items 232, 233.

236. Mellers, Wilfrid. "American Music (An English Perspective)." *Kenyon Review* 5/3 (Summer 1943): 357–75.

Includes a discussion of Ives with comparisons to Whitman and Van Dyke, as well as a consideration of the impact of composing in isolation. Mellers concludes that, in his combination of European traditions with American vernacular substance, Ives was "the distinctive musical voice of America."

237. Metzer, David. " 'We boys': Childhood in the Music of Charles Ives." *19th Century Music* 21/1 (Summer 1997): 77–95.

Investigation of Ives's representations of childhood through quotations, song texts, programs, and form. Metzer links Ives's nostalgia for, and musical recreations of his childhood with, American cultural traditions from the mid nineteenth century through to the 1920s. Includes analyses of "Tom Sails Away" and the Fourth Violin Sonata.

238. Milligan, Terry G. "Charles Ives: Musical Activity at Poverty Flat (1898–1908)." *Journal of Band Research* 20/1 (Fall 1984): 30–36.

Primarily a biographical survey of Ives's musical, professional, and social life until his marriage. Discusses the influence on his compositions of his living arrangements at Poverty Flat and his organist position at Central Presbyterian Church.

239. Milligan, Terry G. "Charles Ives: Musical Activity at Yale." *Journal of Band Research* 19/2 (Spring 1984): 39–50.

Somewhat limited overview of Ives's compositional activity at Yale, with mentions of his music for Center Church, compositional exercises for Parker's classes, and music for fraternity shows and the Hyperion Theater.

240. Moor, Paul. "On Horseback to Heaven: Charles Ives." *Harper's Magazine* 197 (September 1948): 65–73; reprinted in *Charles Ives and His World* (item 36), 408–22.

Substantive survey (with errors) includes details on: Ives's childhood and education; the importance of his father and later wife on his experimental music; and Ives's insurance career, including the influence of Emerson and Thoreau on the pamphlet "The Amount to Carry." Extensive commentary on the reception of the music and Ives's life in the late 1940s.

241. Moore, MacDonald Smith. "Yankee Blues: Musical Culture and American Identity." Ph.D. dissertation, New York University, 1980. Revised as idem, *Yankee Blues: Musical Culture and American Identity.* Bloomington: Indiana University Press, 1985. ISBN 0253368030. ML 200 .M75 1985.

Cultural study comparing Daniel Gregory Mason, Ives, George Gershwin, and Aaron Copland as representatives of opposing ideological camps through the 1920s. Moore asserts that Mason and Ives espoused the primacy of "Yankee" musical thought by drawing on culturally defined ideals of race and gender, and in contrast to contemporary images of jazz.

242. Morgan, Robert P. "Spatial Form in Ives." In *An Ives Celebration: Papers and Panels of the Charles Ives Centennial Festival-Conference* (item 50), 145–158.

Influential article that examines Ives's manipulation of musical space through various techniques including physical placement of performing forces, circular form, fragmentation, serial processes, registral organization, and simulataneity.

243. Moross, Jerome. "Some Thoughts On Ives." In *South Florida's Historic Ives Festival* (item 858), 38.

Reflects on Moross's discovery of Ives's music through the *Concord Sonata* and *114 Songs*; its impact on his own compositions; and the need to discover the music of Ives's contemporaries.

244. Mortenson, Gary C. "Father to Son: The Education of Charles Ives." *Music Educator's Journal* 73/7 (March 1987): 33–37.

Recounts George's musical activities in Danbury, including his experiments, and their impact on his son through his Yale education and later career. Concludes that George prepared his son "to combat the established musical tastes prevalent at this time."

245. Mumelter, Martin. "Zu den Violinsonaten von Charles Ives." *Österreichische Musikzeitschrift* 48/3–4 (March–April 1993): 147–151.

General description of Ives's use of quotations, bi- and polytonality, polyrhythms, and other experimental devices, as well as the influence of Transcendentalism on his music. Concludes with an overview of the four violin sonatas, described individually according to style and quotations.

246. "Musical Whitman." *Newsweek* 43 (31 May 1954): 78.

Obituary with comparisons to Mark Twain and Whitman, a recount of the Pulitzer award, and the statement that Ives "never enjoyed the recognition should have been his." Also mentions his insurance career.

247. Nicholls, David. "Unanswerable Questions/Questionable Answers." *Music and Letters* 75/2 (May 1994): 246–252.

Reviews current issues in Ives scholarship including chronology, editing practices, and the reception of his music.

248. Nicholls, David. "*In Re Con Moto Et Al*: Experimentalism in the Works of Charles Ives (1874–1954)." In *American Experimental Music, 1890–1940*. Cambridge: Cambridge University Press, 1990, 5–88. ISBN 0521345782. ML 200.5 .N55 1990.

Expansive survey of Ives's stylistic diversity and eclecticism through analyses of several choral and chamber works, including (among others) *From the Steeples and the Mountains*, *Trio*, *Three-Page Sonata*, *Set for Theatre or Chamber Orchestra*, *The Unanswered Question*, *Central Park in the Dark*, *Tone Roads No. 3*, *In Re Con Moto Et Al.*, and *Psalm 90*. Nicholls focuses on several aspects of Ives's experimental writing, including bi- and polytonality, musical layering, diatonic and non-diatonic interval structures, ostinati, and polyrhythms, to structure the best known progressive works as well as their utilization in later, less exclusively experimental compositions. Extensively illustrated with both musical examples and diagrammatic summaries.

249. Norris, Christopher. "American Pioneer." *Music and Musicians* 23/2 (October 1974): 36–40.

     General survey of Ives's musical style and output, with consideration of the challenges to the performer, reception of his music, use of quotations, programmatic considerations, and philosophy of music as represented in the *Essays*.

250. O'Reilly, F. Warren. "Charles Ives: American Patriot, Prophetic Genius, Modern Non-Conformist." In *South Florida's Historic Festival* (item 858), 47–49.

     Biographical survey emphasizes Ives's dual lives: between sports and music in childhood, between business and music in adulthood. Briefly comments on reception in the 1930s and 1940s. Originally published as "Charles Ives: All-American." *Clavier* 13/7 (1974): 10–11.

251. Orrey, Leslie. *Programme Music: A Brief Survey from the Sixteenth Century to the Present Day.* London: Davis-Poynter, 1975.

     Although concise, Orrey's discussion of Ives places his use of programs within an historical context. Also considers the issue of "substance" and "manner," as well as the meaning of Ives's quotation and whether a listener needs to recognize and know the history of his sources.

252. Owens, Thomas Clarke. "Charles Ives and His American Context: Images of 'Americanness' in the Arts." Ph.D. dissertation, Yale University, 1999.

     Eloquent and substantial investigation of the changing meaning of "Americanness" throughout Ives's career, stretching from the ideals of American identity as constructed at Yale, to the role played by nationality in the critical reception of Ives's music. Also contextualizes Ives's use of characterization (Aunt Sarah, Rollo, etc.), and compares "Americanist" biographies of Ives and Albert Pinkham Ryder.

253. Pearsall, Ronald. "Ives in Performance." *Music Review* 47/1 (1986–87): 24–28.

     Brief outline of early performances and reviews, especially Slonimsky's 1931 Paris concerts and Philip Hale's review in the *Boston Herald* (excerpt reprinted in *Memos*, item 20, pages 13–14). Pearsall traces the impact of this and other negative published opinions on Ives's later writings, including his dismissal of Sibelius and Wagner.

254. Perkins, Francis D. "Letters: In Defense of Critics." *Harpers* 197 (December 1948): 14.

Letter to the editor in response to item 240. Perkins argues that the inaccessibility of Ives's music in performance and publication has contributed to its "neglect" by critics, and suggests that musicologists might be better equipped to find and promote significant works.

255. Perlis, Vivian. "Charles Ives: Victorian Gentleman or American Folk Hero?" In *Folk Music and Modern Sound*, edited by William Ferris and Mary L. Hart. Center for the Study of Southern Culture Series. Jackson: University Press of Mississippi, 1982, 141–50. ISBN 0878051570. ML 3545 .F63 1982.

Study of the paradox between Ives's Victorian mores and personal behavior, and his modernist musical aesthetics and political views.

256. Perlis, Vivian. "'*Monumenta Americana*' Revisited." In *A Celebration of American Music: Words and Music in Honor of H. Wiley Hitchcock*, edited by Richard Crawford, R. Allen Lott, and Carol J. Oja. Ann Arbor: University of Michigan Press, 1990, 439–48.

Describes the methodology of oral history, illustrated by excerpts from interviews with Ives's family and friends as first published in item 62.

257. Perlis, Vivian. "Ives and Oral History." *Notes* 28/4 (June 1972): 629–42.

Condensed summary of interviews with Ives's family and friends, later published in item 62, including background information on the process and methodology of oral history.

258. Plinkiewisch, Helen E. "A Contribution to the Understanding of the Music of Charles Ives, Roy Harris, and Aaron Copland." Ed.D. dissertation, Columbia University, 1956.

Early work, this education dissertation focuses primarily on teaching selections from these three composers. For Ives, includes techniques for teaching the *Three Harvest Home Chorales, Psalm 67, Symphony No. 3, Concord Sonata, Serenity, Ann Street, Two Little Flowers,* and *Evening*.

259. Porter, Ellen Jane Lorenz. "A Treasure of Camp-Meeting Spirituals." Ph.D. dissertation, Union Graduate School, Cincinnati, Ohio, 1978.

Helpful survey of the background of camp-meeting and revival music through the nineteenth-century includes a cursory discussion of Ives's quotations from this repertoire in works such as the Fourth Symphony.

260. Putz, Werner, Peter Virnich, and Peter Winz-Luckei. "Neue Musik handelnd erfahren: Eine Unterrichtsreihe zu Charles Ives und John Cage." *Musik und Bildung* 19/5 (1987): 350–58.

Translates as "Action-Oriented Experiences with New Music: A Lesson Sequence Using Charles Ives and John Cage." Recounts two approaches to teaching the music of Ives and Cage, one using "active understanding" and the other using Gestalt principles.

261. Rahmanova, Marina. "Charles Ives." *Sovetskaja muzyka* 6 (June 1971): 97–108.

Russian outline of Ives's life and work with emphasis on the *Concord Sonata* and the *Essays*. Discusses the influence of Transcendentalism and compares his music with the poetry of Walt Whitman. This entry listed in Block (item 1, B144) as Rakhmamova, M. "Charl'z Ayvs." *Sovetskaya Muzyka* 35 (June 1971): 97–108.

262. Rathert, Wolfgang. "The idea of potentiality in the music of Charles Ives." In *Ives Studies* (item 55), 105–32.

Relates Ives's uses of musical borrowing, fragmentation, autobiographical programs, open form, and formal interchangeability to the philosophical concept of potentiality, which "is grounded in the act of transcending the constitutive, formal and content-related boundaries of art."

263. Rectanus, Hans. "Wechsel der Unterrichtsformen unter Einbeziehung verschiedener Medien als didaktische Notwendigkeit im Musikunterricht." In *Medieninvasion: die Kulturpolitische Verantwortung der Musikerziehung.* Mainz: Schott, 1985, 101–11. ISBN 3795726492. MT 1 .B95 M4.

Title translates as "Changing Forms of Instruction through Changing Media, a Didactic Necessity in Music Education." Investigates the use of media in middle and secondary schools, and illustrates the educational applications of media through a videotaped session in which *The Unanswered Question* is taught.

264. Rich, Alan. *American Pioneers: Ives to Cage and Beyond.* 20th-Century Composers. London: Phaidon, 1995. ISBN 0714831735. ML 390 .R42 1995y.

General overview of life and works with many distortions and inaccuracies, and lacking citations. Extreme emphasis on experimental procedures.

265. Riedel, Johannes. "The Ives Liturgy: A Mass of the Common Man." *Student Musicologists at Minnesota* 6 (1975–76): 225–36.

Argues that Ives's beliefs are reflected in both his religious and secular works, and that the diverse styles of his compositions convey a realistic image of American life. Concludes with a compilation of writings and music in the form of a Lutheran liturgy.

266. Rinehart, John McLain. "Ives' Compositional Idioms: An Investigation of Selected Short Compositions as Microcosms of his Musical Language." Ph.D. dissertation, Ohio State University, 1970.

Suggests that Ives used short chamber pieces and songs as a means of exploring experimental techniques such as pitch and nonpitch serialism (dynamics, duration and rhythm); combinatoriality; borrowing; spatial relationships; and aleatoric procedures.

267. Ringer, Alexander L. "Amerikanische Musik im Zeitalter des Jazz." In *Bericht über das Internationale Symposion 'Charles Ives und die amerikanische Musiktradition bis zur Gegenwart' Köln 1988*, ed. Klaus Wolfgang Niemöller. Kölner Beiträge zur Musikforschung No. 164. Regensburg: Gustav Bosse Verlag, 1990, 73–87. ISBN 3764924063. ML 200.5 .I58 1990.

Along with Piston, Harris, and others, considers Ives's use of stylistic diversity within the sociopolitical context of the 1920s and 1930s.

268. Rogan, William J. "Vorkämpfer einer neuen Schule? Charles Ives zum vierzigsten Todestag." *Das Orchester* 42/11 (November 1994): 2–5.

Translated as "Pioneer of a New School? For the 40th Anniversary of the Death of Charles Ives," this article generally summarizes Ives's biography, the influence of Transcendentalism, his use of quotation, and the reception of his works and their challenges to the editor and performer.

269. Root, Deane L. "The Pan American Association of Composers (1928–1934)." *Anuario interamericano de investigacion musical/Yearbook for Inter-American Musical Research/Anuario interamerican de pesquisa musical* 8 (1972): 49–70.

Profiles the history and activities of the association that premiered, performed, and recorded several Ives works. Includes excerpts from Ives's correspondence with Slonimsky, plus valuable reviews of the concerts, programs and notes, and a rare list of programs broadcast by radio station WEVD, New York.

270. Rosenfeld, Paul. "A Plea for Improvisation." *Modern Music* 19/1 (November–December 1941): 10–15.

Consideration of the role of improvisation in music both historically and in contemporary music, including a brief endorsement of the improvisatory nature of Ives's use of alternative versions and performer choice.

271. Rosenfeld, Paul. "The Advance of American Music." *Kenyon Review* 1 (Spring 1939): 185–193.

Sequel to item 272. Outlines the challenge of promoting new American music with brief mention of the performance of parts of Ives's Fourth Symphony and the condition of his manuscripts.

272. Rosenfeld, Paul. "The Advent of American Music." *Kenyon Review* 1 (Winter 1939): 46–53.

Part of the article describes *Three Places in New England* and *Concord Sonata* with emphasis on experimentation, precedence over European contemporaries, and the influence of Transcendentalism. Rosenfeld also quotes William Carlos Williams on Ives's neglect. See also item 271.

273. Rosenfeld, Paul. "Ives." In *Discoveries of a Music Critic*. New York: Harcourt, Brace, 1936, 315–24; reprint, New York: Vienna House, 1972.

Informed early essay summarizes Ives's use of quotations and stylistic juxtaposition, and harmonic and rhythmic experimentation. Particular emphasis on Ives as "a nationalistic American composer" through his unique forms of expression. Also considers the influence of Transcendentalism on *Concord Sonata* and the significance of the *114 Songs*.

274. Rosenfeld, Paul. "Charles E. Ives, Pioneer Atonalist." *New Republic* 71 (20 July 1932): 262–64; reprinted in *Charles Ives and His World* (item 36), 363–67.

Review of the 1932 premiere of *Set for Theatre Orchestra* as well as several other orchestral works and songs, emphasizing both their atonal language (compared to Mahler and Schoenberg), polytonality, and use of quotations for extramusical purposes.

275. Rossiter, Frank. "Charles Ives: Good American an Isolated Artist." In *An Ives Celebration: Papers and Panels of the Charles Ives Centennial Festival-Conference* (item 50), 16–28.

Traces the impact of conventional American culture—particularly his Yale education—on Ives's career and self-imposed artistic isolation. Includes a discussion of Ives's political views as a rebellion against Yale values, and the relationship between gender and musical experimentation.

276. Rossiter, Frank. "Charles Ives and American Culture: The Process of Development, 1874–1921." Ph.D. dissertation, Princeton University, 1970.

Rossiter examines Ives as a product of his culture, with particular emphasis on the significance of Ives's isolation in light of dominant social values of the time. Although superceded by item 67, this source includes valuable insights on Ives's life until 1921. For a review by Robert Crunden, see *Yearbook for Inter-American Musical Research* 8 (1972): 181–84.

277. Rothstein, Edward. "Ives Country." *New York Times*, 22 August 1980, section C, 8.

Reports on the opening, purposes, background, and creation of the Charles Ives Center at Canterbury School, CT. Includes comments from Carter on Ives's isolation and compares their works.

278. Sakae, Yoneda. "Charles Ives no ongakukozo ni okeru de-composition." *Ongakugaku* 34/2 (1988): 97–111.

Examines Ives's use of fragments, avoidance of traditional structures, and creation of a unified work through tempo and dynamics. Title translates from the Japanese as "De-Composition in the Structure of Charles Ives's Music."

279. Salzman, Eric. "Charles Ives, American." *Commentary* 46/2 (August 1968): 37–43.

Astute reevaluation of Ives's ideas, compositional style, image, and overall significance. Salzman discusses Ives's relationship to conventional musical traditions, and challenges the myth of the "inspired primitive" and "isolated eccentric individualist."

280. Schafer, William J. "Introducing Charles Ives: A Multi-Media Experience." *Student Musicologists at Minnesota* 6 (1975–76): 5–15.

Description of the interdisciplinary multimedia program "Ives Lives" as presented at Berea College, Kentucky. With commentary on program's pedagogical value.

281. Schoffman, Nachum. "Serialism in the Works of Charles Ives." *Tempo* 138 (October 1981): 21–32.

Studies Ives's use of serial processes through his use of twelve-tone rows, chord series, duration series, tempo and dynamic series, and simultaneous series. Includes discussions of and excerpts from *Tone Roads No. 1*, "On the

Antipodes," "Aeschylus and Sophocles," *Three Harvest Home Chorales*, "The Cage," *Over the Pavements*, "Vote for Names," *String Quartet No. 2*, "Soliloquy," and "The Masses."

282. Schonberg, Harold C. "Natural American, Natural Rebel, Natural Avant-Gardist." *New York Times Magazine*, 21 April 1974, 12–14, 71–73, 78, 82–83.

Extensive profile offers a thorough biography and overview of significant works, emphasizing Ives's isolation from European contemporaries, independent experimentation, and delayed recognition.

283. Schonberg, Harold C. "Stubborn Yankee." *New York Times*, 5 March 1961, section 2, 9.

Details Ives's nationalistic tendencies through his New England influences, overall "Yankee" musical style, and use of quotations. States that Ives's best music "rises triumphantly over the hedges of technical impossibilities and just plain bad writing," including the Second Symphony and the *String Quartet No. 2*.

284. Schonberg, Harold C. "America's Greatest Composer." *Esquire* 50/6 (December 1958): 229–35.

Describes Ives's "Yankee" characteristics, both personal and musical, in contrast to contemporary Europeans. General biography and stylistic survey emphasizing his use of American sources and inspiration, negative audience reactions, and experimentation and accomplishments, despite what Schonberg describes as Ives's "terrible technique."

285. Schrade, Leo. "Charles E. Ives: 1874–1954." *Yale Review* 44 (1955): 535–45; reprinted in *Charles Ives and His World* (item 36), 433–42.

In addition to his general account of Ives's life and works, Schrade profiles the early stages of Ives reception, extensively compares Ives to Debussy, and defends the importance of nineteenth-century musical styles in his later works. A perceptive commentary.

286. Schwarz, K. Robert. "Composers' Closets Open for All to See." *New York Times*, 19 June 1994, section 2, 1.

Overview of scholarship addressing homosexual composers. Discusses Ives's "pathological homophobia" and its origins in late nineteenth-century attitudes toward music and sexuality.

287. Scott, Ann Besser. "Medieval and Renaissance Techniques in the Music of Charles Ives." *Musical Quarterly* 78/3 (Fall 1994): 448–78.

Identifies possible influences in Ives's music from Medieval and Renaissance precedents including stratification, successive composition, use of borrowed material as a cantus firmus, and stylistic heterogeneity. Through excerpts from Horatio Parker's lecture notes, Scott suggests that Ives learned of these historical models in his classes at Yale.

288. Seeger, Charles. "Charles Ives and Carl Ruggles." *Magazine of Art* 32 (July 1939): 396–99 and 435–37.

Praises Ives's integration of diverse idioms, material, and styles, as well as his independence from European influence. Regard Ives's spatial innovations, or in Seeger's term his "musical perspective," as one of his greatest achievements.

289. Seeger, Charles. "Grass Roots for American Composers." *Modern Music* 16/3 (March–April 1939): 143–149.

Very brief mention (p. 144) of Ives's quotations of popular music in orchestral music, placed within the context of developing a uniquely American style.

290. Sherwood, Gayle. "Charles Ives and 'Our National Malady.' " *Journal of the American Musicological Society* 54/3 (Fall 2001): 555–584.

Study of Ives's illnesses of 1906 and 1918 expands on Feder (item 42) by suggesting that Ives did not suffer from heart ailments in the current sense. Posits that Ives was diagnosed with neurasthenia or nervousness, and explores the ramifications of this disease in contemporary America.

291. Shirley, Wayne. "Ives as an Innovator." In *South Florida's Historic Ives Festival, 1974–76* (item 858), 50–52.

In his response to Carter's famous recollection of Ives's revisions (recorded in item 62), Shirley examines the nature of Ives's innovations, and the form and content of his revisions. He concludes that Ives's "radicalism isn't a matter of dressing but goes down to the marrow of the work."

292. Shultis, Christopher. *Silencing the Sounded Self: John Cage and the American Experimental Tradition.* Boston: Northeastern University Press, 1998, 3–4, 14–28, and passim. ISBN 1555533779. ML 410 .C24 S58 1998.

Study of the experimental tradition in America traces one branch to Ives and Emerson. Includes a detailed comparison of Ives's aesthetics and musics with Emerson's philosophy of "dualism, idealism and self." Considers the philosophical significance of Ives's quotations and objections to them by Cage and Carter.

293. Siegmeister, Elie. "Charles Ives: American Expressionist and Populist." In *South Florida's Historic Ives Festival, 1974–76* (item 858), 39–43.

    Determined defense of Ives against criticisms by Thomson, Carter, and others. Considers his espousal of populist materials (through quotations) and ideas. Compares Ives's work with "American expressionists" such as Eugene O'Neill and William Faulkner,

294. Slonimsky, Nicolas. "Charles Ives: The Man and His Music." *Choral Journal* 15/5 (January 1975): 15–16.

    Personal recollections including Slonimsky's impressions of Ives and his music. Details on the organizing and execution of the Pan American concerts that Slonimsky conducted as well as his 1934 recording. Includes a facsimile reprint of Ives's letter to Slonimsky of 26 February 1930.

295. Slonimsky, Nicolas. "Working with Ives." In *South Florida's Historic Ives Festival, 1974–76* (item 858), 35–37.

    Personal recollections includes a brief discussion of Ives's opinions on other composers, and specific details of the premiere and European performances of *Three Places in New England*.

296. Slonimsky, Nicolas. *Music Since 1900*. 5th ed. New York: Schirmer Books, 1994.

    Mentions several Ives premieres as well as dates of several compositions. Also includes correspondence between Slonimsky and Ives.

297. Slonimsky, Nicolas. "Charles Ives—America's Musical Prophet." *Musical America* 74/4 (15 February 1954): 18–19; reprinted in *Charles Ives and His World* (item 36), 430–32.

    Portrayal of Ives as prophet and revolutionary, focusing on the progressive aspects of his compositions. Includes a brief account of the changing reception of Ives's *Three Places in New England*. Excerpts from this article were reprinted under the same title in *Pan Pipes* 47/2 (January 1955): 20–21, with added information concerning gifts by Ives, through Harmony, to the Sigma Alpha Iota Foundation.

298. Slonimsky, Nicolas. "Charles Ives, Musical Rebel." *Américas* 5/9 (September 1953): 6–8 and 41–42.

Slonimsky praises Ives's work as "the most complex music in existence" and emphasizes George's role in encouraging his son's experimentation. Describes Ives's belated recognition and continuing isolation. Concludes with a discussion of his political views and the variability of the music through flexible instrumentation and performer choice.

299. Slonimsky, Nicolas. "Bringing Ives Alive," *Saturday Review*, 28 August 1948, 45 and 49; reprinted in *Charles Ives and His World* (item 36), 347–49.

Profile concentrates on the unjust neglect of Ives's works, and the significance of the *Concord Sonata*. With comments on the work's program and quotations, as well as a pithy biographical sketch.

300. Slonimsky, Nicolas. "Composer Who Has Clung to His Own Way." *Boston Evening Transcript*, 3 February 1934, section 3, 4–5.

Profile discusses Ives's musical innovations as well as his insurance career. Reports the growing interest in the music as "his music began to be performable," and anticipates the long-neglected acceptance of his works.

301. Slonimsky, Nicolas. "Composers of New England." *Modern Music* 7/2 (February–March 1930): 24–27.

Includes a brief summary of Ives's style, based on the Fourth Symphony and *Three Places in New England*, with mention of challenges to the conductor, overall texture, and experimental procedures.

302. Smith, Catherine Parsons. " 'A Distinguishing Virility': Feminism and Modernism in American Art Music." In *Cecilia Reclaimed: Feminist Perspectives on Gender and Music*, edited by Susan C. Cook and Judy S. Tsou. Urbana: University of Illinois, 1994, 90–106. ISBN 0252020367. ML 82 .C42 1994.

Overview of engendered attitudes toward music from late in the first decade of the 1900s through to the 1920s. The discussion of Ives, while brief, offers a significant rereading in light of the feminist literary theories of Gilbert and Gubar. Smith compares the gendered language of the *Memos* to T. S. Eliot's *Wasteland*, and concludes that Ives's writings contributed to the "anti-woman atmosphere" among modernist composers.

303. Starr, Larry. "The Early Styles of Charles Ives." *19th Century Music* 7/1 (Summer 1983): 71–80.

Considers works from 1888–1901 as representative of either the conservative or radical style, including several songs and psalm settings. Starr concludes that despite their internal stylistic consistency, their hetergeneity as a group prefigures Ives's mature musical language in which stylistic juxtaposition is the norm. Extensive analysis supported by musical examples from "Feldein-samkeit," "Memories—Rather Sad," *Psalm 67* and *Psalm 54*.

304. Starr, Larry. "Charles Ives: The Next Hundred Years—Towards a Method of Analyzing the Music." *Music Review* 38/2 (May 1977): 101–11.

Exploration of Ives's use of stylistic heterogeneity to create form, as demonstrated in an overall analysis of the "The Alcotts" movement of *Concord Sonata*. Starr demonstrates that the movement is carefully structured through the alternation of five different styles ranging from simple diatonicism to dense, dissonant polyphony.

305. Starr, Larry. "Style and Substance: "Ann Street" by Charles Ives." *Perspectives of New Music* 15/2 (Spring–Summer 1977): 23–33.

Detailed analysis of "Ann Street" with emphasis on its combination of a coherent, unified musical structure with stylistic hetergeneity. An expanded and revised version appears in item 69.

306. "The Stuff of Success." *Newsweek* 45 (17 January 1955): 90–91.

Review of the Cowell's book (item 37) includes descriptions of George Ives and his Civil War experience, Ives's work in insurance, his connection to Mark Twain, his publication of the *Concord Sonata*, the reception of his works, and the Pulitzer. Concludes that Ives was "a pithy American genius."

307. Swafford, Jan. "'La vita nuova': The Courtship of Charles and Harmony Ives." *American Music* 13/4 (Winter 1995): 470–89.

Slightly revised version of a chapter from *Charles Ives: A Life with Music* (item 70). Details Ives's relationship to Harmony Twichell, their courtship, and marriage. Includes previously unpublished excerpts from their letters.

308. Swafford, Jan. "Ives Thrives." *Musical America* 109/5 (September 1989): 67–70.

Summary of Ives's life and works emphasizing his neglect during his lifetime, and his ongoing recognition. Also discusses a new recording of the Fourth Symphony by the Chicago Symphony.

309. Swed, Mark. "Music Review: Pianist Berman's Strengths Go on Display in Pomona." *Los Angeles Times*, 28 January 2000, section F, 30.

Within a review of a concert by Boris Berman, contemplates the impact of Yale on Ives's music, as well as contemporary attitudes towards American music at the university.

310. Taruskin, Richard. "To the Editor." *Current Musicology* 19 (1975): 33–40.

Strong response to item 846, a critique of the Centennial Festival-Conference by Helms. Taruskin disputes Helms's assessment of Ives's political views based on the text of "An Election" and Ives's performance of "They Are There!" as well as excerpts from his writings.

311. Taubman, Howard. "Forget Posterity." *New York Times*, 23 November 1958, section 2, 11.

In this discussion of the interaction between living composers and neglectful audiences, Taubman speculates on the impact on Ives's music if he had achieved recognition early in his career. Suggests that Ives's "private jokes and calculated difficulties" were his way of "thumbing his nose at a cold and hostile world." Also compares Ives's neglect and belated recognition to Webern.

312. Taubman, Howard. "Posterity Catches Up With Charles Ives." *New York Times Magazine*, 23 October 1948, 15 and 34–36; reprinted in *Charles Ives and His World* (item 36), 423–29.

Significant outline of Ives's life and music, one of the first to reach a national audience. Taubman interweaves standard accounts of Ives's childhood, father's influence, musical training at Yale, career in insurance, independent experimentation, and long-standing neglect with anecdotal information gained in an extended interview with Ives.

313. Taylor, Paul Franklin. "Stylistic Heterogeneity: The Analytical Key to Movements IIA and IIB from the *First Piano Sonata* by Charles Ives." D.M.A. dissertation, University of Wisconsin-Madison, 1986.

Tests Starr's concept of "stylistic heterogeneity" (item 304) by analyzing Movements IIa and IIb of the First Piano Sonata. Taylor concludes that the cooperation of style contrasts and conventional formal elements indicate that Ives appears to be "a better composer than he has been taken to be."

314. Teachout, Terry. "The Anti-Modern Modernist." *Commentary* 103/5 (May 1997): 55–59.

Profile of Ives's life and music and discussion of his place within the modernist movement. Observes (erroneously) that Ives's music is rarely played.

315. Thomson, Virgil. *Selected Letters of Virgil Thomson*, edited by Tim Page and Vanessa Weeks Page. New York: Summit, 1988, 259 and 329. ISBN 0671621173. ML 410 .T452 A41 1988.

Two significant mentions of Ives. In a paragraph-long letter of 16 December 1952 to John M. Conly, music critic and editor of *High Fidelity* magazine, Thomson compares his music to Ives's. In a second item to an unknown correspondent of 20 January 1970, Thomson criticizes the "carelessness and volubility" of Ives's music.

316. Thomson, Virgil. "The Ives Case." *New York Review of Books* 14/10 (May 21 1970): 9–11; reprinted in *American Music Since 1910*. New York: Rinehart and Winston, 1971, 22–30. ISBN 030764653. ML 200.5 .T5; and in *A Virgil Thomson Reader*. Boston: Houghton Mifflin, 1981, 460–67.

Informed discussion of Ives's life and music suggests that his musical style has its origins in his double life in business and music. Thomson observes that a work like *Concord Sonata* "frequently comes out in sound less well than it looks on the page." Concludes that Ives's "divided allegiance" left "fatal scars" on his music because of his haste and "limited reflection."

317. Tick, Judith. "Charles Ives and the Politics of Direct Democracy." In *Ives Studies* (item 55), 133–62.

Compares Ives's political opinions and ideology to the agendas, processes, and beliefs of the Direct Democracy, or "I & R" (initiative and reform), movement. In doing so, Tick places Ives's writings and music (particularly the songs "Vote for Names" and "Majority") within a clear sociopolitical context.

318. Tick, Judith. "Charles Ives and Gender Idealogy." In *Musicology and Difference: Gender and Sexuality in Music Scholarship*, edited by Ruth A. Solie. Berkeley: University of California Press, 1993. ISBN 0520079272. ML 3838 .M96 1993.

Extremely significant source for its analysis, interpretation, and critique of engendered rhetoric in Ives's writings. Tick makes important distinctions between the construction and purposes of Ives's misogynistic and homophobic statements, and concludes that his ferocious attacks on "effeminate" music and musicians served to establishing his independence from the musical establishment.

319. Tick, Judith. "Ragtime and the Music of Charles Ives." *Current Musicology* 18 (1974): 105–13.

Identifies rhythmic, textural, and phrase patterns in chamber and piano music, particularly the First Piano Sonata, as compared with contemporary and earlier ragtime patterns. Tick's detailed documentation of ragtime figurations, based on compositions by Scott Joplin and ragtime practice described by Ben Harney, results in the most scholarly study of ragtime in Ives.

320. Tischler, Barbara L. *An American Music: The Search for An American Musical Identity*. New York: Oxford University Press, 1986, 38–41. ISBN 0195040236. ML 200 .5 .T55 186.

Describes Ives's music within the context of regionalism and nationalism, particularly his identification with New England Transcendentalism in the *Concord Sonata*.

321. Toncitch, Voya. "Contribution a la recherche des origines estetiques de la pensée musicale contemporaine." *Anuario musical* 27 (1973): 189–201.

Examines the "diversity of contemporary musical thought" with consideration of Ives's exploration of musical time and spatial relationships.

322. Tucker, Mark. "Of Men and Mountains: Ives in the Adirondacks." In *Charles Ives and His World* (item 36), 161–96.

Traces Ives's vacations in Keene Valley, Saranac Lake, and Elk Lake in upstate New York. Tucker provides original research on the historical signficance of the Adinrondacks as a source of intellectual and artistic inspiration, and traces their importance in Ives's biography (particularly his marriage to Harmony) and music. Includes rare photographs of the Iveses on vacation.

323. "United States Postal Service Issues Classical Composers and Conductors Stamps." *American Music Teacher* 47/3 (December 1997/January 1998): 6–7.

Mentions the issuing of a 32-cent stamp honoring Ives within the "Legends of American Music" series.

324. Voss, Egon. "Bemerkungen zur Musik von Charles E. Ives (1874–1954)." *Schallplatte und Kirche* 2 (1970): 145–48.

Summary of Ives's style and the influence of Transcendentalism on his work. Also comments on quotations, challenges to the performer, and the need for a published edition of his writings.

325. Walker, Donald R. "The Vocal Music of Charles Ives." *Parnassus: Poetry In Review* 3/2 (Spring/Summer 1975): 329–344.

Part of the Parnassus collection (item 168). General description of the harmony, structure, and style of the published songs and choral music. With emphasis on the dichotomies of "substance" and "manner" and experimentation and conservatism.

326. Wallach, Laurence David. "The New England Education of Charles Ives." Ph.D. dissertation, Columbia University, 1973.

Significant study of Ives's earliest education and influences in Danbury and at Yale, and evaluates contemporary attitudes toward music and musicians. Considers many unpublished musical fragments, as well as the importance of Emerson and Thoreau to shaping Ives's musical thinking during this early period.

327. Ward, Charles W. "Charles Ives: The Relationship between Aesthetic Theories and Compositional Processes." Ph.D. dissertation, University of Texas, 1974.

Examines Ives's uses of experimentation, quotation, and innovative compositional forms in light of his aesthetic ideas. Includes extensive discussions of the influence of Transcendentalism (particularly Emerson's writings) on Ives's experimentation, and the meaning of quotation as musical material and extramusical symbol. Thorough bibliography to 1974.

328. Warren-Findley, Janelle. "American Studies and American Fine-Art Music." *American Studies* 19/2 (1978): 85–87.

Within a review of several books on Ives, recommends the development of a methodology by which cultural historians will fully address issues in American classical music.

329. Watt, Douglas. "Musical Events: Concert Records." *New Yorker* 27/1 (17 February 1951): 97–99.

General review of recent chamber and short orchestral recordings, with a discussion of the "feeling of participation" that the listener experiences. Also considers Ives's use of experimental techniques "to find exact and unformalized means of expressing his ideas," and his integration of popular musics.

330. Weigl, George. "Musical Musings." *Sunday Republican Magazine (Waterbury, CT)*, 21 August 1977, 4.

Obituary of George Roberts, Ives's copyist, details his ideas about and interactions with Ives. Notes Roberts's "uncanny knack of discerning what Ives meant in the weird scores he presented."

331. Westenburg, Richard. "Charles Ives." *Music/AGO-RCCO Magazine* 8/10 (October 1974): 26–29.

   General overview of Ives's life, philosophy, and religious beliefs as revealed in the *Essays*. With additional commentary on the choral and organ music, as well as personal perspectives on Ives's choral music by Westenburg, the organist and choirmaster of Central Presbyterian Church in New York from 1964 to 1974.

332. Whitesell, Lloyd. "Reckless Form, Uncertain Audiences: Responding to Ives." *American Music* 12/3 (Fall 1994): 304–319.

   Whitesell suggests a new approach to listening to Ives, through an appreciation of the formal freedom, or lack of unity, as well as the hetergeneity and associative aspects of musical styles and quotations in the songs "The Things Our Fathers Loved" and "Ann Street."

333. Wickstrom, Fred. "Ives and Percussion, A Forerunner on All Fronts." In *South Florida's Historic Ives Festival, 1974–76* (item 858), 57–58.

   Analyzes what Wickstrom calls the "Ives Percussion Sound" according to instrumentation, rhythm, notation, conducting, and rehearsing. Focuses on the Fourth Symphony and *Three Places in New England*.

334. Wiecki, Ronald V. "Two Musical Idealists—Charles Ives and E. Robert Schmitz: A Friendship Reconsidered." *American Music* 10/1 (Spring 1992): 1–19.

   Description of Ives's relationship to the French pianist Schmitz, including Schmitz's efforts to publicize Ives's music both individually and through the Pro Musica Society, which he founded. Particular emphasis is placed on the aesthetic ground shared by both men, especially their interest in quarter-tone composition. Includes a valuable listing of Pro Musica performances of Ives's works between 1925 and 1942.

335. Winters, Thomas. "Additive and Repetitive Techniques in the Experimental Works of Charles Ives." Ph.D. dissertation, University of Pennsylvania, 1986.

   Intensive study of three additive and repetitive techniques in Ives's experimental music: wedge-palindromes, ostinati, and imitation. Winters traces Ives's use of these procedures by adapting conventional musical language, expanding the technique in an exclusively experimental work, and later incorporating the device on a smaller scale into a larger work. Concludes that the systematic exploration of these and other devices provides an overall structural unity to Ives's compositions.

336. Woodside, Christine. "Pop in the Pews." *New York Times*, 16 April 2000, Connecticut section, 1.

      This profile of Connecticut church musicians and composers mentions Ives as a founder of the flourishing tradition.

337. Wooldridge, David. "Charles Ives and the American National Character 'Musical Spirit of '76'." In *South Florida's Historic Ives Festival, 1974–76* (item 858), 27–29.

      Wide-ranging essay explores Ives's historical position with comparisons to Herman Melville and Thoreau. Extensive commentary on negative reactions to Ives's music, particularly during the 1960s and early 1970s.

338. Wyttenbach, Jürg. "Charles Ives, Musiker, USA." In *Jürg Wyttenbach: Ein Portrait im Spiegel eigener und fremder Texte*. Zurich, Switzerland: Pro Helvetia Zytglogge, 1994, 62–63. ISBN 3729604821. ML410.W988 J8 1994.

      Extremely concise summary of the major points of Ives's life and musical style, emphasizing his experimentation and uniquely American sensibility as seen in his education, quotations, and political views.

339. Yates, Peter. "Charles Ives: An American Composer." *Parnassus: Poetry in Review* 3/2 (Spring/Summer 1975): 318–328.

      Part of the Parnassus collection (item 168). Creative essay describing Ives's importance to American composers, his interactions and similarities with Schoenberg, and his opinions on the First World War. Concludes with a poem by Peyton Houston entitled "Concord: In Memory of C. I."

340. Yates, Peter. "Charles Ives: The Transcendental American Venture, Part 1." *Arts and Architecture* 78/2 (February 1961): 6–8.

      Part of Yates's trilogy (see items 341, 342). Yates's own account of his activities on behalf of Ives's music including the Evenings on the Roof concert series, with a personal perspective on the reception of Ives's music. Includes anecdotes about the ongoing importance of Ives's insurance writings and compares the Transcendentalist views of "The Amount to Carry" with the *Essays*.

341. Yates, Peter. "Charles Ives: The Transcendental American Venture, Part 2." *Arts and Architecture* 78/3 (March 1961): 4.

      Part of Yates's trilogy (see items 340, 342). Overview of the music within Ives's career and in connection with Emerson's writings and the ideas of

John Jay Chapman. With additional comparisons to Debussy and the German Romantic tradition.

342. Yates, Peter. "Charles Ives: The Transcendental American Venture, Part 3." *Arts and Architecture* 78/5 (May 1961): 6–8, 30–31.

Part of Yates's trilogy (see items 340, 341). Wide-ranging discussion of the style and aesthetics of Ives's music with comparisons to Van Gogh, Berg, Schoenberg, and Webern. Considers the applicability of the artistic labels "naïve" and "primitive" to Ives's musical style, and discusses the role of quotation in Ives's approach.

343. Yates, Peter. "Charles E. Ives." *Arts and Architecture* 67/2 (February 1950): 13–17.

Overview of the large orchestral works, violin sonatas, string quartets, and *Concord Sonata*. Compares Ives's radicalism to Schoenberg's and considers the impact of isolation on Ives's musical style. Outlines the difficulties facing performers of the music.

344. Yates, Peter. "Charles Ives." *Arts and Architecture* 61/9 (September 1944): 20, 40.

Profile on Ives's seventieth birthday. Examines the character and environment of the American artist and compares Ives to Wright, Whitman, and Melville. Describes American aspects of the songs "Charlie Rutledge," "The Greatest Man," and "The Swimmers" along with the violin sonatas and *Concord Sonata*. Briefly comments on the reception of the *Concord* in Los Angeles.

345. Yates, Peter. "Charles Ives." *California Arts and Architecture* 57/11 (November 1940): 18.

Biographical profile discusses Ives's insurance career and the musical influence of New England and New York as heard in his works. Describes the *Concord Sonata* and "General William Booth" in limited detail.

346. Zimmerman, Walter. " 'Self-Reliance'—Eigenständigkeit in Charles Ives' Charakter und Musik." *Neuland* 1 (1980): 54–58.

Examines Ives's independence as represented in his writings—the *Memos* and *Essays*—and in his musical experiments, particularly his excursions away from tonality. Traces the origins of his independent ideas to Transcendentalism, especially the writings of Emerson.

4

Topical Studies

TRANSCENDENTALISM

The following studies focus nearly exclusively on the influence of Transcendentalism on Ives's music. For studies that consider other issues as well, see "Transcendentalism" in the Keyword Index. See also item 35 for a thorough investigation of the origins of Ives's Transcendentalist beliefs.

347. Albert, Thomas Russel. "The Harmonic Language of Charles Ives' 'Concord Sonata'." Ph.D. dissertation, Unversity of Illinois, 1974.

    Addresses the issue of "substance and manner" as well as the influence of Emerson and Thoreau on the "artistic independence" of the sonata. Also analyzes the derivation of harmonic structures from melodic motifs.

348. Barnett, Christina Powers. "Charles Ives: '114 Songs' and Transcendental Philosophy." D.M.A. dissertation, University of Texas at Austin, 1986.

    Study of aspects of Transcendental philosophy in the music and Ives's own texts of *114 Songs*. Includes discussions of ambiguity and paradox, inspiration from nonmusical ideas, and representations of both the individual and the universal.

349. Bozynski, Michelle Carole. "Transcendentalism and Social Context as Meaning in the Music of Charles Ives: A Case Study of 'The Things Our Fathers Loved.' " Master's Thesis, University of Alberta, 1995.

    Compares Ives's Transcendentalism with philosophical and literary movements of the turn of the century. Emphasizes his use of quotations and layering as a means of memorializing a specifically "American" past. Includes a detailed study of the text, layers, and quotations of "The Things Our Fathers Loved."

350. Brandt, Rebecca Lynne. "Transcendentalism and Intertextuality in Charles Ives's War Songs of 1917." Master's thesis, University of North Texas, 1998.

Examines primarily the texts of "In Flanders Fields," "He Is There!," and "Tom Sails Away" from two perspectives: their relationship to Transcendentalism; and the intertextuality of the musical borrowings of the songs. First, the songs are considered according to both the original principles of Transcendentalist philosophers, and as a reflection of Ives's interpretation of this philosophy. Second, Brandt considers the songs' intertextuality, or textual interdependence, as manifest through quotation. Based on this interpretation, Brandt critiques Ives's "conflicting views of the morality of war."

351. Cameron, Catherine M. *Dialectics in the Arts: The Rise of Experimentalism in American Music.* Westport, CT: Praeger, 1996. ISBN 0275956105. ML 3845 .C36 1996.

History of experimentalism from the late nineteenth to the mid twentieth centuries. Gives a six-page summary of Ives's aesthetics, particularly the influence of Transcendentalism on his experimental procedures. Also includes an overview of the Fourth Symphony.

352. Chmaj, Betty E. "The Journey and the Mirror: Emerson and the American Arts." *Prospects: An Annual of American Cultural Studies* 10 (1986): 353–408.

Chmaj includes a section detailing the influence of Emerson on Ives's music and writings within a larger study of Emerson's impact on American culture. States that Ives is "the true Emerson of American music" and suggests that "Ives tried to write his music the way Emerson wrote his prose."

353. Chmaj, Betty E. "Sonata for American Studies: Perspectives on Charles Ives." *Prospects: An Annual of American Cultural Studies* 4 (1978): 1–58. E 169.1 .P945.

Study of Emerson's speech "The American Scholar," and its endorsement of American art. Traces the influence of this and other Emersonian ideas on Ives, Walt Whitman, and Frank Lloyd Wright.

354. Davidson, Audrey. "Transcendental Unity in the Works of Charles Ives." *American Quarterly* 22/2 (Spring 1970): 35–44: reprinted as a chapter in idem, *Substance and Manner: Studies in Music and the Other Arts.* St. Paul, MN: Hiawatha Press, 1977, 3–12. ISBN 0930276000. ML 60 .D16.

Concise consideration of the issues of unity, coherence, and completeness as evidenced in Ives's writings, and overall musical style. Addresses criticisms of his work by Carter and Copland, and compares and contrasts Ives's beliefs to those of German and Transcendentalist philosophers, particularly Coleridge. Davidson concludes that Ives's use of quotational fragments, his harmonic and rhythmic structures, and his performance instructions all represent the aesthetic of "a music as free as the person who created it."

355. DiYanni, Robert. "In the American Grain: Charles Ives and the Transcendentalists." *Journal of American Culture* 4/4 (Winter 1981): 139–51.

Suggests that Ives's musical and literary output are "aspects of a larger transcendental unity" through a comparison of specific passages from the *Essays* with writings by Emerson and Thoreau. Considers the influence of Transcendentalism on "The Housatonic at Stockbridge," the Second and Fourth Symphonies, and the *Universe Symphony*.

356. Dujmic, Dunja. "The Musical Transcendentalism of Charles Ives." *International Review of the Aesthetics and Sociology of Music* 2/1 (June 1971): 89–95.

Describes American Transcendentalism as the "continuous source" of Ives's music, and states that Ives "turned to the study of century old transcendentalist postulates with real scholarly care." Considers the relationship of folklore and programs to Ives's use of Transcendentalism.

357. Feder, Stuart. "Charles Ives and Henry David Thoreau: 'A Transcendental tune of Concord.' " In *Ives Studies* (item 55), 163–76.

Discusses the influence of Thoreau's life, work, and ideas on the *Concord Sonata, Tone Roads No. 3,* and on several songs. Also suggests that Thoreau served as a psychological substitute for Ives's father George. Includes previously unknown correspondence from the 1940s between Ives and Walter Harding.

358. Geselbracht, Raymond H. "Transcendental Renaissance in the Arts: 1890–1920." *New England Quarterly* 48 (December 1975): 463–86.

Discusses the influence of Transcendentalism on Ives, Frank Lloyd Wright, and Isadora Duncan, particularly in their rejection of European values and the importance of nature.

359. Girgus, Sam B. "Charles Ives and the Transcendentalists." *Research Studies* 43/1 (1975): 19–25.

Discusses Ives's Transcendentalist views in general, and examines their influence on his music and writings.

360. Goudie, Andrea. "Exploring the Broad Margins: Charles Ives's Interpretation of Thoreau." *Midwest Quarterly* 13/3 (Spring 1972): 309–17.

Informed comparison both of the "Thoreau" movement of the *Concord Sonata* and of the *Essays* with Thoreau's own writings, beliefs, personality, and musical activities and attitudes. With extensive quotations that are unfortunately not provided with citations.

361. Hunnicutt, Ellen. "The Practical Uses of Emerson: Charles Ives." *Soundings* 70/1–2 (1987): 189–198.

Discusses the influence of Emerson specifically and Transcendentalism in general on Ives's aesthetics, writings, and compositions.

362. Mauk, David C. "New England Transcendentalism Versus Virulent Nationalism: The Evolution of Charles Ives' Patriotic March Music." *American Studies in Scandinavia* 31/1 (1999): 24–33.

Analyzes the second movement of the Fourth Symphony as a rejection of war through the distortion of traditional marches. Suggests that the third movement reflects the power of Transcendentalism through hymn tunes.

363. Mellers, Wilfrid. "Realism and Transcendentalism: Charles Ives as American Hero." In *Music in a New Found Land: Themes and Developments in the History of American Music*. London: Barrie and Rockliff, 1964; reprinted New York: Alfred A. Knopf, 1965; reprinted with a new introduction, 1987, 38–64. ISBN 019520526X. ML 200 .M44 1987.

In his balanced and highly sympathetic overview, Mellers discusses Ives's work according to two influences: realism, through the recreation of childhood experiences and "life-as-it-is, in all its apparent chaos and contradiction"; and Transcendentalism, through the unification of that chaos. Includes an extensive discussion of the *Concord Sonata* as "Ives's most developed exploration" of the two viewpoints, as well as descriptions of several songs, symphonies, chamber, and choral works.

364. Rathert, Wolfgang. "Der amerikanische Transzendentalismus." In *Musik und Religion*. Laaber, Germany: Laaber Verlag, 1995, 189–214. ISBN 3890072658. ML 3845 .M9765.

In the section, translated as "American Transcendentalism," is a brief, two-page consideration of Ives's beliefs—as evidenced in his writings and compositions—and their relationship to the Transcendentalism of Thoreau. Expanded in item 45.

365. Rathert, Wolfgang. "Philosophische Grundlagen der Musik von Charles Ives." In *Entgrenzungen in der Musik*, edited by Otto Kolleritsch. Studien zur Wertungsforschung Vol. 18. Graz: Universal, 1987, 123–37. ISBN 3702401873. ML 60 .E63 1987.

Translated as "Philosophical Bases for the Music of Charles Ives" in the collection *Removing Borders in Music*, Rathert compares Ives's musical aesthetics with Emerson's writings on Transcendentalism. He suggests that Ives's work attempts to break from European musical history by achieving artistic autonomy. Available in a Serbian translation by Pavlusko Imsirovic as "Filozofske osnove Ajzove muzike." *MT: Muzicki Talas* 3/4 (1996): 106–111.

366. Robinson, David B. "Children of the Fire: Charles Ives on Emerson and Art." *American Literature* 48 (January 1977): 564–76.

Discusses the influence of Emerson and Thoreau on Ives's music, writing, and aesthetics.

367. Rosa, Alfred F. "Charles Ives: Music, Transcendentalism, and Politics." *New England Quarterly* 44/3 (September 1971): 433–443.

Analyzes the *Essays Before A Sonata* focusing on Ives's ideas on program music, his awareness of Emerson's writings and principles, his descriptions of Thoreau, and his use of quotation. Concludes with a brief discussion of the influence of Thoreau on Ives's political writings.

368. Rycenga, Jennifer Joanne. "The composer as a religious person in the context of pluralism." Ph.D. dissertation, Graduate Theological Union, 1992.

Includes a consideration of Ives's Transcendentalist philosophy and its relationship to his music. Rycenga suggests that composers such as Ives, Pauline Oliveros, John Cage, Ornette Coleman, and others "adopt a religio-aesthetic strategy by virtue of their creativity, when it involves a direct interaction with materiality in a manner which implies that material can be and is a location for relationship, including both ethics and ontology."

369. Staebler, Roger. "Charles Ives: An Evaluation of His Aesthetic Philosophy." Master's thesis, College-Conservatory of Music of Cincinnati, 1959.

Early study of the influence of Emerson and Thoreau on Ives's personal philosophy, and particularly on the *Concord Sonata*.

370. Ward, Charles W. "Charles Ives's Concept of Music." *Current Musicology* 18 (1974): 114–19.

Compares Ives's metaphysical concept of music with Thoreau's ideas about music. Argues that his evocation of "natural" music is particularly close to Thoreau's metaphor of the telegraph harp and, ultimately, the music of the universal Over-Soul. Available in Serbian as "Ajvzov koncept muzike [Ives's Concept of Music]." *MT: Muzicki Talas* 3/5–6 (1996): 82–84.

MUSICAL QUOTATION OR BORROWING

See also "borrowings and quotations" in the keyword index; and book-length studies including items 34 and 47.

371. Austin, William. *"Susanna," "Jeanie," and "The Old Folks at Home": The Songs of Stephen C. Foster from His Time to Ours.* New York: Macmillan, 1975. ISBN 0-02-504500-8. ML 410 .F78 A9.

In Chapter 13, "Composers of 'New Music' " (pp. 317–330), Austin summarizes Ives's quotations from Foster with extended descriptions of the Second Symphony, the First Piano Sonata, *Concord Sonata*, "The 'St. Gaudens' in Boston Common," and *Elegy for Stephen Foster*. Austin also relates the importance of Foster to Ives and his father, and assigns both musical and programmatic significance to Ives's choice of quotations.

372. Averill, Ron. "The Use of Quotation in 20th-Century Works by Ron Averill, Charles Dodge, and Charles Ives." D.M.A. document, University of Washington, 1995.

Discusses quotations in the songs "The Housatonic at Stockbridge," "In Flanders Fields," "Old Home Day," and "Grantchester," according to their content, recognizability, method of utilization, and compositional context. Also questions the ultimate "level of originality" that exists in quotation-based compositions.

373. Ballantine, Christopher. "Charles Ives and the Meaning of Quotation in Music." *Musical Quarterly* 65 (1979): 167–84.

Important discussion of the various ways that Ives uses quotations associatively, including texted and untexted quotations, and webs of associations. Also considers the relationship between borrowings and programs, as well

as their "musico-philosophical" significance. Available in a Serbian translation by Ivana Misic as "Ajvz i znacenje citiranja u muzici [Ives and the
Meaning of Quotation in Music]." *MT: Muzicki talas* 4/1–2 (1997): 88–94.

374. Brinkmann, Reinhold. "Wirkungen Beethovens in der Kammermusik."
     Beitrage zu Beethovens Kammermusik: Symposion Bonn 1984, edited by
     Sieghard Brandenburg and Helmut Loos. Munich: Henle, 1987, 79–110.
     ISBN 3873280485. ML 410 .B42 B46 1987.

     Briefly discusses Ives's quotations from Beethoven in his chamber music,
     and places these borrowings within the larger context of Beethoven recep-
     tion and influence. Brinkmann also examines the cause of Beethoven's con-
     tinuing importance. Translates as "Beethoven's influence on chamber
     music."

375. Burkholder, J. Peter. " 'Quotation' and Paraphrase in Ives's Second Sym-
     phony." *19th Century Music* 11/1 (Summer 1987): 3–25; reprinted in *Music
     at the Turn of the Century*, edited by Joseph Kerman. Berkeley: University
     of California Press, 1990, 33–56. ISBN 0520068556. ML 196 .K45 M8.

     Consideration of borrowed materials and their combination, alteration, and
     transformation in the Second Symphony. Burkholder identifies and exam-
     ines Ives's employment of both American vernacular and European classi-
     cal sources, and finds that paraphrase technique was crucial to the musical
     and aesthetic integration of both influences within the art music idiom.

376. Burkholder, J. Peter. " 'Quotation' and Emulation: Charles Ives's Use of His
     Models." *Musical Quarterly* 71/1 (1985): 1–26.

     Outlines several different types of musical borrowing, including modeling,
     paraphrase, cumulative setting, quoting, and quodlibet, then focuses on
     Ives's different uses of musical models throughout his work. Concludes
     that borrowings in Ives function on musical, programmatic, and "musico-
     philosophical" levels, creating a complex network of meaning. Much of this
     material is expanded in item 34.

377. Cooper, Jack Thomas. "Three Sketches for Jazz Orchestra Inspired by
     Charles Ives Songs." D.M.A. dissertation, University of Texas at Austin,
     1999.

     Three compositions for jazz orchestra based on Ives's songs, with an an-
     alysis and summary of Ives's influence. Includes a comparison of musical
     borrowings—their purpose, utilization, and sources—by Ives and jazz
     composers.

378. Cyr, Gordon. "Intervallic Structural Elements in Ives's Fourth Symphony." *Perspectives of New Music* 9/2–10/1 (1971): 291–303.

     Explores shared intervallic structures in the quotations, as well as Ives's manipulation and alteration of these elements to form the thematic and harmonic structure of the work. Concludes that the resulting musical "cell" unifies the work and justifies the choice of quotations on a purely musical basis.

379. Ellison, Mary. "Ives' use of American 'popular' tunes as thematic material." In *South Florida's Historic Festival 1974–1976* (item 858), 30–34.

     Discusses Ives's adaptation of quotations in the Third Symphony and *Three Places in New England* through melodic, rhythmic, harmonic, and formal processes.

380. Harrison, Lou. "On Quotation: New Attitude Towards Quoted Material Taken from Life." *Modern Music* 23/3 (Summer 1946): 166–169.

     Comparison of the use, purpose, and meaning of preexisting material in music primarily by Ives but also Mahler, Virgil Thomson, and Stravinsky. Includes a somewhat detailed comparison of Ives with James Joyce.

381. Henderson, Clayton W. "Ives' Use of Quotation." *Music Educator's Journal* 61/2 (October 1974): 24–28.

     Examines Ives's transformation of borrowed materials through melodic, metrical, rhythmic, and harmonic alterations. Briefly discusses Ives's utilization of quotations for descriptive, formal, and thematic purposes.

382. Henderson, Clayton W. "Structural Importance of Borrowed Music in the Works of Charles Ives: A Preliminary Assessment." In *Report of the Eleventh Congress of the International Musicological Society Held at Copenhagen, 1972*, edited by Henrik Glahn et al. Copenhagen: Edition W. Hansen, 1974, 437–46. ISBN 8774550268. ML 36 .I628 1972.

     Signficant source that draws on item 383. Discusses the structural and programmatic aspects of Ives's quotations, particularly their role in unifying traditional forms including rondo, verse and refrain, and ternary forms. Concludes that Ives chose his quotations carefully to function on many levels.

383. Henderson, Clayton Wilson. "Quotations as a Style Element in the Music of Charles Ives." Ph.D. dissertation, Washington University, 1969.

Important early consideration of the significance of quotations in Ives's music. Henderson categorizes their use as thematic, structural, or descriptive; describes their melodic, rhythmic, and harmonic alterations; and analyzes their relationship to overall form, and Ives's musical philosophy and experimentation.

384. Hepokoski, James. "Temps Perdu." *Musical Times* 135 (December 1994): 746–51.

Examines the Ives's use of quotations, the "connotationally loaded memory-fragment" through the process of what Hepokoski calls "teleological genesis" (Burkholder's "cumulative form"). Hepokoski asserts that as Ives moved further into adulthood, his quotation-based music became increasingly complex in order to briefly regain his lost childhood.

385. Johnson, Timothy A. "Chromatic Quotations of Diatonic Tunes in Songs of Charles Ives." *Music Theory Spectrum* 18/2 (Fall 1996): 236–61.

Explores Ives's chromatic alterations of diatonic hymn tunes in the songs "The Innate," "The Camp-Meeting," "At the River," "Nov. 2, 1920," "Hymn," and "Old Home Day." The author focuses on how Ives transforms his material intervallically, establishes "linked diatonic areas" within quotations, and how the altered quotations retain "diatonic orientations" of the original hymn tunes. Extensive analysis, primarily of melodic lines in comparison with source materials.

386. Magers, Roy V. "Charles Ives's Optimism, or, The Program's Progress." In *Music in American Society, 1776–1976: From Puritan Hymn to Synthesizer*, edited by George McCue. New Brunswick, NJ: Transaction Books, 1977, 73–86. ISBN 0 87855 209X. ML 200 .1 .M9.

Argues that Ives's choice of quotations in the Fourth Symphony create a concealed program that parallels his belief in the ultimate triumph of human progress. Magers maintains that this optimism is supported through the harmonic and thematic structure of the work as well.

387. Marshall, Dennis. "Charles Ives's Quotations: Manner or Substance?" *Perspectives of New Music* 6/2 (Spring-Summer 1968): 45–56.

Examines the formal and intellectual purposes of quotations in *First Piano Sonata* and "The Fourth of July." Marshall concludes that, while the quotations' programmatic aspects are a significant factor in their selection, the musical structure of the borrowed tunes is fundamental to the form and unification of the works, and thereby form the substance of Ives's art.

388. Mays, Kenneth Robert. "The Use of Hymn Tunes in the Works of Charles Ives." Master's thesis, Indiana University, 1961.

Early study of Ives's borrowings from hymn tunes in the Third Violin Sonata, and Second, Third, and Fourth symphonies, second movement. Most of the work is summarized in a table form that lists each significant appearance of each hymn, with a general description of its character and form. Concludes with a consideration of the cultural and aesthetic significance of the quoted hymn tunes.

389. Morgan, Robert. "American Music and the Hand-Me-Down Habit." *High Fidelity/Musical America* 26/6 (June 1976): 70–72.

Consideration of the use of quotation by American composers including Ives, Anthony Philip Heinrich, and Ernest Bloch within a review of recent recordings. Morgan concludes that the habit of quotation occurs both in European and American music, and that the "manner and aesthetic meaning" of quotation in both traditions varies considerably.

390. Rabinowitz, Peter J. "Fictional Music: Toward a Theory of Listening." In *Theories of Reading, Looking, and Listening*, edited by Harry R. Garvin. Bucknell Review 26, no. 1. Lewisburg: Bucknell University Press, 1981, 193–208.

Suggests analyzing quotation-based music by Ives and others based on a listener's knowledge of those quotations, the impact of that knowledge on the listening experience, and the creation of "fictional" music, or "music that pretends to be a different performance of some other music."

391. Saylor, Bruce. "Looking Backwards: Reflections on Nostalgia in the Musical Avant-Garde." *Centerpoint* 3 (Spring 1975): 3–7.

In this study of the past as an element of musical expression, Saylor considers Ives's influence on contemporary American composers as manifest through his invocation of quotation-based nostalgia.

392. Sterne, Colin. "The Quotations in Charles Ives's Second Symphony." *Music and Letters* 52/1 (January 1971): 39–45.

Sterne offers an intriguing interpretation of the quotations in the Second Symphony. He suggests that Ives intended the work as both an elegy to European symphonic music, and a celebration of American music through the gradual ascendency of borrowings from hymn and patriotic tunes over Beethoven, Brahms, and Wagner. Sterne concludes that the work announces

Ives's "indebtedness to, and at the same time his rebellion against, an entrenched European tradition."

393. Tibbe, Monika. "Musik in Musik. Collagetechnik und Zitierverfahren." *Musica* 25/6 (June 1971): 562–63.

Briefly discusses Ives's use of popular music sources as quotations in comparison with works by Mahler, Beethoven, and Weber.

394. Ward, Charles. "Hymn Tunes as 'Substance and Manner' in Charles Ives." Master's thesis, University of Texas, 1969.

Analyzes the relationship of hymn texts to quoted tunes in Ives's works. Ward asserts that the discarded texts often contribute extramusical information amounting to a hidden program or narrative.

CHRONOLOGY

395. Baron, Carol K. "Dating Charles Ives' Music: Facts and Fictions." *Perspectives of New Music* 28/1 (1990): 20–56.

In her response to Solomon (item 404), Baron presents a handwriting study based on three manuscripts, and applies her methodology to Ives's "Putnam's Camp" sources. Also considers the nature, impact, and chronology of revisions to *The Unanswered Question* and "The Alcotts" from *Concord Sonata*. For related correspondence, see items 396 and 405.

396. Baron, Carol K. "Correspondence." *Perspectives of New Music* 28/(Summer 1990): 333–34.

Response to Zahler's correspondence (item 405) concerning the analysis and dating of *The Unanswered Question*.

397. Burkholder, J. Peter. "Charles Ives and His Fathers." *Institute for Studies in American Music Newsletter* 18/1 (November 1988): 8–11.

In an informed response to Solomon (item 404), Burkholder reviews Ives's successful efforts to misrepresent himself as an independent, isolated composer who owed nothing to the European tradition. He also asserts that Solomon's arguments constitute "an important corrective to received wisdom."

398. Henahan, Donal. "The Polysided Views of Ives's Polytonality." *New York Times*, 10 June 1990, section H, 23, 28.

Reports on Baron's 1990 article (item 395) with comparison to Solomon's original (item 404). Also comments on reactions to the controversy within the scholarly community.

399. Lambert, J. Philip. "Communications." *Journal of the American Musicological Society* 42/1 (Spring 1989): 204–9.

Lambert's reply to Solomon (item 404) questions Solomon's interpretations of date contradictions found in Ives chronology, particularly the memos, addresses, and phone numbers found on the musical manuscripts. Lambert suggests that many such notations are associative, and should not be used as chronological evidence.

400. Roos, James. "A Fresh, Tough Look at a Legendary Composer." *Miami Herald*, 13 November 1988.

Reports on premieres of the critical editions of the first and fourth symphonies by Michael Tilson Thomas and the New World Symphony at Miami's Gusman Center. Also discusses recent scholarship (including item 404), and recounts reactions to it by John Kirkpatrick, Nicolas Slonimsky, and Tilson Thomas.

401. Sherwood, Gayle. "Redating Ives's choral sources." In *Ives Studies* (item 55), 77–101.

Analyzes the chronological redistribution of Ives's choral works. Establishes two choral "periods." The first (c. 1887–c. 1903) includes Ives's many conservative works and early experiments for chorus, while the second period (c. 1909–c. 1927) encompasses Ives's mature progressive compositions.

402. Sherwood, Gayle. "Questions and Veracities: Reassessing the Chronology of Ives's Choral Works." *Musical Quarterly* 78/3 (Fall 1994): 403–21.

Reconsiders Solomon's arguments (item 404) and the chronology established by Kirkpatrick by redating Ives's choral works through analysis of music paper types and handwriting. Concludes that, although a full revised chronology is necessary, the preliminary results "verify Ives's reputation as an innovator."

403. Solomon, Maynard. "Communications." *Journal of the American Musicological Society* 42/1 (1989): 209–18.

See entry for items 399 and 404.

404. Solomon, Maynard. "Charles Ives: Some Questions of Veracity." *Journal of the American Musicological Society* 40/3 (Fall 1987): 443–70.

In his controversial article and "Communications" response to Lambert (item 399), Solomon reconsiders Ives's assertion of his compositional isolation. In this context, Solomon presents a number of archival examples involving conflicts between the accepted chronology and other documentation. This evidence includes contradictory notations on Ives's manuscripts referring to addresses, dates, or events, in addition to heavily revised scores, references to unsubstantiated early works or performances, and contradictions within Ives's lists and prose writings. Solomon concludes that a revised chronology is necessary to determine Ives's relationship to his European and American contemporaries.

405. Zahler, Noel. "Correspondence." *Perspectives of New Music* 28/2 (Summer 1990): 331–32.

Criticism of item 395 regarding the analysis and dating of *The Unanswered Question*. For a rebuttal, see item 396.

INSURANCE

See also the keyword index under "Insurance" for more entries.

406. "Charles Ives: Insurance Innovator." In *South Florida's Historic Festival* (item 858), 45–46.

Survey of Ives's insurance activities compiled by the Mutual Life Insurance Company of New York. Suggests that Ives's biographical circumstances influenced his insurance policies, and describes some of his interactions with Mutual executives.

407. Rhodes, Russell. "America's Top Musical Composer." *Eastern Underwriter*, 25 February 1949, 8.

Profile in a major insurance journal contains: quotations from Julian Myrick, Ives's insurance partner; a discussion of his business accomplishments and approaches; and a summary of his father's influence, education, and musical style.

408. Schultz, Gordon A. "A Selected Bibliography of Charles Ives' Insurance Writings." *Student Musicologists at Minnesota* 6 (1975–76): 272–79.

Annotated bibliography of thirteen items written by Ives, many of which were published in *The Eastern Underwriter*. Includes articles, pamphlets, letters, and memoranda, as well as a bibliography of thirteen advertisements for the Ives & Myrick Agency between 1918 and 1929.

COMPARISONS WITH OTHER COMPOSERS, ARTISTS,
AND WRITERS

409. Angermann, Klaus, and Barbara Barthelmes. "Die Idee des klingenden
Raumes seit Satie." In *Musik zwischen E und U: ein Prolog und sieben Kon-
gressbeiträge*, edited by Ekkehard Jost. Veröffentlichungen des Instituts für
Neue Musik und Musikerziehung Darmstadt Vol. 25. Mainz: Schott, 1984,
107–26. ISBN 3795717655. ML 5 .D29.

Translates as "The Idea of the Sounding Space Since Satie." The first part of
the essay discusses the creation of musical space by Satie, Ives, and Varèse
and the new demands imposed on the listener as a result.

410. Baldwin, Philip. "An Analysis of three violin sonatas by William Bolcom."
D.M.A. document, Ohio State University, 1996.

Discusses Bolcom's early fascination with the music of Ives and the impact
of this influence on his later music.

411. Block, Geoffrey. "Ives and the 'Sounds that Beethoven Didn't Have.' " In
Charles Ives and the Classical Tradition (item 33), 34–50.

Explores Ives's relationship with Beethoven as evidenced through his Second String Quartet and *Concord Sonata*, his transcription of the Adagio
movement of Beethoven's *Piano Sonata in F Minor, Op. 2, No. 1*, and his
prose writings.

412. Bonham, Robert John. "Some Common Aesthetic Tendencies Manifested in
Examples of Pioneer American Cabins and Old Harp Music and in Selected
Works of H. H. Richardson and Charles E. Ives." Ph.D. dissertation, Ohio
University, 1981.

Broad ranging comparison of Ives's works with contemporary and earlier
American art and architecture in an attempt to define indigenous characteristics. Bonham concludes that these characteristics include the transformation of European models, inclusion and adaption of local materials,
inventiveness, and improvisation.

413. Botstein, Leon. "Innovation and Nostalgia: Ives, Mahler, and the Origins of
Modernism." In *Charles Ives and His World* (item 36), 35–74.

In this wide-ranging and provocative essay, Botstein interweaves culture
and reception studies with musical analysis to explore five points: 1, Understanding the Career of Charles Ives; 2, Ives and Mahler: Parallel Careers
and Twin Revivals; 3, Religion and Art: The Emerson Connection; 4, Ives

and Modernism in New York; 5, Music and Morals. He suggests that both Ives and Mahler manipulated contrasts between musical nostalgia and innovation to preserve nineteenth-century moral agendas.

414. Bruce, Neely. "Ives and 19th-Century Music." In *An Ives Celebration: Papers and Panels of the Charles Ives Centennial Festival-Conference* (item 50), 29–43.

Primarily a comparison of Ives's songs with those of Stephen Foster, with secondary discussions of Dudley Buck, Anthony Philip Heinrich, and others. Emphasis on similarities of texts, instrumentation, accompaniment, and quotation.

415. Buchman, Andrew. "Ives and Stravinsky: Two Angles on 'the German Stem.' " In *Charles Ives and the Classical Tradition* (item 33), 131–49.

Compares the relationship of Ives and Stravinsky to both the Western European tradition and their native folk and popular musics. Buchman suggests that the two composers' integration of classical and vernacular musics not only stems from a shared heritage, but also serves to establish a unique identity for each.

416. Burkholder, J. Peter. "Ives and the 19th-Century European Tradition." In *Charles Ives and the Classical Tradition* (item 33), 11–33.

Burkholder asserts that Ives, despite his experimentation and American musical identity, remained rooted in the European tradition. Analyzes Ives's modelings on Donizetti and Dvořák, and compares his resetting of "Ich Grolle Nicht" with the original by Schumann.

417. Burkholder, J. Peter. "Rule-Breaking as a Rhetorical Sign." In *Festa Musicologica: Essays in Honor of George J. Buelow*, edited by Thomas J. Mathiesen and Benito V. Rivera. Stuyvesant, NY: Pendragon, 1995. ISBN 094519370X. ML 55 .B92.

Examination of how composers such as Monteverdi, Mozart, and Ives use innovation as a rhetorical device to enforce musical meaning. Includes a brief consideration of *The General Slocum* plus Ives's description of his *Yale-Princeton Football Game*.

418. Call, William Anson. "A Study of the Transcendental Aesthetic Theories of John S. Dwight and Charles E. Ives and the Relationship of These Theories to Their Respective Work as Music Critic and Composer." D.M.A. dissertation, University of Illinois, 1971.

Compares the influence of Transcendentalism on Dwight and Ives's *Essays*. Applies Ives's aesthetics to a detailed Schenkerian analysis of the Fourth Symphony, fourth movement.

419. Crunden, Robert Morse. *Ministers of Reform: The Progressives' Achievement in American Civilization 1889–1920.* New York: Basic Books, 1982. ISBN 0465046312. E 661 .C945 1982; reprint, Urbana: University of Illinois Press, 1984. ISBN 0252011678. E 661 .C945 1984.

Compares the "innovative nostalgia" of Ives and Frank Lloyd Wright, and considers their relationship to Progressivism alongside other figures such as Woodrow Wilson, Jane Addams, and John Dewey.

Reviews: *Choice* 20 (December 1982): 639; Fred H. Matthews, *Historical Reflections* 10/2 (1983): 245–267.

420. Davidson, Colleen. "Winston Churchill and Charles Ives: The Progressive Experience in Literature and Song." *Student Musicologists at Minnesota* 3 (1968–69): 168–94 and 4 (1970–71): 154–80.

Extended comparison of biographies, political beliefs, and output with emphasis on parallels in Churchill's books to Ives's song (mostly texts and subjects). Davidson concludes that while both started as Progressives, the First World War shattered their optimism, as reflected in Churchill's *The Dwelling Place of Light* and Ives's "A Farewell to Land."

421. Davis, Ronald L. "MacDowell and Ives." In *A History of Music in American Life, Vol. 2: The Gilded Years, 1865–1920.* Huntington, NY: Robert Krieger, 1980, 108–38. ISBN 0898740037. ML 200 .D26.

Unintegrated comparison of the two composers except for brief comments on their reception and influence. Discusses Ives's education, innovations, Transcendentalist beliefs, and divided life.

422. Denhoff, Michael. "*Stille und Umkehr*: Betrachtungen zum Phänomen Zeit." *MusikTexte* 24 (1988): 27–38.

Translates as "*Stille und Umkehr*: Observations on the Phenomenon of Time." Explores the textural and time aesthetics of Bernd Alois Zimmermann as expressed in his orchestral work *Stille und Umkehr*. Applies these ideas to *The Unanswered Question*, as well as in Schubert's *String Quintet in C major* and Boulez's *Rituel.*

423. Eger, Joseph. "Ives and Beatles!" *Music Journal* 26/9 (September 1968): 46, 70–71.

Comparison of the musical qualities, reception, and social identification of Ives and the Beatles. Some parallels include the rejection of established values, experimentation, collage, and eclecticism.

424. Feder, Stuart. "Homesick in America: The Nostalgia of Antonin Dvořák and Charles Ives." Chapter in *Dvořák in America, 1892–95*, edited by John C. Tibbetts. Portland: Amadeus Press, 1993. ISBN 0 931340 56 X. [*?ML 780.92 D98 T].

Discusses similarities, and musical and personal connections between the two composers. Feder suggests that nostalgia was central to each composer's musical language through quotation, in Ives's case, and the less specific integration of folk idioms by Dvořák. Also traces their connection through Ives's teacher and Dvořák's one-time colleague, Horatio Parker, with suggestions on the psychological and musical impact of this association on Ives.

425. Feith, Michel. "La commemoration: traduction ou trahison? Saint-Gaudens, Ives, Lowell." *Revue Francaise d'Etudes Américaines* 80 (1999): 69–81.

Translates as "Commemoration: Tradition or Treason," Feith analyzes two artistic works inspired by the Saint-Gaudens sculpture: Ives's composition and Robert Lowell's poem "For the Union Dead." Considers the means and effectiveness of each tribute, and their contextual significance.

426. Fine, Elaine. "Review of Ives, *Trio* (Sound Recording)." *American Record Guide* 63/6 (November–December 2000): 124.

Review of a recent recording of Ives's *Trio* along with a trio by Rebecca Clarke (1886–1979). Includes stylistic comparisons of both works, including the nationalistic sound and paraphrasing of folk-music materials.

427. Fouse, Kathryn Lea. "Surrealsim in the Piano Music of Representative 20th-Century American Composers with Three Recitals of Selected Works of Ives, Cowell, Crumb, Cage, Antheil, and Others." D.M.A. dissertation, University of North Texas, 1992.

Summary of the aesthetics and characteristics of the art and literature of Surrealism, and their appearances in the piano music of Ives and others. Fouse isolates the following factors as Surrealist techniques: "(1) the practice of automatism; (2) the juxtaposition of unrelated themes or images; and (3) the creation of dream-like atmospheres."

428. Gillespie, Don. "John Becker, Musical Crusader of St. Paul." *Musical Quarterly* 62/2 (April 1976): 195–217.

Outlines Becker's interactions with Cowell and, later, Ives. Discusses the personal dimensions of the friendship between Becker and Ives, their musical collaborations, as well as Becker's heroic efforts on behalf of avant-garde music—his own and others—in St. Paul. Several excerpts from their correspondence. An earlier version appears as "John Becker, The Musical Crusader of St. Thomas College" in *Student Musicologists at Minnesota* 6 (1975–76): 31–65.

429. Gruhn, Wilfried. "Die Bedeutungskonstitution in textgebundener Musik: Ansatze zu einer strukturellen Hermeneutik präsentativer Symbole." In *Wort und Ton im Europäischen Raum: Gedenkschrift für Robert Schollum*, edited by Hartmut Krones. Wien, Austria: Bohlau, 1989, 23–40. ISBN 3205052005. ML 55 .S368.

Title translates as "Constituting Meaning in Texted Music: Approaches to a Structural Hermeneutics of Presentative Symbols." Compares settings of Heine's poem "Ich grolle nicht" by Schumann and Ives for their "constitutive meaning." Concludes that both composers "view the text as a component of a musical structure with immanent meaning."

430. Hansen, Chadwick. "The 54th Massachusetts Volunteer Infantry As A Subject for American Artists." *Massachusetts Review* 16/4 (1975): 745–759; revised as "One Place in New England: The Fifty-Fourth Massachusetts Volunteer Infantry As A Subject for American Artists." *Student Musicologists at Minnesota* 6 (1975–76): 250–71.

Historical background on the infantry unit that inspired the original sculpture, and the program of "The 'St. Gaudens' in Boston Common." Also includes a description of the commissioning and unveiling of the sculpture, and a consideration of Ives's intentions in his accompanying poem.

431. Harley, Maria Anna. "An American in Space: Henry Brant's 'Spatial Music.' " *American Music* 15 (Spring 1997): 70–92.

Within a discussion of Brant's use of sound placement, discusses the influence of Ives as a precursor and founder of the idiom.

432. Harrison, Lou. "Ruggles, Ives, Varèse." *View* 5/4 (November 1945): 11; reprinted in *Soundings: Ives, Ruggles, Varèse. Soundings* (Spring 1974): 1–4.

Refers to the three as "founders of the art tradition in Usonian music," and compares Ives to the painter Eilshemius. Complains about the lack of performances of Ives's music, which is described as "of great interest and delight."

433. Hertz, David Michael. *Angels of Reality: Emersonian Unfoldings in Wright, Stevens, and Ives*. Carbondale: Southern Illinois University Press, 1993. ISBN 080931746X. NX 504 .H47 1993.

Admirable and well-executed consideration of the influence of Emerson on Ives, Frank Lloyd Wright, and Wallace Stevens. The book is divided into two parts. Part 1, "The Conflict of Creativity," examines the precursors and influences on each artist, and includes a chapter on "Ives, Emerson and Rival Composers" as well as a consideration of the use of quotation by all three figures. The second part, "Metaphors of Value in Three Modern Transcendentalists" looks at the interaction of gender discourse and Americanism, as well as the importance of nature for the three. Although many of Ives's compositions are discussed, particular attention is given to the *Concord Sonata* and "Washington's Birthday."

434. Jacobson, Bernard. "The 'In' Composers: Mahler, Ives, Nielsen, Sibelius, Vivaldi, Berlioz—Are They Permanent Classics or Just Temporary Fads?" *High Fidelity/Musical America* 19/7 (July 1969): 54–57.

Contains only the briefest mention of Ives within a larger consideration of the mechanisms through which composers rise to prominence or fade into oblivion. States that Ives's popularity "has been helped by the rising tide of American musical consciousness, in a period that thinks of itself as a cultural explosion."

435. Johnston, Walter. "Style in W. C. Williams and Charles Ives." *20th Century Literature* 31 (Spring 1985): 127–36.

Comparison with the writer William Carlos Williams, who was a near contemporary of Ives. Johnston concludes that both artists shared certain similarities, including the use of local conditions for inspiration; employing dissonance to "defeat conventional response"; and the lack of a sense of finality in their works.

436. Kakinuma, Toshie, and Mamoru Fujieda. " 'I Am One of Mr. Ives' Legal Heirs': An Interview with Lou Harrison." *Sonus: A Journal of Investigations into Global Musical Possibilities* 9/2 (Spring 1989): 46–58.

Includes only a brief mention of Ives at the beginning of the article and within the title.

437. Kay, Norman. "Aspects of Copland's Development." *Tempo* 95 (Winter 1970–71): 23–29.

Includes brief but informed comparisons of Ives and Copland (pp. 23–24, 26), which contrast their biographies, musical styles, and relationships to the musical public. Kay concludes that despite commonalities, they are "the antitheses of American music."

438. Konold, Wulf. "Arkadien in Neuengland: Zum hundersten Geburtstag von Charles Edward Ives." *Musica* 28/5 (1974): 468–69.

Centennial reflection on Ives's music and life compares his musical experimentation and impact on later generations with that of Schoenberg. Comments on the similarities between the *Universe Symphony* and Stockhausen's multimedia works.

439. Koppenhaver, Allen J. "Charles Ives, Winslow Homer, and Thomas Eakins: Variations on America." *Parnassus: Poetry in Review* 3/2 (Spring/Summer 1975): 381–393.

Part of the Parnassus collection (item 168). Overall comparison of biography, output, masculine themes, and attitudes of the three. Includes valuable excerpts from primary and secondary sources, which are unfortunately not provided with full citations.

440. Kostelanetz, Richard. *John Cage (ex)plain(ed)*. New York: Schirmer, 1996, 104 and passim. ISBN 002864526X. ML 410 .C24 K73 1996.

Several passing references to Ives as Cage's predecessor in the American experimental tradition, in addition to a paragraph comparing Cage's *HPSCHD* to the *Universe Symphony*.

441. Kostelanetz, Richard, ed. *Conversing with Cage*. New York: Limelight, 1988, 39–40, 47 and passim. ISBN 087910100. ML 410 .C14 K87 1988.

Includes Cage's comments on the character and music of Ives collected from various interviews. With brief comparisons to Satie and Mao Tse-tung.

442. Lambert, Philip. "Ives and Berg: 'Normative' Procedures and Post-Tonal Alternatives." In *Charles Ives and the Classical Tradition* (item 33), 105–130.

Lambert analyzes works by both composers, emphasizing their creation of new "normative" procedures—that is, "principles and relations that operate in the same basic form in various musical contexts," including harmonic distortion, stylistic heterogeneity, and exploitation of structural models including intervallic cycles and chromatic sets. Exceptionally perceptive in-depth analysis.

443. Lambourn, David. "Grainger and Ives." *Studies in Music* 20 (1986): 46–61.

Compares both composers in terms of early musical education and influences, aesthetic philosophy, use of nature and popular music, innovative musical techniques, gendered language and imagery, compositional and notational habits, and overall musical vocabulary. Includes a comparison of Grainger's *The Warriors* with Ives's Fourth Symphony with special emphasis on instrumentation and scoring.

444. La Motte-Haber, Helga de. "Zum Raum wird hier die Zeit." *Österreichische Musikzeitschrift* 41/6 (June 1986): 282–88.

Translated as "Here Time is Turning into Space," this article considers the historical use or creation of space within music from Gabrieli and Schutz to Ives and Cage. Discusses the use of space in *Universe Symphony* particularly in comparison to the spatial works of Satie and Bill Fontana's "Soundsculptures."

445. Lea, Henry. *Gustav Mahler: Man on the Margin*. Modern German Studies, Vol. 15. Bonn: Bouvier, 1985, 75–78.

Includes a three-page comparison of Mahler's and Ives's use of folk materials.

446. Liebenau, Horst. "Bernhard [sic] Herrmanns Filmmusik für Psycho." *Musikpädagogische Forschungsberichte* 1993: 356–69.

Briefly discusses Ives's influence on Herrmann's 1936 composition "Sinfonietta" as well as Hermann's later use of sections of this composition in the soundtrack of the film *Psycho*.

447. Mack, Dieter. "Auf der Suche nach einer amerikanischen Musik? Zur Musiksprache von Charles Ives anhand der Three-Page-Sonata." Chapter in *Visionen und Aufbruche: Zur Krise der modernen Musik 1908–1933*, edited by Gunther Metz. Hochschuldokumentationen zu Musikwissenschaft und Musikpädagogik Musikhochschule Freiburg No. 5. Kassel: Bosse, 1994, 201–33. ISBN 3-7649-2515-9. ML 197 .V57 1994.

Translates as "The Search for an American Music? The Musical Language of Charles Ives as Seen in the Three-Page Sonata," this article considers the uniquely American qualities of the work, including its stylistic and technical diversity, and textural stratification. Also discusses the influence of Transcendentalism and existentialism on the work.

448. Manfred, Frederick. "Ives and Faulkner." *Student Musicologists at Minnesota* 6 (1975–76): 1–4.

Compares aspects of regionality, reception, isolation, and personal expression in the works of both artists.

449. Marcotte, Gilles. "L'amateur de musique: Des musiques qui parlent." *Liberté* 39/231 (June 1997): 180–186.

Discusses the ability of Ives to express musically what remains inexpressible through words, in *The Unanswered Question*. Compares the two versions of this work, and both versions with Mahler's symphonies. In French.

450. McCalla, James W. "Structural and Harmonic Innovations in the Music of Schoenberg, Stravinsky and Ives Prior to 1915." Master's thesis, New England Conservatory of Music, 1973, 59–83 and passim.

Compares the technical devices, aesthetic principles, and general compositional approaches as evidenced in *Pierrot lunaire, Le sacre du printemps,* and *Concord Sonata.* Emphasizes the central role of Transcendentalist philosophy in Ives's work, and compares available literary writings by each composer.

451. Morgan, Robert P. "Ives and Mahler: Mutual Responses at the End of an Era." *19th Century Music* 2 (1978–79): 72–81: reprinted in *Charles Ives and the Classical Tradition* (item 33), 75–86.

Landmark essay, among the first to suggest extensive parallels between Ives and the European tradition. Morgan discusses musical and aesthetic commonalities, focusing on both composers' employment of tonality, popular and folk materials, and formal disjunction and juxtaposition.

452. Morgan, Robert P. "Rewriting Music History: Second Thoughts on Ives and Varèse." *Musical Newsletter* 3/1 (January 1973): 3–12 and 3/2 (April 1973): 15–23.

Critiques music history accounts from the 1950s to the early 1970s, suggesting that Ives and Varèse represent an experimental mainstream that was ignored by earlier commentators. Much of Part I of the article outlines Ives's anticipations of later compositional techniques including melodic and rhythmic serialism, musical borrowing, and eclecticism. Also considers the question of Ives's technical competence and training, and concludes that Ives's work represents an extension of historical traditions.

453. Nicholls, David. "Transethnicism and the American Experimental Tradition." *Musical Quarterly* 80 (Winter 1996): 569–94.

Compares the use of specifically "American" materials by Ives and Copland with composers who use transethnic materials such as Cowell, Harrison, Partch, Riley, and Young. Also considers how the reception of these two groups reveals much about American cultural values.

454. Parthun, Paul. "Concord, Charles Ives, and Henry Bellamann." *Student Musicologists at Minnesota* 6 (1975–76): 66–86.

Parthun explores the relationship between Ives and Bellamann, one of his earliest supporters, as evidenced primarily through their correspondence. Includes little-known details on Bellamann's later life and interactions with the Iveses, as well as a thorough bibliography of his own writings and a chronological summary of his life.

455. Rathert, Wolfgang. "Aspekte asthetischer Modernität bei Mahler und Ives." In *Das Gustav-Mahler-Fest Hamburg 1989*, edited by Matthias Theodor Vogt. Kassel, Germany: Barenreiter, 1991, 333–343. ISBN 3761810156. ML 410 .M23 I58 1989.

Comparison of "aesthetic modernity" in Ives and Mahler, as demonstrated in their approaches to form (summation in Mahler, fragmentation in Ives) and relationship to tradition.

456. Rathert, Wolfgang. "Mahler und Ives: Gibt es eine 'geheime Zeitgenossen-schaft'?" *Neue Zeitschrift für Musik* 151/10 (Oct 1990): 7–12.

Title translates as "Mahler and Ives: Were they 'secret contemporaries'?" Comparison of aesthetic similarities between Ives and Mahler and speculation on their reported 1910 meeting. Expanded in item 455.

457. Reed, Joseph W. *Three American Originals: John Ford, William Faulkner and Charles Ives*. Middletown, CT: Wesleyan University Press, 1984. ISBN 0819551015. NX 504 .R4.

Integrated comparison that considers the impact of Americanism on the films, literature, and music of the three artists, including regionalism, individualism, isolation, creation of a canon, and free adaptation of existing genres. Except for Ives's "A Song—For Anything," contains little musical discussion.

Reviews: Arthur Kinney, *Modern Fiction Studies* 31 (Summer 1985): 411–13; Corey Field, *Notes* XLII/4 (June 1986): 783–85.

458. Retallack, Joan, ed. *Musicage: Cage Muses on Words, Art, Music*. Hanover, NH: University Press of New England, 1995, 283. ISBN 0819552852. ML 410 .C24 A5 1995.

Brief but interesting passage reports Cage's comparison of his use of spatial approaches with that of Ives, and Cage's comments on Ives's microtonal music.

459. Romine, Thomas Howard. "Double String Quartet: Musical Score and Analysis." D.M.A. dissertation, Ohio State University, 1984.

The second movement is based on quotations from Ives's two string quartets. Includes a brief discussion of Ives's use of quotations and his influence on Romine's compositional language.

460. Rossiter, Frank. "The 'Genteel Tradition' in American Music." *Journal of American Culture* 4/4 (Winter 1981): 107–15.

Applies the highbrow/lowbrow dichotomy voiced by Van Wyck Brooks to American music of the early twentieth century, and compares the approaches of Ives and Daniel Gregory Mason. Original and convincing scholarship indicates that Ives knew Mason's writings and was influenced by them.

461. Schiff, David. *The Music of Elliot Carter.* London: Eulenberg Books, 1983, 17–19 and passim. ISBN 0903873060. ML 410 .C255 S33.

Discusses Ives's influence on Carter's music both generally and in specific pieces and passages. Considers Carter's writings on Ives, and finds philosophical parallels within Ives's own writings.

462. Schwartz, Elliott. "Directions in American Composition Since the Second World War: Part I—1945–1960." *Music Educator's Journal* 61/6 (February 1975): 29–39.

Discusses Ives's influence on composers such as Elliot Carter, Henry Brant, and John Cage, whose experiments with metrical complexity, spatial relationships, and contrapuntal interactions are "directly related" to Ives.

463. Schwarz, Boris. "Schoenberg—und Ives—Tagunen in den USA." *Österreichische Musikzeitschrift* 30 (January–February 1975): 67–68.

Report on centennial celebrations for both composers briefly compares their aesthetics and musical style. Describes the New York Philharmonic's Mini-Festival around Ives as well as the papers, panels, and concerts of the Centennial Conference in New York and New Haven.

464. Shreffler, Anne Chatoney. "Elliott Carter and his America." *Sonus* 14/2 (Spring 1994): 38–66.

Includes an overview of the Carter-Ives relationship, as well as a very specific assessment of Ives's influence on Carter, particularly through quotations of Ives's First Violin Sonata in Carter's First Quartet. Also discusses the legacy of Ives's textures and collages as heard in Carter's *Symphony of Three Orchestras*, and *Mirror on Which to Dwell*.

465. Spackman, S. G. F. "The American Musical Avant-Garde and Europe." *European Contributions to American Studies* 10 (1986): 189–202.

Discusses the interactions between Ives, Cowell, Ruggles, and Riegger with European musical ideas and audiences. Suggests that the modernists attempted to gain European acceptance through performance tours while building a uniquely "American" musical tradition that rejected British and German influences.

466. Stambler, Bernard. "Four American Composers." *Juilliard Review* 2/1 (Winter 1955): 7–16.

Comparison of Ives, Copland, Schuman, and Barber focuses on musical training, relationship to performers and audiences, and career choices. Ultimately, Stambler concludes that "the sad paradox of Ives" was his commitment to business that left little energy and dedication to his music. As a result, his music is that "of a great amateur."

467. Starr, Larry. "Ives, Gershwin, and Copland: Reflections on the Strange History of American Art Music." *American Music* 12 (Summer 1994): 167–87.

Suggests common ground between the three composers, with an emphasis on their conscious desires to create American as opposed to European concert music through stylistic diversity and synthesis. Also considers the often negative reactions of American critics and audiences to the work of Ives and Gershwin. Includes analysis of and excerpts from "Majority."

468. Stern, Karen. "Notes in Passing." *Adirondack Life* 20/2 (1989): 48–51.

Compares the use of folk music in works of Ives and Bartók, both of whom were inspired by the Adirondack mountains.

469. Tawa, Nicholas E. "Ives and the New England School." In *Charles Ives and the Classical Tradition* (item 33), 51–72.

Somewhat limited overview suggesting parallels in musical style, cultural background, and philosophy between Ives and Horatio Parker, George Chadwick, John Knowles Paine, and others.

470. Teachout, Terry. "Cross Over, Beethoven." *Time* 149/13 (31 March 1997): from www.time.com.

     In this profile of composer Michael Daugherty, the composer states, "Crossover is American. . . . Sometimes I think maybe what I'm doing is what Charles Ives would be doing if he were alive today. He used the music he heard—hymn tunes, band marches—and I use TV and Muzak."

471. Vinay, Gianfranco. "Charles Ives e i musicisti europei: Anticipazioni e dipendenze." *Nuova Rivista Musicale Italiana* 7/3–4 (July–December 1973): 417–29.

     Wide-ranging comparison of Ives's compositional techniques with those of roughly contemporary European composers including Mahler, Debussy, and the early works of Hindemith. Concludes that, while his experiments anticipate modernist techniques, Ives was shrewdly manipulating European styles and models.

472. Ward, Keith C. "Ives, Schoenberg and the Musical Ideal." In *Charles Ives and the Classical Tradition* (item 33), 87–104.

     Investigation of parallels in musical thought, values, and compositional techniques (particularly developing variation) between Schoenberg and Ives. Ward concludes that, despite their many differences, both composers sought unique solutions to their common challenges.

473. Ward, Keith Charles. "Musical Idealism: A Study of the Aesthetics of Arnold Schoenberg and Charles Ives." D.M. dissertation, Northwestern University, 1986.

     Suggests that the philosophy of idealism lies behind the musical experiments of Schoenberg and Ives, through three main elements: dualism, expressive need, and "an acceptance of the eternal artistic spirit of constant change." Includes a comparison of their respective philosophies and brief analyses of several short piano pieces by each composer.

     Reviews: Michael Saffle, *Bulletin of the Council for Research in Music Education* 100 (Spring 1989): 34–39.

5

Individual Studies by Genre

ORCHESTRAL AND BAND WORKS

474. Ahlstrom, David. "The Problem of the Unfinished: A Cart, a Deity, and Ives's *Universe Symphony.*" *Sonus* 11/2 (Spring 1991): 65–76.

A very brief comparison of Ives's work to the Festival of the Cart of Jagannath in India, alongside twentieth-century Vedantic interpretations of the festival. Not recommended.

475. Atlas, Allan W. *The Wheatstone English Concertina in Victorian England.* Oxford: Clarendon, 1996. ISBN 0198165803. ML 1083 .A84.

Includes a paragraph on Ives's use of the concertina in *Orchestral Set No. 2* within a larger discussion of contemporary uses of the instrument.

476. Austin, Larry. "The Realization and First Complete Performances of Ives's *Universe Symphony.*" In *Ives Studies* (item 55), 179–232.

Extensive discussion of the sources of the *Universe Symphony* and Austin's realization of this unfinished work that premiered in 1994. Austin explains his interpretation of the sketches, particularly the structural format, instrumentation, and overall effect of the rhythmic cycles for percussion orchestra, here labeled *Life Pulse Prelude* or *LPP*. Includes plates of sixteen primary sources.

477. Badolato, James. "The Four Symphonies of Charles Ives: A Critical, Analytical Study of the Musical Style of Charles Ives." Ph.D. dissertation, Catholic University of America, 1978.

General overview of the four symphonies. Each movement is described according to thematic design (including quotations), formal-tonal structure, orchestration, texture, and rhythm. Badolato's traditional approach is most successful for the first two symphonies.

478. Bergman, Timothy. "*Symphony No. 2* by Charles Ives: A Basis for Interpretation." D.M.A. dissertation, University of Miami, 1993.

A complete study of the sources, reception, and structure of the Second Symphony as the preparation for interpretation by an orchestra conductor. Details the work's premiere, as well as its compositional and editorial history. Each movement is analyzed according to harmonic, thematic, and quotational structure. Includes an extensive discussion of tempo relationships and errata in the published score.

479. Bond, Victoria. "Towards Creating a Composer-Friendly Environment." *Journal of the Conductors' Guild* 12/1–2 (Winter–Spring 1991): 64–70.

Although otherwise insubstantial, this source includes an interview with Nicolas Slonimsky, who discusses conducting the premiere and arranging for the publication of *Three Places in New England*.

480. Brooks, William. "A Drummer-Boy Looks Back: Percussion in Ives's *Fourth Symphony*." *Percussive Notes* 22/6 (1984): 4–45.

Thorough discussion of the use of pitched and nonpitched percussion primarily in the second and fourth movements, with slight mention of the first movement. Includes an overview of the reception of the work (focusing on the 1927 performance) as well as consideration of the manuscript sources and editing challenges for the percussion parts. Perhaps most helpful is Brooks's detailed account of the notational peculiarities for pitched percussion (celesta, timpani, and bells) and of the utilization of nonpitched percussion for pulse, accent, and cadence. Concludes with a consideration of cyclic structure in the percussion parts, and two appendices summarizing the second movement's use of percussion.

481. Brooks, William Fordyce. "Sources and Errata List for Charles Ives' *Symphony No. 4*, Movement II." D.M.A. dissertation, University of Illinois, 1976.

Discusses the manuscript sources for the work, and includes a detailed comparison and list of significant errata with the 1965 Associated edition.

482. Brooks, William. "Unity and Diversity in Charles Ives's Fourth Symphony." *Anuario interamericano de investigacion musical/Yearbook for Inter-American Musical Research* 10 (1974): 5–49.

Somewhat misleading title, because the article analyzes only the first movement in great detail. After introducing the concepts of "substance" and "manner," Brooks considers the creation of unity and diversity within the movement from two perspectives, by recognizing sequential sectional structure built on orchestration, tonality, meter, and melody; and using laminar analysis, or the isolation of families of layers, in the work's orchestration, prominence, pulse, pattern, tonality, melody, and the pitch class E-sharp. Includes several discussions of the use of borrowed material.

483. Charles, Sydney Robinson. "The Use of Borrowed Materials in Ives' Second Symphony." *Music Review* 28/2 (May 1967): 102–11.

Analyzes Ives's direct borrowings and paraphrases in the Second Symphony. Divides Ives's quotations into three categories: unessential; structurally essential; and material that appears in more than one movement. Concludes that "there is really no reason to posit any other basis of selection, any sentimental, emotional, or evocative intention on Ives's part" other than purely musical considerations.

484. Cooney, Denise Von Glahn. "New Sources for 'The 'St. Gaudens' in Boston Common (Colonel Robert Gould Shaw and His Colored Regiment)." *Musical Quarterly* 81/1 (Spring 1997): 13–50.

Valuable consideration of the work within a new context. Cooney suggests that poetic tributes to Shaw by Emerson, William Vaughn Moody, and Robert Underwood Johnson, descriptions of Shaw's final battle, and the monument itself contributed greatly to the musical structure and quotations of the work and Ives's own attached poem.

485. Crane, Frederick. "How Should the Jew's Harp Part of 'Washington's Birthday' be played?" *Verundzwanzigsteljahrsschrift der Internationalen Maultrommelvirtuosengenossenschaft* 1 (1982): 49–57.

Brief examination of the Jew's harp part of "Washington's Birthday" based on manuscript sources, the *New Music* published edition, the peculiarities of Ives's notation, the construction of the instrument, and the appropriate number of players. Suggests that the written score should be interpreted as a "guide for improvisation." Concludes with an evaluation of the Jew's harp performances on several commercial and noncommercial recordings. See also item 501.

486. Debruyn, Randall Keith. "Contrapuntal Structure in Contemporary Tonal Music: A Preliminary Study of Tonality in the 20th Century." D.M.A. dissertation, University of Illinois, 1975.

Applies Schenkerian analysis to the third movement of the Fourth Symphony as well as works by Hindemith, Bartók, Stravinsky, and Hovhaness.

487. Echols, Paul. "The Music for Orchestra." *Music Educator's Journal* 61/2 (October 1974): 29–41.

Stylistic survey of orchestral music with extensive musical examples. Focuses on the variety of musical forms, styles, and techniques found in the symphonies and sets including quotation, programmatic elements, and experimentation.

488. Franceschini, Romulus. "A Postscript on Ives's Fourth." *American Record Guide* 32/3 (November 1965): 223.

Commentary by a staff member of the Fleisher Collection who helped prepare the score for the premiere of the Fourth Symphony. Emphasizes the experimental aspects of Ives's music and their problematic representation in notation, with an example from the finale of the Fourth Symphony.

489. Herrmann, Bernard. "Four Symphonies by Charles Ives." *Modern Music* 22/4 (May–June 1945): 215–222; reprinted in *Charles Ives and His World* (item 36), 394–402.

Important early overview of the symphonies with a summary of the influences, organization, significant quotations, and overall style of each work illustrated by musical excerpts.

490. Hilliard, John Stanley. "Charles Ives' *Robert Browning Overture*: Style and Structure." D.M.A. dissertation, Cornell University, 1983.

Primarily a structural analysis focusing on Ives's use of repetition, dynamic and tempo structures, thematic transformation and synthesis, harmonic and linear aspects, and imitation and fugal procedures.

491. Hüsken, Renata. "Charles Ives' 'Robert Browning Overture.' " *Neuland* 1 (1980): 16–24.

This two-part discussion of the work begins with an extensive comparison of the attitudes, approaches, and output of Ives and Browning, including their tendency toward stylistic juxtaposition and multiplicity. The second section is an analysis of the work focusing on thematic and motivic content. Identifies a possible quotation from Wagner's *Ring des Nibelungen* in the trumpet theme.

492. Josephson, Nors. "The Initial Sketches for Ives's 'St. Gaudens in Boston Common.' " *Soundings* 12 (1984–85): 46–63.

Reproduces facsimiles of two early sketches for the work, along with transcriptions and detailed musical analysis. Josephson concludes that the underlying harmonic structure of the work was present in the earliest sources, although later revisions altered phrase and cadential stucture, and introduced more contrapuntal material.

493. Josephson, Nors S. "Zur formalen Struktur einiger später Orchesterwerke von Charles Ives (1874–1954)." *Die Musikforschung* 27/1 (1974): 57–64.

   Detailed analysis of orchestral works dating from 1911–1916 through formal, key, rhythmic, and interval analysis. Josephson divides these works into three distinct periods: abstract ("The 'St. Gaudens' in Boston Common" and *Robert Browning Overture*); realist (programmatic works including "Decoration Day," "Putnam's Camp" and "The Fourth of July"); and symbolic ("From Hanover Street North" and the Fourth Symphony, fourth movement). Concludes with a brief comparison to the works of Berg.

494. Knight, John Wesley. "Graphic Analyses of the Conducting Techniques for Irregular Meters and Nonmetrical Organizations Found in Selected 20th-Century Band Literature." Ph.D. dissertation, Louisiana State University, 1979.

   Includes passages from Ives's *Scherzo: Over the Pavements* along with ten other twentieth-century pieces in an educational survey of five noted college band conductors. Conductors were asked to specify which conducting patterns they would use for each; their responses are used to construct recommended teaching techniques as well as graphic representations for conducting patterns.

495. Kopetz, Barry E. "Charles Ives's *Variations on 'America.'* " *Instrumentalist* 45/9 (April 1991): 20–28, 75–79.

   Detailed analysis of the band arrangement directed at wind band directors with specifics for dynamics, phrasing, balance, conducting patterns, cues, and rehearsal techniques. Concludes with a long and very precise list of errata in the published score and parts.

496. Kramer, Jonathan D. "Postmodern concepts of musical time." *Indiana Theory Review* 17/2 (Fall 1996): 21–61.

   Presents an investigation of "Putnam's Camp," along with works by Beethoven and Mahler, according to the writer's theory of "multiple musical time," or music that "can enable listeners to experience different sense of directionality, different temporal narratives, and/or different rates of motion, all *simultaneously*." The writer concludes that the intertextual references in "Putnam's Camp," multiple narratives including Ives's own program and the interpretation of musical borrowings, and multilayered textural, dynamic and formal structures combine to anticipate "postmodern temporal multiplicity."

497. Lambert, Philip. "Ives's Universe." In *Ives Studies* (item 55), 233–59.

Lambert places Ives's *Universe Symphony* within its intellectual context through a wide-ranging survey of philosophical, artistic, and musical representations of the cosmos throughout history. Special emphasis on similarities in the concepts, musical structures, and procedures of the *Universe*, Scriabin's *Mysterium,* and Schoenberg's *Die Jakobsleiter.*

498. Lipkis, Laurence Alan. "Aspects of Temporality in Debussy's 'Jeux' and Ives' 'Symphony No. 4,' Fourth Movement." Ph.D. dissertation, University of California, Santa Barbara, 1984.

Brief consideration of Ives's innovative use of temporal processes in the final movement of the Fourth Symphony. Lipkis's primary conclusion is that the work rejects traditional markers of temporality—such as regular phrases and cadences—in favor of a more "organic" structure.

499. Magers, Roy Vernon. "Aspects of Form in the Symphonies of Charles Ives." Ph.D. dissertation, Indiana University, 1975.

A somewhat limited study of the thematic structures of the four symphonies divided into two parts: first, a summary of the form of each movement based on thematic analysis; and second, a comparison of all four works based on general formal organizations used (sonata, ternary, etc.), and characteristic thematic and formal features.

500. Maisel, Arthur. "*The Fourth of July* by Charles Ives: Mixed Harmonic Criteria in a 20th-Century Classic." *Theory and Practice* 6/1 (August 1981): 3–32.

A detailed Schenkerian analysis of "The Fourth of July," with emphasis on demonstrating Ives's coherent use of specific motivic and harmonic structures from foreground to background. Includes Ives's description of the work, and extensive graphs.

501. Mihura, Brian L. "The Great Jew's Harp Hunt of 1954." *Verundzwanzigsteljahrsschrift der Internationalen Maultrommelvirtuosengenossenschaft* 1 (1982): 44–48.

Entertaining account of the auditions for a Jew's harp player to perform in a 1954 concert of "Washington's Birthday" conducted by Stokowski. Includes a basic description of the instrument itself. See also item 485.

502. Moomaw, Charles J. "A PL/1 Program for the Harmonic Analysis of Music by the Theories of Paul Hindemith and Howard Hanson." Master's thesis, University of Cincinnati, 1971.

     Gives sample results for a computer-generated analysis of a section of "Washington's Birthday," as well as portions of Stravinsky's *L'Histoire du Soldat* and Bartók's *Music for Strings*. Data primarily measures guide tones, roots, and chord groups based on Hindemith, as well as basic intervals and pitch content.

503. Myers, Betty Dustin. "The Orchestral Music of Charles Ives." Master's thesis, Indiana University, 1951.

     Early, limited general overview of the four symphonies and orchestral sets, focusing on their overall thematic form and unconventional instrumentation, harmonic language, and rhythmic structures. Includes transcriptions from two letters from Cowell to Myers on behalf of Ives (12/15/50 and 5/12/51), one of which briefly discusses Ives's "Long Green Organ Book."

504. Nelson, Mark D. "Beyond Mimesis: Transcendentalism and Process of Analogy in Charles Ives' 'The Fourth of July.' " *Perspectives of New Music* 22/1–2 (1983–84): 353–84.

     Examines the work as an intricate web of philosophic, acoustic, and quotational meanings. With emphasis on quotation, program, and musical structure, Nelson explores "The Fourth of July" as a manifestation of Ives's Transcendental beliefs; an evocation of both specific acoustical events (parades, marches) and nonacoustic or natural phenomena (a smoking fuse, fireworks); and a subtle and complex realization of the psychological process of everyday experience. Available in a Serbian translation by Mirjana Detelic as "Iznad mimezisa: Transcendentalizam i analoski procesi u Cetvrtom julu Carlsa Ajvza." *MT: Muzicki Talas* 3/4 (1996): 84–97.

505. Rathert, Wolfgang. "Zur Entwicklung des symphonischen Werkes von Charles Ives." In *Bericht über das Internationale Symposion "Charles Ives und die amerikanische Musiktradition bis zur Gegenwart' Köln 1988*, edited by Klaus Wolfgang Niemöller. Kölner Beiträge zur Musikforschung No. 164. Regensburg: Gustav Bosse Verlag, 1990, pp. 53–70. ISBN 3-7649-2406-3. ML 200.5 .I58 1990.

     Compact discussion in which Rathert traces the evolution of Ives's symphonic language through the programs, styles, and aesthetics of the four symphonies and selected other symphonic movements including parts of the *Universe Symphony*. Concludes that Ives's late works paradoxically present musical time as both unified and fragmented.

506. Rathert, Wolfgang. "Charles Ives: Robert Browning Overture." *Neue Zeitschrift für Musik* 148/4 (April 1987): 28–31.

Stylistic, formal, and aesthetic analysis. Available in a Serbian translation by Vlastimir Pericic as "Uvertira Robert Brauning [Robert Browning Overture]." *MT: Muzicki Talas* 4/1–2 (1997): 84–87.

507. Rathert, Wolfgang. "Charles Ives: Symphonie Nr. 4, 1911–1916." *Neuland* 3 (1982–83): 226–41.

Outlines the philosophical program of the work, in comparison with the *Universe Symphony*, Transcendentalism in general, and Emerson's writings in particular. Rathert's main focus is an analysis of the work highlighting the formal arrangement of each movement; the motivic and thematic relationships (specifically quotations and ostinati); and specific details of phrase, rhythmic, metrical, contrapuntal, canonic, and harmonic elements.

508. Roller, Jonathan. "An Analysis of Selected Movements from the Symphonies of Charles Ives Using Linear and Set Theoretical Analytical Models." Ph.D. dissertation, University of Kentucky, 1995.

Detailed analyses of three movements using varied approaches: First Symphony, second movement, using Schenkerian analysis; Third Symphony, third movement, using both Schenkerian and adapted linear analysis; and Fourth Symphony, first movement, using set-theory analysis. Numerous graphs and diagrams for each analysis.

509. Rossomando, Fred E. "A Conductor's Guide to the Third Symphony of Charles Ives." Master's thesis, Indiana University, 1971.

A basic overview of each movement with advice as to conducting patterns, tempi, articulation, phrasing, and bowing. Very general information on quotations, form, and harmony.

510. Schnepel, Julie. "The Critical Pursuit of the Great American Symphony, 1893–1950." Ph.D. dissertation, Indiana University, 1995, 527–41.

Looks at critical reception of American symphonies and the criteria voiced by critics such as Virgil Thomson and Olin Downes necessary to establish a great American symphonic tradition. In her conclusion, Schnepel suggests that Ives's Second Symphony may have satisfied the necessary criteria, but was unknown until after the debate had waned.

511. Schonberg, Harold. "Complex and Yet Simple." *New York Times*, 2 May 1965, Section 2, 11.

Discusses the Fourth Symphony in terms of its American character and experimental writing. Also speculates on the effect of isolation and lack of contemporary performances on his musical style.

512. Shirley, Wayne. " *'The Second of July'*: A Charles Ives Draft Considered as an Independent Work." In *A Celebration of American Music: Words and Music in Honor of H. Wiley Hitchcock*, edited by Richard Crawford, R. Allen Lott, and Carol J. Oja. Ann Arbor: University of Michigan Press, 1990, 391–404. ISBN 0 472 094009. ML 200 .C44 1989.

In-depth comparison of the sketch-score of Ives's "The Fourth of July" to the final version, with emphasis on overall form, orchestration, textures, layering, and later revisions and additions. Shirley concludes that, while the original sketch is not as complex as the final version, the textural, intervallic, and quotational structure of the earlier source is nevertheless remarkably radical on its own terms.

513. Snapp, Kenneth. "Build a Band—And Educate It, Too." *Instrumentalist* 32/2 (September 1977): 52–53.

Introductory comments and study guide for *Overture and March "1776"* aimed at a college-level band. General description of the work's form, rhythmic characteristics, and quotations.

514. Taruskin, Richard. "Out of Hibernation, Ives's Mythical Beast." *New York Times*, 2 June 1996, section 2, 26.

Considers the historical and biographical importance of the *Universe Symphony*, and previews the premiere of Johnny Reinhard's version in June of 1996.

515. Taruskin, Richard. "Away With the Ives Myth: The 'Universe' Is Here at Last." *New York Times*, 23 October 1994, section H, 42.

Comments on Larry Austin's realization of the *Universe Symphony* with discussion of the work's signficance, structure, and sources. With illustrations and photos.

CHAMBER WORKS

516. Bader, Yvette. "The Chamber Music of Charles Edward Ives." *Music Review* 33/4 (November 1972): 292–99.

Survey of the complete chamber works beginning with a consideration of Ives's instructions to performers and continuing through a general discussion of the overall style and content of the string quartets and works for violin and piano.

517. Budde, Elmar. "Anmerkungen zum Streichquartett Nr. 2 von Charles E. Ives." In *Bericht über den internationalen musikwissenschaftlichen Kongress Bonn 1970*, edited by Carl Dahlhaus et al. Kassel: Bärenreiter, 1971, 303–7.

Budde discusses Ives's unconventional writing in the first movement of the Second String Quartet, and gives a general stylistic overview. Emphasizes that this work contains many compositional techniques typically associated with Ives.

518. Cantrick, Susan. "Charles Ives's String Quartet No. 2: An Analysis and Evaluation." Master's dissertation, Peabody Conservatory, 1983.

Thorough analysis of the work's compositional language, form, and particularly stylistic heterogeneity. Also includes a detailed comparison of manuscript sources with the published edition.

519. Carter, Elliott. "Stravinsky and Other Moderns in 1940." *Modern Music* 17/3 (March–April 1940): 164–170.

Includes a brief but telling commentary on the premiere of the *Sonata No. 4 for Violin and Piano*. Carter notes the "terrific, obvious faults of construction," recognizes its use of American themes, and suggests that it would have been better if written for viola.

520. Christensen, Erik. *The Musical Timespace: A Theory of Music Listening.* Alborg, Denmark: Alborg University Press, 1996. ISBN 8773075256. MT 6 .C465 1996.

Analyzes Ives's manipulation of musical time in *The Unanswered Question* and *Central Park in the Dark*. Includes listening guides for both pieces (pp. 51–56) and a more intensive discussion of the works' musical soundspace. Illustrated with musical excerpts and a "soundscape" graph of *The Unanswered Question* that summarizes interval structures (pp. 119–25).

521. Enke, Heinz. "Charles Ives' *The Unanswered Question*." In *Versuche musikalischer Analysen*, edited by Peter Benary. Veroffentlichungen des Institut für Neue Musik und Musikerziehung, Darmstadt, Vol. 8. Berlin: Merseburger, 1967, 30–34. ML 5 .D29 V8.

Analyzes the work in terms of rhythm and performance problems with an emphasis on the three strata. Briefly critiques the use of programs in Ives's music.

522. Gaudibert, Eric. "A propos de *From the steeples and the mountains* d'Ives." *Dissonanz/Dissonance* 29 (August 1991): 14–15.

Description of the work's thematic, harmonic, rhythmic, and formal structure with emphasis on its symmetrical features. Includes several examples and a basic formal diagram.

523. Goss, Glenda Dawn. *Music and the Moderns: The Life and Works of Carol Robinson.* Metuchen, NJ: Scarecrow Press, 1993. ISBN 0810826267. ML 417 .R65 G67 1993.

Although not a substantial source, does include a discussion of Robinson, an active performer of new music. Includes a description of her performances with Madeleine Carabo of the Third Violin Sonata in 1946–47, with a reprint of the program, program notes, and excerpts from the Robinson-Ives correspondence.

524. Gratovich, Eugene. "Ives Second Violin Sonata: Performance Alternatives." *American String Teacher* 29/2 (Spring 1979): 46–49.

Discusses sources and substantial variants for each movement, particularly the phrasing, bowing, and meter changes of "In the Barn." Expands on Gratovich's earlier essay (item 525).

525. Gratovich, Eugene. "The Violin Sonatas." *Music Educator's Journal* 61/2 (October 1974): 58–63.

Describes the four sonatas with emphasis on the second and fourth. Includes some motivic, harmonic, and formal analysis, and identifies the most prominent quotations throughout.

526. Gratovich, Eugene. "The Sonatas for Violin and Piano by Charles Ives: A Critical Commentary and Concordance of the Printed Editions and the Autographs and Manuscripts of the Yale Ives Collection." D.M.A. dissertation, Boston University, 1968.

Discusses the four violin sonatas with a description of sources, revisions, marginalia, quotations, and general style and compositional techniques. Also traces early performances.

527. Hitchcock, H. Wiley, and Vivian Perlis, eds. "On Performing the Violin Sonatas." In *An Ives Celebration: Papers and Panels of the Charles Ives Centennial Festival-Conference* (item 50), 127–140.

Transcription of a panel discussion on the sonatas for violin and piano between Nancy Mandel, Alan Mandel, Eugene Gratovich, Regis Benoit, Daniel Stepner, and John Kirkpatrick.

528. Hitchcock, H. Wiley, and Noel Zahler. "Just What *Is* Ives's Unanswered Question?" *Notes* 44/3 (March 1988): 437–43.

Study of the source of *The Unanswered Question* with a focus on the main trumpet theme in its two versions, one from 1906 and another from the 1930s. By comparing extant sources, the authors conclude that both variants are valid and justify the offering of two editions.

529. Jolas, Betsy. "Sur *The Unanswered Question.*" *Musique en jeu* 1 (1970): 13–16.

Discussion of the work's outline and critique of Ives's program based on the author's response.

530. Lambert, J. Philip. "Another view of *Chromâtimelôdtune.*" *Journal of Musicological Research* 11/4 (September 1991): 237–62.

Comparison of three realizations by Gunther Schuller, Gerard Schwarz, and Kenneth Singleton with particular emphasis on Ives's experimental use of pitch-class aggregates as "a comprehensive pitch resource." The author's analysis of the original source content, marginalia, and revisions suggest that *Chromâtimelôdtune* represents one of Ives's "most clearly structured experiments," despite the lack of a definitive, complete source.

531. McCandless, William Edgar. "Cantus Firmus Techniques in Selected Instrumental Compositions, 1910–1960." Ph.D. dissertation, Indiana University, 1974.

Discussion of Ives's use of quotations in the Fourth Violin Sonata (pp. 155–75). With a descriptive outline of the main themes and general discussion of motivic development, harmony, and texture. McCandless suggests that Ives's use of complete quotations only at the end of movements is related to his Transcendentalist belief that truth "is an ultimate goal, not a point of departure."

532. Milligan, Terry Gilbert. "Charles Ives: A Study of the Works for Chamber Ensemble Written between 1898 and 1908 Which Utilize Wind Instruments." D.M.A. dissertation, University of Texas, 1978.

Overview of twenty-five works that "use wind instruments in a prominent way," with a focus on three works: *From the Steeples and the Mountains*, *Scherzo: Over the Pavements*, and *Central Park in the Dark*. Outlines the origins, instrumentation, and general style of these and several other chamber and small orchestra works.

533. Pozzi, Raffaele. "Polemica antiurbana ed isolamento ideologico in Central Park in the Dark di Charles Ives." *Nuova rivista musicale italiana* 19/3 (July–September 1985): 471–81.

   Interprets *Central Park in the Dark* within the context of growing urbanization and the loss of agrarian culture in the United States at the turn of the century. Concludes that the work represents an "antiurban polemic" that also reflects Ives's Transcendental beliefs.

534. Rottermund, Krzysztof. "Filozofia, estetyka i warsztat w utworze Charlesa Ivesa *The Unanswered Question*." *Zeszyty naukowe* 28 (1989): 199–202.

   Translated from the Polish as "Philosophy, Aesthetics, and Form in Charles Ives's *The Unanswered Question*," this article examines the aesthetic basis of the work as well as its experimental aspects.

535. Shirley, Wayne. "Once More Through *The Unanswered Question*." *Institute for Studies in American Music Newsletter* 18/2 (May 1989): 8–9, 13.

   Intriguing reading of *The Unanswered Question* through the lens of an Emerson poem entitled "The Sphinx." The poem includes the line, "Thou art the unanswered question." Shirley speculates not only that Ives knew the poem, but that his composition uses Emerson's phrase as a hidden program in which the musical question represents the riddle of the sphinx.

536. Walker, Gwyneth. "Tradition and the Breaking of Tradition in the String Quartets of Ives and Schoenberg." D.M.A. dissertation, University of Hartford, 1976.

   Comparison of the compositional techniques and aesthetics of both composers, with a focus on their string quartets. Summarizes the works' structure, harmonic language, rhythm, meter, texture, and themes.

KEYBOARD WORKS

   See keyword index under individual listings, and items 29 and 32 for book-length studies.

537. Alexander, Michael J. "Bad Resolutions or Good? Ives's Piano 'Take-Offs.' " *Tempo* 158 (September 1986): 8–14.

   Examines the improvisatory nature of many of the studies and take-offs for piano, and Ives's early exposure to experiential listening through his father's influence. Includes brief excerpts from *Study #8* and *Study #20*, as well as *Seen And Unseen*. Some of this material is expanded in item 29.

538. Baron, Carol Kitzes. "Ives on His Own Terms: An Explanation, a Theory of Pitch Organization, and a New Critical Edition for the *Three Page Sonata*." Ph.D. dissertation, City University of New York, 1987.

Examines the interaction of extramusical program and musical structure, with a focus on the pitch organization of the *Three-Page Sonata*. Baron identifies cyclic organization throughout the work, as well as the use of "partially ordered 12-note sets" as the structural basis for the third movement.

539. Bellamann, Henry. "Reviews: 'Concord, Mass., 1840–1860' (A Piano Sonata by Charles E. Ives)." *Double Dealer* 2 (October 1921): 166–69; reprinted in *Charles Ives and His World* (item 36), 280–84.

First significant published review of the *Concord Sonata* with brief comments on the *Essays*. Bellamann considers the nationalistic aspects of the work with general descriptions of the style and program of each movement. Concludes that the work is "an essay of lofty thought and feeling" with "moments of achievement [that are] elevating and greatly beautiful."

540. Belland, Anna. "Charles Ives: *Varied Air and Variations*." In "Piano Variations by Ives, Valen, Lutoslawski, Dallapiccola: A Discussion of Their Styles and Forms." D.Mus. dissertation, Indiana University, 1981, 3–20.

A basic descriptive analysis of the piece outlining the general style and content of each variation. With conventional biographical material and transcriptions of Ives's marginalia from the sources, plus a discussion of the unique demands the work places on a pianist's technique.

541. Birkby, Arthur. "Ives, the Organist." *Clavier* 13/7 (1974): 29–30.

Overview of the works for organ focuses on the *Variations on "America"* and gives performance recommendations for the work.

542. Block, Geoffrey. "Remembrance of Dissonances Past: The Two Published Editions of Ives's *Concord Sonata*." In *Ives Studies* (item 55), 27–50.

Through intensive source study and musical analysis, Block suggests three purposes for many of Ives's revisions in the second edition of the *Concord Sonata*: first, the restoration of previously discarded musical ideas; second, both corrections and revisions aimed at making the work more "performer-friendly"; and third, enhancements of the "Beethoven motive," particularly in the "Emerson" movement.

543. Bruderer, Conrad. "The Studies of Charles Ives." Ph.D. dissertation, Indiana University, 1968.

Primarily a detailed discussion of the editorial and performance challenges of the studies, with general comments on the works' structure and harmony. Bruderer describes the sources for each study with commentary on illegibility, possible errors, alternate readings, and omissions, as well as practical solutions. Reprints several of Magee's transcriptions (item 558), plus the author's transcriptions for studies 9 and 22.

544. Burk, James M. "Ives Innovations in Piano Music." *Clavier* 13/7 (1974): 14–16.

Describes innovative piano techniques in the piano works (particularly the *Concord Sonata*) such as quarter-tones, polytonality, polyrhythms, cluster chords, atonality, use of ragtime, formal innovations, performer's choices, unusual dynamics, and quotations. Discusses accompanying writings such as the *Essays*.

545. Clark, Sondra Rae. "Ives and the Assistant Soloist." *Clavier* 13/7 (1974): 17–20, 30.

Discussion of variants of the *Concord Sonata* (building on item 547) is aimed at the performer. Offers several variants in transcription, including a suggestion from Ives that the performer use an assistant for some passages.

546. Clark, Sondra Rae. "The Element of Choice in Ives's 'Concord Sonata'." *Musical Quarterly* 60/2 (April 1974): 167–86.

Considers variants in the *Concord Sonata* based on careful analysis of manuscript sources as well as Ives's revisions to the first printed edition (some reproduced in facsimile). Clark presents a well-documented argument that Ives did not intend to create a fixed score, but intended to have performers choose among notational, dynamic, and tempi variables. Condenses Clark's 1972 dissertation (item 547).

547. Clark, Sondra Rae Scholder. "The Evolving Concord Sonata: A Study of Choices and Variants in the Music of Charles Ives." Ph.D. dissertation, Stanford University, 1972.

Extensive, detailed discussion of the variants in the *Concord Sonata* based primarily on Ives's revisions to the first printed edition. Clark's argument, that Ives intended to have performers choose among numerous variables, is condensed in item 546.

548. Coleman, Donna Jeanne. "A Source Study of the Fifth Movement of Charles Ives's First Piano Sonata: Toward a Critical Edition." D.M.A. document, Eastman School of Music, 1986.

Thorough examination of manuscript sources including layers of revision, compared with the Peer 1979 edition. Also reviews the work's premiere and first recording. Uses correspondence and interviews with Lou Harrison, William Masselos, and Paul Echols.

549. Conen, Hermann. " 'All the Wrong Notes are Right'—Zu Charles Ives' 2. *Klaviersonate 'Concord, Mass. 1840–60.'* " *Neuland* 1 (1980): 28–42.

Extensive consideration of the sonata's origins, manuscript sources, relationship to the *Essays*, interactions with Transcendentalism, overall structure, experimental techniques and use of quotations. Includes motivic, thematic, harmonic, and stylistic analysis of the "Emerson" and "Thoreau" movements.

550. Cowell, Henry, and Richard F. Goldman. "Current Chronicle: New York." *Musical Quarterly* 35 (1949): 451–465.

The second section (pp. 458–62) includes a description by Cowell of the *Three-Page Sonata* and the First Piano Sonata, both of which had been recently premiered by William Masselos. Most of this portion is devoted to a general motivic and melodic analysis of the *Three-Page Sonata*.

551. Dumm, Robert. "Performer's Analysis of an Ives Piano Piece." *Clavier* 13/7 (1974): 21–25.

Detailed performance directions for *Study #22* includes a full reprint of the Kirkpatrick edition. With formal analysis and recommendations for tempi, practice methods, and pedaling.

552. Evseeva, Marina. "Fortepiannaja sonata v tvorcestve kompozitorov SSA XX veka: Carl'z Ajvz, Aaron Koplend, Vinsent Persiketti." Ph.D. dissertation, Gosudarstvennaja konservatorija, Moscow, 1989.

Translated from the Russian as "The Piano Sonata as Cultivated by 20th-Century Composers in the United States: Charles Ives, Aaron Copland, Vincent Persichetti." Brief overview of the *Concord Sonata* with attention to its uniquely American elements.

553. Feinberg, Alan. "An Ives premiere." *American Record Guide* 61/6 (November–December 1998): 6–8.

Discusses Ives's pianistic style as heard in the *"Emerson" Concerto*. Also outlines the importance of Emerson's life and ideas on the work.

554. Fruehwald, Robert Douglas. "Motivic Transformation in the 'Thoreau' Movement of Charles Ives' 'Concord Sonata.' " Ph.D. dissertation, Washington University, 1985.

Detailed motivic analysis of the 'Thoreau" movement based on the premise that the work is based on four generative ideas. Fruehwald suggests that the constant transformations of these four basic motives unify this superficially diverse work. Includes numerous comparative graphs and musical excerpts.

555. Hertz, David Michael. "Ives's *Concord Sonata* and the Texture of Music." In *Charles Ives and His World* (item 36), 75–117.

Extensive comparison of the *Concord Sonata* with works by Beethoven, Liszt, Chopin, Debussy, and Scriabin. Hertz equates Ives's accomplishments to those of Walt Whitman, stating that both artists claimed more from the European tradition than their "mediocre," "nondescript," and "forgotten" American precursors.

556. Hinson, Maurice. "The Solo Piano Music of Charles Ives (1874–1954)." *Piano Quarterly* 88 (Winter 1974–75): 32–35.

Somewhat uneven summaries of First Piano Sonata, *The Anti-Abolitionist Riots*, *Some South-Paw Pitching*, *Three Protests*, *Varied Air and Variations*, *Study #22*, and the *Concord Sonata*. For each, includes a brief background (including Ives's own descriptions), overall form, descriptive analysis, and notes on unique pianistic techniques.

557. Kolosick, J. Timothy. "A Computer-Assisted, Set-Theoretic Investigation of Vertical Simultaneities in Selected Piano Compositions by Charles E. Ives." Ph.D. dissertation, University of Wisconsin, 1981.

Uses an Apple II program to analyze brief excerpts from five published piano pieces including *Study No. 22* and *Varied Air and Variations*. Summarizes vertical and horizontal intervallic relationships with varying success.

558. Magee, Noel H. "The Short Piano Works of Charles Ives." Master's thesis, Indiana University, 1966.

Comprehensive catalogue with detailed musical descriptions of all of Ives's complete short piano works, namely the studies, *Three-Page Sonata*, *Rough and Ready*, *The Seen and Unseen*, *Waltz-Rondo*, *Song Without Words*, *Scene Episode*, *Bad Resolutions*, *Varied Air*, and *Three Protests*. For each work, Magee provides a general history, formal outline, melodic and harmonic analysis, and memoranda and other comments on the work by Ives. Also includes performance-quality transcriptions of unpublished works, many of which are reprinted in Bruderer (item 543).

559. Mandel, Alan. "Charles Ives's Music for the Piano." *Student Musicologists at Minnesota* 6 (1975–76): 201–17.

Overview of published and select unpublished piano works, particularly the studies. Considers variants, revisions, errata, Ives's humor, quotations, polytonality, and unconventional keyboard techniques and notation.

560. McCrae, Elizabeth. "The Piano Music." *Music Educator's Journal* 61/2 (October 1974): 53–57.

Cursory introduction to the technical challenges of the piano music including dense melodic and contrapuntal lines, polyrhythms, syncopations, pedalling, chord clusters, harmonic structure, motivic usages, rapid chord shifts, and polytonality. With examples from *Three Protests*, the first and second piano sonatas, and the *Three-Page Sonata*.

561. McDonald, Charlene Harb. "Trends in Selected Piano Sonatas of the First Quarter of the 20th Century: Formal Processes and Pianism." DMA dissertation, Indiana University, 1978.

Includes a discussion of the First Piano Sonata (pp. 80–105) with an overview of the work's historical background, outline of "stylistic processes" (general form, key areas, musical quotations), and summary of the work's challenges to the performer. Draws heavily on Masselos's descriptions of the work as well as Harrison's preface to the Peer edition.

562. Mumper, Dwight Robert. "The First Piano Sonata of Charles Ives." Ph.D. dissertation, Indiana University, 1971.

Detailed formal, harmonic, and melodic analysis of the First Piano Sonata with emphasis on the varied appearances of musical quotations. An appendix presents original sources for many of the quotations (hymn tunes and popular songs), while the introduction gives a general overview of the work's origin based primarily on the Cowells's biography (item 37), first edition, and Ives's *Essays* (item 21).

563. Newman, Ron. "Ragtime Influences in the Music of Charles Ives." *Jazz Research Papers* 5 (1985): 145–56.

Examines Ives's use of ragtime elements in the First Piano Sonata. Traces the history of Ives's introduction to ragtime, and presents several musical examples illustrating ragtime syncopation, accents, meter changes, and melodic and accompanying patterns in the various movements.

564. Osborne, William. "Charles Ives the Organist." *American Organist* 24/7 (July 1990): 58–64.

Excellent, detailed study of Ives's training and performances as an organist. Reconstructs his studies and offers new evidence connecting John Cornelius Griggs to Dudley Buck. Also investigates Ives's later interactions with E. Power Biggs concerning the *Variations on "America"* through their correspondence. Concludes with a listing of registrations for the organs of Ives's New Haven and New York churches.

565. Palmer, Kenneth Robert. "A Performer's Guide to Charles Ives' *Piano Sonata No. 2 'Concord Mass., 1840–1860.'*" Ph.D. dissertation, Washington University, 1986.

Study of the challenges to the performer of the *Concord Sonata*. Based in part on discussions with John Kirpatrick and Easley Blackwood, as well as the author's own experiences. Includes detailed discussions of difficult passages, as well as an overview of the work's formal structure, motivic unity, and melodic continuity.

566. Pappastavrou, George. "Ives's Quarter-Tone Pieces." *Clavier* 13/7 (1974): 31–32.

Performer's guide to the *Three Quarter-Tone Pieces* includes specific technical guidance on retuning the piano, and interpretative suggestions.

567. Perison, Harry. "The Quarter-Tone System of Charles Ives." *Current Musicology* 18 (1974): 96–104.

Recounts Ives's ideas concerning quarter-tone composition, then analyzes the chord structure and intervals of *Three Quarter-Tone Pieces*. Includes a discussion of quotations from *America* and *La Marseillaise*, as well as overall melody, harmony, and diatonic and quarter-tone mixtures.

568. Rasmussen, Jane E. "Charles Ives's Music for the Piano." *Student Musicologists at Minnesota* 6 (1975–76): 201–17.

General summary of published and unpublished works for piano with commentary on the challenges of transcribing and editing Ives's works.

569. Reichert, Linda. "Charles Ives and Quarter-Tone Music: A Transcription of *Three Quarter-Tone Pieces* for Two Pianos." D.M.A. document, Temple University, 1996.

Intriguing consideration of the *Three Quarter-Tone Pieces*. Includes a history of the work's composition and premiere, plus an analytical overview. Perhaps most valuable is a transcription of the work for one performer at two electronic keyboards, with commentary on the unique challenges of using electronic instruments.

570. Rostkowski, David. "America's Greatest Composer: The Piano Works of Charles Ives." In *Piano music. VII: Muzyka fortepianowa. VII*, edited by Janusz Krassowski. Prace specjalne Vol. 42. Gdansk: Akademia Muzyczna im. St. Moniuszki, 1987, 119–42.

Survey of Ives's piano works with emphasis on *Concord Sonata, Three-Page Sonata,* and the First Piano Sonata.

571. Sadoff, Ronald Hayden. "The Solo Piano Music of Charles Ives: A Performance Guide." Ph.D. dissertation, New York University, 1986.

Analyzes the published works for solo piano in terms of sound, harmony, rhythm, and melody, and presents a "timeline" chart for each, summarizing overall organization. Also presents a detailed analysis of *Concord Sonata* using the phenomenological method of Lawrence Ferrara, and discusses the relationship of *Essays before a Sonata* to the composition.

572. Schubert, Giselher. "Die *Concord-Sonata* von Charles Ives. Anmerkungen zur Werkstruktur und Interpretation." In *Aspeckte der musikalischen Interpretation. Festschrift z. 70 Geburtstag von Sava Savoff*, Hermann Danuser, ed. Hamburg: K. D. Wagner, 1980, 121–138.

Study of the history, aesthetics, and motivic structure of the *Concord Sonata* and the related works including *Emerson Concerto* and *The Celestial Railroad*. Also considers the paradoxical influence of Romanticism on this modernist work, and compares the two published editions.

573. Stearns, David Patrick. "Beyond Grave, Still Premiering Composers' 'New' Works Emerge." *USA Today*, 18 November 1998, section D, 8.

Study of premieres of unfinished and reconstructed works includes a description of the *"Emerson" Concerto* premiere as "an act of graverobbing."

574. Stover, Harold. "Charles Ives's Variations on 'America.' " *American Organist* 31/11 (November 1997): 72–75.

Compares Ives's variation techniques with similar works by Dudley Buck and John Knowles Paine, and speculates on whether Ives knew the other works. Also includes comparisons to march and ragtime, and observations on Ives's use of the polonaise.

575. Thomas, Phillip. "Music for One or More Alternately Tuned Acoustic Pianos, 1920–1993: Trends in Melody, Harmony, and Technique." Ph.D. dissertation, University of Cincinnati, 1996.

Briefly considers *Three Quarter-Tone Pieces* within an historical context, and considers the work's aesthetics and technical demands in comparison with works by Busoni and Harry Partch.

576. Toncitch, Voya. "Dodecaphonie et systemes de 24 et 31 tons." *Schweitzerische Musikzeitung/Revue musicale suisse* 113/5 (September-October 1973): 274–78.

Discusses Ives's *Three Quarter-Tone Pieces* within the context of historical alternatives to the tonal system, and compares his usage with the theories of William Pole (1814–1900).

577. Toncitch, Voya. " 'Three Page Sonata' by Charles Ives." *Mélos* 5 (September–October 1972): 277–79.

German source, includes a very general description of the work without musical examples, followed by a brief biography and summary of Ives's musical aesthetics and historical precedence over European contemporaries. Published earlier in French as "Charles Ives: Three-Sonata [sic] pour piano." *Revue musicale de Suisse romande* 3 (August–September 1969): 3–5.

578. Wasson, Jeffrey. "The Organ Works of Charles Ives: A Research Summary." *Student Musicologists at Minnesota* 6 (1975–76): 280–89.

Annotated list of all organ works organized by condition (complete works, incomplete works, lost works). Also compares manuscript sources with published editions and identifies the reuse of lost organ works in later compositions.

579. Wilson, Lawrence. "Ragtime: Its Roots, Style, and Influence." D.Mus. dissertation, Indiana University, 1981, 90–92.

Within the context of ragtime-related compositions, Wilson briefly discusses the use of ragtime elements in the First Piano Sonata. Illustrated by musical excerpts.

580. Wuellner, Guy S. "The Smaller Piano Works of Charles Ives." *American Music Teacher* 22/5 (April-May 1973): 14–16.

Describes the overall organization, style, and programs of *Three-Page Sonata, The Anti-Abolitionist Riots, Some South-Paw Pitching, Three Protests,* and *Three Quarter-Tone Pieces.* With some excerpts of Ives's own descriptions.

CHORAL WORKS

581. Alwes, Chester L. "Formal Structure as a Guide to Rehearsal Strategy in *Psalm 90* by Charles E. Ives." *Choral Journal* 25/8 (April 1985): 21–25.

Analysis of *Psalm 90* focusing on text painting, palindromic structures, whole-tone clusters, and the recurrence of the opening chords throughout. With advice on teaching the work to choirs through whole-tone scales and arpeggiated chords exercises.

582. Christiansen, Larry A. "Charles E. Ives and the Sixty-Seventh Psalm." *Music/AGO-RCCO Magazine* 3/2 (February 1969): 20–21.

Examines the relationship between text, musical phrase, and texture for *Psalm 67*. Christiansen divides the work into an ABCBA symmetrical form. With several musical examples.

583. Crunden, Robert. "Charles Ives: The Man and His Music." *Choral Journal* 25/4 (December 1974): 7–12.

Subtitled "Charles Ives's Innovative Nostalgia," this article presents a surprisingly detailed biography and critical summary of works. Emphasizes Parker's role in Ives's education, and describes the use of "process" and "form" to recreate the experience of nostalgia in works like *Yale-Princeton Football Game*, "Putnam's Camp," and *Universe Symphony*. Listed in Block as B163.

584. Engel, Lehman. *This Bright Day.* New York: Macmillan, 1974. ISBN 0 025361104. ML 410 .E56 A3.

Engel's autobiography includes a brief but valuable recollection of his contact with Ives (pp. 115–18), primarily through early performances of *Psalm 67* and Arrow Press. A complete transcription of Ives's letter to Engel (5/18/37) concerning several choral works is included.

585. Grantham, Donald. "A Harmonic 'Leitmotif' System in Ives's *Psalm 90*." *In Theory Only* 5/2 (May–June 1979): 3–14.

Detailed analysis of *Psalm 90* based on the five opening chords, labeled "The Eternities," "Creation," "God's wrath against sin," "Prayer and Humility," and "Rejoicing in Beauty and Work" by Ives. Grantham traces reoccurences of these structures throughout the work in both choral and organ parts, which illustrate a close but not rigid text-music relationship.

586. Groh, Jack C. "A Conductor's Analysis of and Preparation and Approach to Polyrhythms: With Particular Attention to Polyrhythms in Certain of the Choral Works of Charles E. Ives." D.M.A. dissertation, University of Missouri, 1978.

Outlines techniques for teaching, rehearsing, and conducting polyrhythms in Ives's choral works, especially the second of the *Three Harvest Home Chorales*. Groh's practical approach includes a step-by-step account of introducing the second chorale to a choir and preparing for a performance.

587. Hitchcock, H. Wiley. "Ivesiana. The Gottschalk Connection." *Institute for Studies in American Music Newsletter* 15/1 (November 1985): 5.

Identifies a quotation from Gottschalk's *The Last Hope* in *Psalm 90*, and speculates on its significance. For an expansion, see item 593.

588. Kumlien, Wendell C. "The Music for Chorus." *Music Educator's Journal* 61/2 (October 1974): 48–52.

Useful survey of the choral works divided into three categories: early works; Psalm settings; and unison choir songs with orchestra. Kumlien summarizes the melodic and harmonic style, text, and other salient characteristics of each significant work within each category.

589. Kumlien, Wendell Clarke. "The Sacred Choral Music of Charles Ives: A Study in Style Development." D.M.A. thesis, University of Illinois, 1969.

First extensive study of every complete sacred choral work, including source information, editorial suggestions, text sources and treatments, and structural analyses. In some cases, Kumlien's transcriptions remain the only available edited sources.

590. Lamb, Gordon H. "Charles Ives: The Man and His Music. Interview with Robert Shaw." *Choral Journal* 15/8 (April 1975): 5–7.

Wide-ranging interview records Shaw's recollections of performing Ives's choral works (*Harvest Home Chorales*, *Psalm 67*, and *Psalm 90*), his commentary on orchestral and chamber works, and his experiences with the opinions of audiences and performers on Ives.

591. Lamb, Gordon H. "Charles Ives 1874–1954." *Choral Journal* 15/2 (October 1974): 12–13.

    Overview of several of Ives's published choral works including *Psalm 90, Three Harvest Home Chorales, Psalm 150, Psalm 67,* and *The Celestial Country.* With brief comments on level of difficulty, instrumentation, and content. Includes brief discography.

592. Lynn, Debra Jo. "Learning Sequences for the Experimental Choral Psalm Settings of Charles Ives." D.A. dissertation, Ball State University, 1999.

    Presents specific choral exercises and drills for rehearsing and teaching *Psalm 67, Psalm 14, Psalm 24, Psalm 25, Psalm 54, Psalm 100, Psalm 135,* and *Psalm 150* to an advanced choir. Includes a case-study application of these methods to a rehearsal of *Psalm 25* and a review of the results. Also contains an interview with Gregg Smith discussing his experiences editing, rehearsing, and performing these experimental psalms.

593. Offergeld, Robert. "More on the Gottschalk–Ives connection." *Institute for Studies in American Music Newsletter* 15/2 (May 1986): 1–2, 13.

    Response to item 587 clarifying that Gottschalk's *The Last Hope* existed in an adaptation as a popular hymn tune that Ives may have known, and that may have been the source for the *Psalm 90* quotation.

594. Sabin, Robert. "20th-Century Americans." In Jacobs, ed., *Choral Music: A Symposium.* Baltimore: Penguin Books, 1963; reprint, 1978: 371–72.

    Brief descriptions of *Psalm 67* and *Three Harvest Home Chorales* as "ahead of our time," along with a general biographical statement.

595. Sherwood, Gayle. " 'Buds the Infant Mind': Charles Ives's *The Celestial Country* and American Protestant Choral Traditions." *19th Century Music* 23/2 (Fall 1999): 163–89.

    Using a revised chronology and musical analysis, compares Ives's church music—the anthems, service music, and the cantata *The Celestial Country*—to that of his teachers Horatio Parker and Dudley Buck. Concludes that Ives's early sacred choral compositions reflect the creative and cultural tensions in late nineteenth-century American Protestant choral music, as well as Ives's contemporary biographical circumstances and musical environment.

596. Sherwood, Gayle. "The Choral Works of Charles Ives: Chronology, Style, Reception." Ph.D. dissertation, Yale University, 1995.

Redates Ives's choral works and reconsiders his compositional career in light of the results. Final section reviews the reception of the choral works to 1974. Includes transcriptions of several unpublished choral works.

597. Smith, Gregg. "Charles Ives: The Man and His Music; Charles Ives and His Music For Chorus." *Choral Journal* 15/3 (November 1974): 17–20.

Brief biography followed by an overview of Ives's sacred and secular choral music. Includes a listing of works arranged by performing forces and publisher, as well as a note on recordings.

598. Tipton, Julius R. "Some Observations on the Choral Style of Charles Ives." *American Choral Review* 12/3 (July 1970): 99–105.

Brief melodic, harmonic, and rhythmic analyses of *Psalm 24* and the *Harvest Home Chorales*, plus commentary on Ives's setting of the texts. Tipton concludes that the two works are representative of Ives's style and worthy of serious attention.

599. Vinquist, Mary Ann. "The Psalm-Settings of Charles Ives." Master's thesis, Indiana University, 1965.

Uneven discussion of the psalm settings as well as the *Three Harvest Home Chorales* with highly selective comments on their melody, harmony, rhythm, and form. Most valuable for the discussion of texts with comparison to biblical and prayer book sources.

SONGS

600. Argento, Dominick. "A digest analysis of Ives' 'On the Antipodes.' " *Student Musicologists at Minnesota* 6 (1975–76): 192–200.

Analyzes the melody, tempo, meter, rhythm, counterpoint, harmony, and form in the song, with attention to Ives's text illustration throughout the work. Based on student notes taken during a lecture.

601. Boatwright, Howard. "The Songs." *Music Educator's Journal* 61/2 (October 1974): 42–47.

Survey of the songs mentions Ives's text sources and stylistic diversity. Boatwright's primary focus is on the songs' reception and publication history, in volumes paid for by Ives and later copyrighted editions.

602. Briggs, John. "24 Ives Songs." *New York Times*, 5 June 1955, section 2, 11.

Review of the Overtone recording by Helen Boatwright and John Kirk-patrick, with brief descriptions of "Abide with Me" and "Autumn."

603. Burr, Raymond A. "The Art Songs of Charles Ives." In *South Florida's Historic Festival* (item 858), 53–56.

Summarizes Ives's views on the nature and purpose of songs. With a survey of songs based on family and political themes.

604. Copland, Aaron. "One Hundred and Fourteen Songs [*114 Songs*]." *Modern Music* 11/2 (January–February 1934): 59–64; reprinted in *Charles Ives and His World* (item 36), 307–312.

Substantial review of *114 Songs* including commentary on Ives's preface and a general description and analysis of several songs. Copland addresses Ives's attitude towards the professional composer as well as his public, concluding that the weaknesses in the music "arise from a lack of that kind of self-criticism which only actual performance and public reaction can bring."

605. Cox, Paul Wathen. "An Analysis of Sonority Types in Selected Songs of Charles Ives." Master's thesis, Indiana University, 1970.

Classifies sonority types in the *114 Songs* according to structure, including: tertian sonorities (triads, seventh chords, ninth chords, etc.); polychords; nontertian sonorities (clusters, quartal and quintal chords); and hybrid sonorities of irregular structure.

606. Euteneuer-Rohrer, Ursula Henrietta. "Charles E. Ives' 'The Cage': Eine Werkbetrachtung." *Neuland* 1 (1980): 47–52.

Analysis of the song's formal, rhythmic, harmonic, intervallic, and melodic organization, and the relationship of these musical elements to the text.

607. Friedberg, Ruth C. "Charles Ives (1874–1954)." In *American Art Song and American Poetry, I: America Comes of Age*. Metuchen, NJ: Scarecrow, 1981, 43–89. ISBN 0810814609. ML 2811 .F75.

Unique survey of twelve of Ives's songs that use text by Americans, including Longfellow, Whittier, Holmes, Sprague, Emerson, Whitman, Lindsay, Thoreau, Untermeyer, Cooper, and Aldrich. Each song is analyzed with regards to Ives's treatment of the poetry, with brief biographies of the poet as well.

608. Gilman, Janet Lynn. "Charles Ives—Master Songwriter: The Methods Behind His Madness." Ph.D. dissertation, University of Southern California, 1994.

Categorizes all published songs according to texts, as: the European art song; sacred songs; nature songs; philosophical songs; political songs; "common man" songs; sentimental songs; and comical songs. Gilman identifies similarities of musical structure within each category using a variety of analytical tools, including Schenkerian and set-theory analysis, identification of musical borrowings, and tonal analysis.

609. Green, Douglass M. "Exempli gratia: A Chord Motive in Ives's 'Serenity.' " *In Theory Only* 4/5 (October 1978): 20–21.

Through analysis, asserts that the structure of the work is generated from the opening chord progression. Also briefly addresses the effectiveness of word painting in Ives's setting.

610. Gregg, Thomas Andrew. "Song Composers and Their Poetry Choices: An Analysis of the Literary Background and Textual Selections of Twelve Composers." D.M.A. dissertation, Ohio State University, 1989.

Includes a very general summary of Ives's text choices with an overview of his education and sources for song texts arranged by author's date of birth, use of non-English texts, contact with text author, etc. Also a brief percentage-based comparison of Ives's texts with those of Samuel Barber, Ned Rorem, and Dominick Argento.

611. Hitchcock, H. Wiley. "Ives's *114 [+15]* Songs and What He Thought of Them." *Journal of the American Musicological Society* 52/1 (Spring 1999): 97–144.

Thorough examination of Ives's published song collections: *114 Songs*, *Thirty-Four Songs*, *Nineteen Songs* and *Fifty Songs*. Hitchcock critiques Ives's choices for each volume, his published and unpublished comments on their purposes, and, in some cases, revisions and restorations in some reprinted songs. Extensively illustrated with musical excerpts and comprehensive tables correlating contents, overlap, and revisions for all four collections.

612. Hitchcock, H. Wiley. " 'A grand and glorious noise!': Charles Ives as Lyricist." *American Music* 15/1 (Spring 1997): 26–44.

Analyzes Ives's lyrics in the collections *114 Songs*, *34 Songs,* and *19 Songs*. Hitchcock concludes that Ives continuously spoke "with his own voice," whether he was working with his own lyrics, or setting texts by others.

613. Hitchcock, H. Wiley. "Charles Ives and the Spiritual 'In the Morning' / *Give Me Jesus.*" In *New Perspectives on Music: Essays in Honor of Eileen Southern*, edited by Josephine Wright with Samuel Floyd, Jr. Warren, MI: Harmonie Park Press, 1992, 163–71. ISBN 0 89990 042 6. ML 55 .S6877 1992.

Overview of Ives's setting of the spiritual based primarily on correspondence, with information on his collaboration with Mary Evelyn Stiles who introduced him to the song. Also includes a history of published variants of the spiritual in hymnbooks through the 19th century with comparisons to the melody of Ives's setting.

614. Hitchcock, H. Wiley. "Charles Ives's book of *114 Songs.*" In *A Musical Offering: Essays in Honor of Martin Bernstein*, edited by E. H. Clinksale and C. Brook. New York: Pendragon, 1977, 127–36. ISBN 76053128. ML 55 .B384 1977.

Summarizes the *114 Songs* as representing four song categories: experimental songs; "household" songs; songs influenced by the Euro-American "cultivated" tradition; and songs influenced by American vernacular musics. Also compares Ives's songs to those by his contemporaries and predecessors.

615. Houtchens, Alan, and Janis P. Stout. " 'Scarce heard amidst the guns below': Intertextuality and Meaning in Charles Ives's War Songs." *Journal of Musicology* 15/1 (Winter 1997): 66–97.

Examines "In Flanders Fields," "He Is There!," "Tom Sails Away," and "They Are There!" in context of Ives's conflicted views on war. Also analyzes the influence of Harmony Twichell Ives, Joseph Hopkins Twichell, and Mark Twain on Ives's war songs and attitudes.

616. Kämper, Dietrich. "Die '114 Songs' von Charles E. Ives." In *Amerikanische Musik seit Charles Ives: Interpretation, Quellentexte, Komponistenmonographien* (item 38), 135–145.

Survey of the *114 Songs* with particular attention to the "Four German Songs," "The Cage," "Mists," "Nov. 2, 1920," and "Tom Sails Away." Discusses harmonic, melodic, and rhythmic experimentation, use of quotations, political beliefs, pianistic technique, and stylistic heterogeniety. Also discusses the importance of Walt Whitman and the influence of Transcendentalism.

617. Kelly, Kevin. "The Songs of Charles Ives and the Cultural Contexts of Death." Ph.D. dissertation, University of North Carolina, 1989.

Thorough consideration of cultural images of death in nineteenth-century American culture, and their resonance in Ives's songs, especially in his choices of texts and use of multiple styles. Particular emphasis on the importance of death in mid- and late-century American literature. Kelly concludes that in his choices of text Ives reflected his own time—the late nineteenth century—and that even his most progressive musical settings are a result of the influence of the text.

618. Morgan, Robert P. "The Things Our Fathers Loved': Charles Ives and the European Tradition." In *Ives Studies* (item 55), 3–26.

A thorough analysis of the song "The Things Our Fathers Loved" frames Morgan's discussion of Ives and the disintegration of tonality in early twentieth-century music. Morgan concludes that Ives's unique solutions nonetheless drew heavily on the conventions of the European tradition. For an earlier, condensed version of this in German, see idem, "Charles Ives und das europaische Tradition." In *Bericht über das Internationale Symposion "Charles Ives und die amerikanische Musiktradition bis zur Gegenwart' Köln 1988*, ed. Klaus Wolfgang Niemöller. Kölner Beiträge zur Musikforschung No. 164. Regensburg: Gustav Bosse Verlag, 1990, 17–36. ISBN 37649 2406 3. ML 200.5 .I58 1990.

619. Newman, Philip. "The Songs of Charles Ives (1874–1954)." Ph.D. dissertation, University of Iowa, 1967.

Ambitious survey of 205 song titles. Volume 1 is an analytical survey discussing experimental procedures, text choices, manuscript and published comments, quotations, and overall musical philosophy. Volume 2 is a catalogue of the songs including date, text source, publication information, marginalia, voice range, etc.

620. Schoffman, Nachum. *From Chords to Simultaneities: Chordal Indeterminacy and the Failure of Serialism.* Contributions to the Study of Music and Dance, No. 17. Westport, CT: Greenwood Press, 1990, 51–52, 57, 61–62 and 64. ISBN 0 313 266468. ML 197 .S265 1990.

Examines the serial structure of "The Cage," and the voice-leading and nonfunctional chords of "Grantchester," with musical examples from both works.

621. Schoffman, Nachum. "Charles Ives's Song 'Vote for Names.' " *Current Musicology* 23 (1977): 56–68.

Realization of the unfinished sketch of "Vote for Names," including a facsimile of the score and the completed transcription. Briefly summarizes the history of the song, drawing on Ives's marginalia, followed by a discussion of the editorial challenges and the author's solutions.

622. Schoffman, Nachum. "The Songs of Charles Ives." Ph.D. dissertation, Hebrew University, 1977.

Study of the songs in three parts. Part 1 thoroughly analyzes twenty songs spanning Ives's career and representing a variety of genres and styles. Part 2 offers an overview of Ives's compositional language as seen in his song output (including harmonic and formal structures, programs, texts, etc.), while Part 3 assesses his historical significance.

6

Editing Practices and Selected Reviews of Published Editions

623. Bales, Richard. "Charles Ives: Third Symphony. [Review of *Symphony No. 3* by Charles Ives.]" *Notes* 5/3 (June 1948): 413.

Brief review of the 1947 Arrow edition of the Third Symphony identifies it as a "remarkable and beautiful little work," and as a "true gem, home-fashioned so long ago."

624. Baron, Carol K. "Review of *Symphony No. 3 (The Camp Meeting)* by Charles Ives." *Notes* 48/4 (June 1992): 1436–38.

Review of the 1990 Associated publication edited by Kenneth Singleton. Discusses the manuscript sources with emphasis on correspondence between Ives, Lou Harrison, and Bernard Herrmann.

625. Block, Geoffrey. "Review of *Symphony No. 1* by Charles Ives." *Notes* 57/2 (December 2000): 461–64.

Review of the 1999 Peer edition by James Sinclair has extensive commentary on the work's origins in Parker's classroom, Ives's descriptions, its style, quotations, and reception.

626. Cowell, Henry. "Charles Ives: Second Pianoforte Sonata, 'Concord, Mass., 1840–1860.' Second edition. [Review of Second Pianoforte Sonata by Charles Ives.]" *Notes* 5/3 (June 1948): 413.

Brief review of the second edition does not comment on the music but rather on the reception of Ives through the 1920s and 1930s, emphasizing the activities of Cowell, Schmitz, Bellamann, and Kirkpatrick.

627. Cyr, Gordon. "Review of *Scherzo, All the Way Around and Back* by Charles Ives." *Notes* 29/2 (December 1972): 332.

With comments on the instrumentation and ostinato structure, along with recommendations for performance level.

628. Cyr, Gordon. "Review of *Symphony no. 1* by Charles Ives." *Notes* 29/2 (December 1972): 319.

Brief review of the Peer publication with comments on the similarity of the work's orchestration to organ registration.

629. Dickinson, Peter. "Ives Source. *Country Band March* for Theatre Orchestra. [Review of *Country Band March* by Charles Ives.]" *Musical Times* 125/1695 (May 1984): 278.

Brief review of the Merion edition comments on Ives's representation of amateur music-making: "wrong entries, copyists' mistakes and poor ensemble, as well as references to popular songs."

630. Hamm, Charles. "Review of *Forty Earlier Songs* by Charles Ives." *Notes* 51/2 (March 1995): 1124–25.

Reviews the critical edition by John Kirkpatrick with a preface by H. Wiley Hitchcock with basic commentary on the edition itself and the songs' style.

631. Henck, Herbert. "Aus zweiter Hand: Charles E. Ives' 'Study No. 20.' [Review of *Study No. 20* by Charles Ives.]" *Neuland* 3 (1982–83): 242.

Review of the 1981 Merion publication includes a discussion of the difficulties of creating an authoritative edition in the face of corrections, revisions, and incomplete sources.

632. Henck, Herbert. " 'Waltz-Rondo' und andere Klavierstücke von Charles Ives. [Review of *Waltz-Rondo* by Charles Ives.]" *Neuland* 1 (1980): 44–46.

Review of the 1978 edition of *Waltz-Rondo* by Associated includes an analysis of the work, comparison of the edition with other published piano works, and commentary on the methodology of editing Ives's works.

633. Hitchcock, H. Wiley. "Editing Ives's 129 Songs." In *Ives Studies* (item 55), 51–76.

Account of the challenges facing an editor of Ives's songs. Hitchcock introduces text and musical variants, particularly for "The Cage," "Tolerance," and "Like A Sick Eagle." Compares published editions and Ives's manuscripts, as well as annotations made by Ives on his own published copies.

634. Hitchcock, H. Wiley, and Vivian Perlis, eds. "Three Realizations of *Chromâtimelôdtune*." In *An Ives Celebration: Papers and Panels of the Charles Ives Centennial Festival-Conference* (item 50), 87–109.

Panel discussion about different editions of *Chromâtimelôdtune* between John Kirkpatrick, Gunther Schuller, Gerard Schwarz, and Kenneth Singleton.

635. Lambert, J. Philip. "Review of *Three Improvisations* and *The Unanswered Question* by Charles Ives." *Notes* 44/2 (December 1987): 352–55.

Review of the 1984 Associated edition of *Three Improvisations* and the 1985 Peer edition of *The Unanswered Question*. Contains analytical insights into the motivic and rhythmic structures of the improvisations, as well as comments on the revisions to *The Unanswered Question*.

636. Mandel, Alan, with Lou Harrison, John Kirkpatrick, and James Sinclair. "Editors' Experiences." In *An Ives Celebration: Papers and Panels of the Charles Ives Centennial Festival-Conference* (item 50), 67–85.

Transcription of a panel discussion between Lou Harrison, John Kirkpatrick, James Sinclair, and Alan Mandel on the challenges of editing Ives's compositions, including the *Concord Sonata*, *Three Places in New England*, the First Piano Sonata, "They Are There!," and the Third Symphony.

637. Rathert, Wolfgang. "The Unanswered Question of the Ives Edition. [Review of *The Unanswered Question* and *Trio for Violin, Cello, Piano* by Charles Ives.]" Translated by James Lum. *Musical Quarterly* 73/4 (1989): 575–584.

Review of Ives Society critical editions of *The Unanswered Question* and the *Trio* comments on the Ives Society's editorial approach. Compares manuscript sources and published editions for both works and examines the editors' choices.

638. Sapp, Allen. "Review of *String Quartet No. 2* by Charles Ives." *Notes* 12/4 (June 1955): 489–92.

Review of the Peer edition contains an evolution of the work that states, "its merits are impressive, its aberrations appalling." Sapp also complains of "the irritation [of its] harmonic stasis and textural density."

639. Siebert, Robert. "Review of 'They Are There!' by Charles Ives." *Notes* 20/4 (1963): 565–66.

General description of the work mentions quotations and the patriotic tone, which "fully reflected the spirit of the time."

640. Starr, Larry. "Review of 'Decoration Day' by Charles Ives." *Notes* 47/3 (March 1991): 959–961.

    Reviews the 1989 Peer edition of the second movement of the *Holidays Symphony*, edited by James B. Sinclair. Comments on the style of the work, the strengths of the edition, and current controversies over chronology and editing practices.

641. Ulrich, Homer. "Review of *Trio for Violin, Cello, Piano* by Charles Ives." *Notes* 13/3 (June 1956): 527.

    Review of the Peer edition mentions the style and structure of the work including quotations. Complains of the impossible page turn in the Scherzo stating, "perhaps it would do just as well to play the page twice instead of turning it; I don't believe that anyone would notice."

7

Textbook Accounts, Encyclopedia Entries, and Dictionary Entries

642. Austin, William W. *Music in the 20th Century*. New York: W. W. Norton, 1966, 57–61. ML 197.A8 M8.

Brief, occasionally harsh evaluation of Ives's significance with excerpts from the *Essays* and minimal analysis of "Soliloquy" and "The Innate." Austin states that knowing the identity of Ives's quotations is crucial to understanding the works, and that the composer's own melodies "are not memorable," his rhythms "are often sluggish, or jerky," and that "his command of musical materials is deficient."

643. Bauer, Marion. *20th Century Music: How It Developed, How to Listen to It*. New York: G. P. Putnam's Sons, 1933, 278; reprint, New York: Da Capo Press, 1978, 278. ISBN 0306775035. ML 197 .B29 1978.

Significant mention because of its very early date. Bauer includes a one-page description of Ives outlining his use of specifically New England influences, and notes that Ives's "fine musical training" and "rhythmic curiosity" form the basis of his experimentation.

644. Broyles, Michael. "Art Music from 1860 to 1920." In *The Cambridge History of American Music*, edited by David Nicholls. Cambridge: Cambridge University Press, 1998, 244–49. ISBN 0521454298. ML 200 .C36 1998.

Well-informed overview presents brief descriptions of a variety of works from throughout Ives's career including *The Celestial Country*, "General William Booth," "Fourth of July," *The Unanswered Question*, the Second Violin Sonata, and the Fourth Symphony. Discusses experimentation, musical borrowing for programmatic and musical purposes, cumulative form, layering, and spatial techniques.

645. Burkholder, J. Peter. "Ives, Charles Edward." In *New Grove Dictionary of Music and Musicians*, edited by Stanley Sadie. 2nd edition. London: MacMillan, 2001. ISBN 1561592390. ML 100 .N48 2001.

Substantial overview significantly updates Kirkpatrick's entry from the previous edition (item 662). Divided into the following sections: Unusual aspects of Ives's career; Youth, 1874–94; Apprenticeship, 1894–1902; Innovation and synthesis, 1902–8; Maturity, 1908–18; Last works, 1918–1927; Revisions and premières, 1927–54. Numerous musical examples and extensive bibliography. Work list prepared with James B. Sinclair and Gayle Sherwood includes all complete and several nearly complete works with publication information, compositional interrelationships, and dates.

646. Chase, Gilbert. "Composer from Connecticut." In *America's Music*. New York: McGraw Hill, 1955. 2nd ed., 1966; 3rd ed., 1987, 429–46. ISBN 0 252 00454 X. ML 200 .C5 1987.

Standard overview with emphasis on Ives's early education, his use of popular musics and other borrowings, and the influence of George Ives and Transcendentalism. Summary of the four symphonies and *114 Songs*. With numerous quotations from Ives's writings.

647. Crawford, Richard. "To Stretch Our Ears: The Music of Charles Ives." In *America's Musical Life: A History.* New York: W. W. Norton, 2001, 495–523. ISBN 0-393-04810-1. ML 200 .C69 2000.

Substantial and informed coverage of Ives with emphasis on his connections to American culture and music, both popular and classical. Considers the "Ives Legend" and its origins, as well as the standard mention of the influence of George Ives. Summarizes the *Concord Sonata* and surveys the songs "The Circus Band," "Memories," "Serenity," "Soliloquy," "Charlie Rutlage," and "The Housatonic at Stockbridge."

648. Crawford, Richard. "To Stretch Our Ears: The Music of Charles Ives." In *An Introduction to America's Music*. New York: W. W. Norton, 2001, 495–523. ISBN 0 393 97409 X. ML 200 .C72 2000.

Textually abridged version of item 647 with the addition of brief listening guides for "The Circus Band," "Serenity," and "The Housatonic at Stockbridge."

649. Ewen, David. "Charles Ives." Chapter in *Composers of Tomorrow's Music*. New York: Dodd, Mead, 1971, 1–23. ML 197 .E85.

Standard biography based primarily on Cowell, unfortunately without citations. Overstates the ideas of neglect and isolation, particularly in his later life (for example, "he never contacted a performer or publisher"), but does contain some interesting information on the premieres of the Second Symphony and the Fourth Symphony.

650. Finney, Theodore M. *A History of Music.* New York: Harcourt, Brace, 1935, 601–2; revised edition, 1947, 645; reprinted, Westport, CT: Greenwood Press, 1976. ISBN 0837172705. ML 160 .F49 1976.

Brief but significant early mention of Ives as "an American counterpart of Stravinsky and Schónberg." Ives is grouped alongside Daniel Gregory Mason, John Alden Carpenter, and David Stanley Smith as art music composers of the early century. Mentions Ives's use of "New England folk idioms" and his modesty in promoting his works. The revised edition adds no further information.

651. Gann, Kyle. *American Music in the 20th Century.* New York: Schirmer, 1997, 7–17 and passim. ISBN 0 02 864655 X. ML 200.5 G36 1997.

In the chapter entitled "Forefathers," Ives is grouped along with Carl Ruggles. Biographical summary includes father's influence, Yale education, and reception in the late 1920s and '30s. Discussion of the *Essays* and *Concord Sonata* focuses on the "Alcotts" movement, and concludes with a brief summary of *Three Places in New England.*

652. Goldman, Richard. "American Music: 1918–1960." *New Oxford History of Music,* Band 10. London: Oxford University Press, 1974, 574–83. ISBN 0193163101. ML 160 .N44.

Focuses on experimental approaches (polyrhythms, dissonances, performance challenges) as well as the New England sources of quotations. With numerous and extensive excerpts from the *Concord Sonata, Three Places in New England,* and *Variations on "America."*

653. Griffiths, Paul. *A Concise History of Avant-Garde Music.* New York: Thames and Hudson, 1978. ISBN 0195200446. ML 197 .G74 1978. Reprinted as *Modern Music: A Concise History from Debussy to Boulez.* New York: Oxford University Press, 1985. ISBN 0500201641. ML 197 .G74 1985. Revised edition, *Modern Music and After.* Oxford: Oxford University Press, 1995. ISBN 0198165110. ML 197 .G74 1995.

Brief summary of Ives's musical experimentation, with a comparison to Schoenberg and mention of the influence of American materials and attitudes on his music (pp. 51–56 and passim).

654. Hamm, Charles. "The Search for a National Identity." In *Music in the New World*. New York: W. W. Norton, 1983, 424–37. ISBN 0 393 95193 6. ML 200 .H17.

Unusually expansive overview of Ives's life and works. Works surveyed include the two string quartets; the four symphonies, with emphasis on the fourth; *Unanswered Question* and *Central Park in the Dark*; the First Piano Sonata; and the *Three Places in New England*. Discusses Ives's training at Yale, his choice of an insurance career, use of borrowing and ragtime styles, and later performances of his works.

655. Hansen, Peter S. "Music in the United States." In *An Introduction to 20th Century Music*. Boston: Allyn and Bacon, 1961, 77–84; 2nd ed., 1967, 81–88; 3rd ed., 1967; 4th ed., 1978, 86–96.

Summary of life and works including descriptions of *Concord Sonata* and *Unanswered Question*, with emphasis on programs and experimental procedures. Concludes with an outline of "Style Characteristics" including Ives's use of dissonances and complex rhythms. The fourth edition adds a detailed section on the Fourth Symphony including a full-page excerpt.

656. Hitchcock, H. Wiley. "Charles E. Ives." In *Music in the United States: A Historical Introduction*. Englewood Cliffs, NJ: Prentice Hall, 1969, 148–74; reprinted, 1974; 3rd ed., 1988, 161–86.

Concise overview with a brief biography, description of Ives's musical thought (based on the *Memos* and *Essays*), and summary of his output. Concentrates on the songs but also includes pithy commentary on chamber and orchestral works.

657. Howard, John Tasker. *Our American Music: Three Hundred Years of It*. New York: Thomas Y. Crowell, 1931, 576–78.

Sympathetic early discussion with emphasis on education and reception during the 1920s. Mentions *114 Songs* and *Concord Sonata* and its relationship to Transcendentalism.

658. "Ives, Charles Edward." In *Who is Who in Music*, edited by J. T. H. Mize. 5th ed. Chicago: Who is Who in Music, Inc., 1951.

Biographical and works survey mentions the influence of his father, education and activities at Yale, insurance career, and belated musical career and recognition. Many inaccuracies but significant for its early date and relative length.

659. "Ives, Charles Edward." In *Current Biography 1947*. New York: H. W. Wilson, 1947, 330–32. CT 100 .C98.

Summarizes education, experimental musical style, and use of quotations. Notes recent recognition by the National Institute of Arts and Letters, as well as the Pulitzer Prize. Musical description of the Third Symphony and *Concord Sonata*, with mention of the *Essays*. With photo.

660. Karolyi, Otto. "Businessman and Musical Genius: Charles Ives." In *Modern American Music: From Charles Ives to the Minimalists*. London: Cygnus Arts; Rutherford, NJ: Fairleigh Dickinson University, 1996, 9–20. ISBN 0 8386 3725 6; 1-900541-00-9. ML 200.5 .K37

General biography and overview of the orchestral works and songs, plus specific descriptions of *Central Park in the Dark*, *Three Places in New England*, the four symphonies, *Holidays Symphony*, *Universe Symphony,* and *Concord Sonata*. Emphasis on the use of quotations and influence of Transcendentalism. Although the author draws on some scholarly sources, the essay does not include citations.

661. Kingman, Daniel. *American Music: A Panorama*. New York: Schirmer, 1979; 2nd rev. ed., 1990, 504–29. ISBN 0028733703. ML 200 .K54 1990.

Extensive coverage with a biographical profile emphasizing George's influence and Ives's divided life. Focuses on several songs to show his range such as "The Cage," "Majority," "Charlie Rutledge," and "General William Booth." Includes extensive text excerpts and outines his use of quotations, simultaneity, and attitudes towards performance.

662. Kirkpatrick, John. "Ives, Charles E." In *New Grove Dictionary of Music and Musicians*, edited by Stanley Sadie. New York: Macmillan, 1980. Revised entry with Paul C. Echols in *New Grove Dictionary of American Music*, edited by Stanley Sadie and H. Wiley Hitchcock. New York: Macmillan, 1985. Reprinted in John Kirkpatrick et al., *The New Grove 20th-Century American Masters*. London: Macmillan; New York: W. W. Norton, 1988. ISBN 0333457773. ML 390 .N544 1988.

Biographical survey divided by periods: up to 1899; 1899–1910; 1911–20; and 1920–54. Emphasizes George's influence and the origins of several large orchestral works including the Fourth Symphony and the *Universe Symphony*. Concludes with a discussion of the musical styles employed (especially quotations) and a thorough list of works and bibliography.

663. Levy, Alan Howard. *Musical Nationalism: American Composers' Search for Identity*. Westport, CT: Greenwood Press, 1983. ISBN 0 313 23709 3. ML 200 .5 L48 1983, passim.

Noteworthy for its inclusion of Nadia Boulanger's assessment of Ives as having more flair than genius (p. 55), according to Kirkpatrick.

664. Mellers, Wilfrid. "American Music and an Industrial Community." In *Music and Society*. New York: Roy Publishers, 1950, 191–203.

Somewhat unfocused discussion in which Mellers argues that Ives is more important as a personality than as a composer. Describes his musical aesthetics and technical procedures, and repeatedly describes the music as "naïve" and "crude," "unreasoning and immature." Includes some examples from *34 Songs*.

665. Morgan, Robert. "Charles Ives and American Music." In *20th-Century Music*. New York: W. W. Norton, 1991, 137–48. ISBN 039395272X. ML 197 .M675 1991.

Perceptive survey of Ives's life and major works with emphasis on progressive compositional techniques. Morgan discusses a broad spectrum of works, including *Over the Pavements*, *The Unanswered Question*, the Fourth Symphony, and several songs. Analyses focus on conceptions of tonality, harmonic language, use of quotation, collage, employment of rhythmic and melodic series, and experiments in spatial form. The section concludes with an overview of Ives reception to 1965.

666. Nichols, Janet. *American Music Makers: An Introduction to American Composers*. New York: Walker & Co., 1990. ISBN 0802769578. ML390 .N58 1990.

Aimed at middle and secondary school students. Chapter on Ives with basic biography and style analysis focuses on quotation and experimentation.

667. O'Grady, Terence J. "Critical Perspectives in Early 20th-Century American Avant-Garde Composers." *Journal of Aesthetic Education* 27/2 (Summer 1993): 15–28.

Survey of published histories and textbooks discusses the appearance of Ives and Cowell, in comparison to conventional composers such as Horatio Parker and Edward MacDowell. O'Grady suggests that descriptions of Ives and Cowell emphasize their role as innovators who represent a specific American style, rather than as composers who were influential on their contemporaries.

668. Salzman, Eric. "Ives." In *20th-Century Music: An Introduction*. Englewood Cliffs, NJ: Prentice Hall, 1967, 143–47; reprinted 1974, 128–31. ISBN 0139350152. ML 197 .S17 1974.

Condensed summary of Ives's relationship to American and European "avant-garde" traditions, including a brief analysis of *The Unanswered Question* and mention of reception and ongoing influence to the present. The same entry is reprinted in the third edition of Salzman's volume, published in 1988.

669. Saminsky, Lazare. *Music of Our Day: Essentials and Prophecies.* New York, Thomas Y. Crowell, 1939; reprint, Freeport, NY: Books for Libraries Press, 1970, 151, 166, 167, 170, 173–75. ISBN 8369 1682 4. ML 197 .S18 1970.

Significant early source that celebrates Ives as America's "sharpest instinct for newness rising from the soil." Focuses on the songs including "Evening" and "Down East," as well as giving a general description of the *Concord Sonata*. Particularly intriguing is Saminsky's treatment of Ives alongside younger composers such as Roy Harris and Roger Sessions.

670. Slonimsky, Nicolas. "Ives, Charles Edward." In *Baker's Biographical Dictionary of Musicians.* 8th rev. ed. New York: Schirmer, 2001. ISBN 0028724151. ML 105 .B17 2001.

Revised and slightly expanded version of the sixth edition (1978) entry, which emphasizes the "slow realization of the greatness of Ives and the belated triumphant recognition of his music" through the centennial celebrations and the emergence of "a veritable Ives cult." Musical discussion of the *Concord Sonata, Universe Symphony,* and *114 Songs.* Ives first appears in the fourth edition (1941) with a basic outline of his education, insurance business, and large works.

671. Slonimsky, Nicolas. "Ives, Charles." In *Die Musik in Geschichte und Gegenwart,* edited by Friedrich Blume. Translated by Wilhelm Pfannkuch. Kassel: Bärenreiter, 1957, 1574–80.

Compact life and works survey includes brief family background extending through later reception and the Pulitzer Prize. Musical discussion focuses on modernist techniques such as polytonality and polymeters, as well as use of quotation. With a facsimile of the first page of the *Three-Page Sonata.*

672. Struble, John Warthen. "Charles Ives (1874–1954)." In *The History of American Classical Music.* New York: Facts On File, 1995, 47–63 and passim. ISBN 0 8160 2927 X. ML 200 .S95 1995.

Thorough, balanced, and well-researched summary of Ives's life includes comments on his life and the reception of his works through mid century.

Brief stylistic summary and remarks on Ives's use of nostalgia and his attitudes towards gender. Makes the questionable statement that "Ives is probably the most written-about of any American composer."

673. Yates, Peter. "An Introduction to Charles Ives." In *20th Century Music: Its Evolution from the End of the Harmonic Era into the Present Era of Sound.* New York: Pantheon, 1967, 252–70.

Balanced life-and-works survey. Based on Cowell (item 37), includes excerpts from the *Essays*, manuscript notes, and the author's personal recollections. Also briefly considers later performances by Kirkpatrick and Slonimsky, as well as interest in Ives's music by Mahler, Klemperer, and Schoenberg.

8

Selected Reviews of Premieres, Significant Performances, and Recordings

PREMIERES AND SIGNIFICANT PERFORMANCES

674. Abdul, Raoul. "Cleveland premieres Ives' *Emerson Concerto*." *Amsterdam News*, 15 October 1998, 20.

   Reviews the premiere by the Cleveland Orchestra with a brief history of the work and comments on the reconstruction.

675. "Amusements. The German Dramatic Association." *Danbury Evening News*, 17 January 1888, 3; reprinted in *Charles Ives and His World* (item 36), 274–75.

   Includes a review of the performance of *Holiday Quickstep* at the Danbury Opera House. The writer praises Ives as "a musical genius. . . . We shall expect more from this talented youngster in the future." For a more complete notice, see item 36.

676. Bender, William. " 'New' Ives Work: Bravo." *New York Herald Tribune*, 27 April 1965, 13.

   Review of the premiere of the Fourth Symphony with comments on the assembling of the score. Describes Ives's style as "neurotic," stating that "his music is full of the flavor of old newsreels, or old clothes hanging in the closet."

677. "Berlin Cheers Slonimsky Music." *Boston Herald*, 6 March 1932, 1.

   Brief report of audience reactions to Slonimsky's Pan-American concerts in Berlin: "Wild applause mingled with catcalls and hisses . . . . Some of the audience seemed bewildered at the cacophony of the contemporary offerings."

678. Brozan, Nadine. "Chronicle." *New York Times*, 31 October 1992, 22.

Brief interview with Michael Tilson Thomas and Riely Francis, a percussionist who played the Theremin in Ives's Fourth Symphony in a concert by the New World Symphony.

679. Brozen, Michael. "A Week for Charles Ives: Recitals by Esther Glazer/Easley Blackwood and Alan Mandel." *High Fidelity/Musical America* 18/6 (June 1968): MA 17.

Reports the performance of the four violin sonatas by Glazer and Blackwood on 21 March 1968 at Town Hall, as well as Mandel's 23 March performance of several piano pieces including *Five Take-Offs* and several studies. This brief notice also comments on the unfortunate circumstances of Ives's neglect since his music "could have exerted a healthful influence on our music at a time when it was badly needed."

680. Chanler, Theodore. "Forecast and Review: New York, Spring, 1934." *Modern Music* 11/4 (May–June 1934): 206–7.

Stinging condemnation of Ives's music as heard in two recent New York concerts of songs, choral works, and orchestral movements. Chanler states that the "shoddiness and vulgarity" of the music "only confirmed previous impressions of this composer's music."

681. "Charles E. Ives' Concert and New Cantata, 'The Celestial Country.' " *Musical Courier* 44/17 (23 April 1902): 34; reprinted in *Charles Ives and His World* (item 36), 276–77.

Review of the premiere of *The Celestial Country* comments on individual movements. Identifies Ives as a student of Parker's, and states that "the work shows undoubted earnestness in study and talent for composition."

682. Citkowitz, Israel. "Experiment and Necessity—New York, 1932." *Modern Music* 10/2 (January-February 1933): 110–14; excerpt reprinted in *Charles Ives and His World* (item 36), 307.

Includes a one-paragraph, mostly negative reaction to "Washington's Birthday" citing the work's "confusion in its intention," and criticizing it as "trite and stupidly devotional."

683. Cohn, Arthur. "Americans at Rochester." *Modern Music* 17/4 (May–June 1940): 55–58.

Briefly describes fifteen Ives songs performed in the 1940 Festival of American Music at Eastman with basic musical analysis, comparisons to Schoenberg and Cowell, and commentary on the audience's reaction.

684. Commanday, Robert. "Adventurous Night for San Jose." *San Francisco Chronicle*, 20 November 1989, section F, 2.

   Review of a performance of the Third Symphony by George Cleve and the San Jose Symphony. Comments that the "performances of Ives' work are becoming fewer, his music perhaps [is] entering a slack period. There may be several good reasons for that. In the long run, his music may not hold up." With brief comments on the work.

685. "Composers: Cantankerous Yankee." *Time* 85/19 (7 May 1965): 56.

   Reports on the premiere of the Fourth Symphony. Includes a profile of Ives that emphasizes his isolation and musical innovations. With photo.

686. "Concerts in New York." *Musical America*, 25 April 1934, 33.

   In a review of the Pan-American Association concert, mentions the premieres of "The New River" and "December" in their choral versions, along with a performance of "In the Night." Although highly critical of the choral works, the chamber orchestra work is described as "impressionistically lovely."

687. Cowell, Henry. "Review of Second Symphony, First Performance." *Musical Quarterly* 37/3 (July 1951): 399–402.

   Report on the premiere by Bernstein and the New York Philharmonic at Carnegie Hall. In program-note style, the essay focuses on each movement's main themes with excerpts.

688. Crutchfield, Will. "American Symphony And the Ives Fourth." *New York Times*, 15 October 1984, section C, 14.

   Reviews a performance of the Fourth Symphony by Jose Serebrier and the American Symphony Orchestra. Recounts the performance history of the work including its 1965 premiere, and discusses issues of preparation and conducting with or without an assistant.

689. Davidson, Justin. "The Expansion of a Charles Ives Sonata." *Newsday*, 28 February 1996, B7.

   Review of Brant's orchestration of the *Concord Sonata* states that "*The Concord Symphony* is more than a transcription; it's a metamorphosis."

690. Downes, Olin. "Symphony by Ives is Played in Full." *New York Times*, 23 February 1951, 33; excerpted as "Symphony No. 2 by Charles Ives: New

York 1951 Reading by Leonard Bernstein." *Pan Pipes* 44/2 (January 1952): 8.

Reviews the premiere of the Second Symphony by Leonard Bernstein and the New York Philharmonic. Describes the work as "rudely, tenderly, fantastically and cantankerously Yankee" and highlights its origins at the turn of the century.

691. Downes, Olin. "Tardy Recognition." *New York Times*, 14 April 1946, section 2, 5; reprinted in *Charles Ives and His World* (item 36), 403–7.

Review of the premiere of the Third Symphony by Lou Harrison and the New York Little Symphony underscores Ives's originality and experimentation, delays in performing his works and the American identity of his compositions, described as "sturdy, luxurious, savorous and thorny too."

692. Downes, Olin. "Concert Devoted to Music by Ives." *New York Times*, 25 February 1939, 18; reprinted in *Charles Ives and His World* (item 36), 326–28.

Important review of John Kirkpatrick's performance of the *Concord Sonata* at Town Hall on 24 February 1939 is somewhat noncommital regarding the quality of the piece.

693. Downes, Olin. "English Singers Delight Audience." *New York Times*, 13 December 1937, 22.

Reviews an early performance of *Psalm 67* by the Lehman Engel Singers as part of a WPA-sponsored concert. Downes describes the work as "very carefully thought, deeply felt, individual in expression and not simple to perform."

694. "The Four O'Clock Concert." *Journal and Courier (New Haven)*, 8 May 1902, no page; copy available in the Ives archives, Yale University.

Mentions a performance of the "Intermezzo" for string quartet from *The Celestial Country* by the Kaltenborn String Quartet. The reviewer states that the work "is well worth its place on the excellent program."

695. Freed, Richard D. "Stokowski Leads Symphony by Ives." *New York Times*, 20 December 1968, 50.

Review of an early performance of the Fourth Symphony by Stokowski and the American Symphony Orchestra in a concert dedicated to Henry Cowell.

696. Gann, Kyle. "Heaven Enough." *Village Voice* 41/26 (25 June 1996): 62.

Reviews Johnny Reinhard's performance of the *Universe Symphony* at Alice Tully on 6 June 1996.

697. Gann, Kyle. "Master of the Universe." *Village Voice* 41/23 (4 June 1996): 58.

Preview of Johnny Reinhard's premiere of his version of the *Universe Symphony* includes an interview with Reinhard and background on the history of the piece.

698. Gann, Kyle. "Now in Technicolor." *Village Voice* 41/11 (12 March 1996): 66.

Discusses the premiere of Brant's orchestration of the *Concord Sonata* by the American Composers Orchestra at Carnegie Hall. For a preconcert article, see item 753.

699. Gilman, Lawrence. "A Masterpiece of American Music Heard Here for the First Time." *New York Herald Tribune*, 21 January 1939, 9; reprinted in *Charles Ives and His World* (item 36), 316–21.

Influential review of John Kirkpatrick's performance of the *Concord Sonata* at Town Hall on 20 January 1939. Gilman's extended commentary discusses the work's structure, style, and program with excerpts from Ives's *Essays*.

700. "Goldstein Completes "Modernist' Recital at Aeolian Hall." *New York Herald Tribune*, 19 March 1924, 15; reprinted in *Charles Ives and His World* (item 36), 290–91.

Reviews the premiere of the Second Violin Sonata. States that the work was played from manuscript although it was written fifteen years earlier. The review states that Goldman described the work "as embodying the transcendental idea of the Concord group, but 'shot through with modern ideas.' "

701. Goodman, Peter. "Ives' Chaotic Human Comedy." *Newsday*, 13 April 1992, 49.

Review of a performance of the Fourth Symphony by Seiji Ozawa and the Boston Symphony Orchestra. Goodman describes the work as possibly "the most powerful statement of Ives's questions," and as the product of a "cunning, Connecticut Yankee naivete that dwells cheek-by-jowl with philosophic-religious questing."

702. Griffiths, Paul. "American Music That Rattled Berlin." *New York Times*, 14 January 2001.

Preview of the American Composers Orchestra concert commemorating Slonimsky's European concerts. Refers to Ives's financial sponsorship of the original concerts, audience, and critical reaction, and Slonimsky's comments on *Three Places in New England*.

703. Griffiths, Paul. "Greeting Ives as an Old, Familiar Friend." *New York Times*, 17 October 2000.

Reviews a performance of the *Concord Sonata* by Marilyn Nonken with discussion of her approach to the final moments of the piece.

704. Henahan, Donal. "Ives and Brahms by Cleveland Orchestra." *New York Times*, 16 May 1987, 15.

Reviews a performance of the Fourth Symphony by Christoph von Dohnanyi and the Cleveland Orchestra. Recounts the performance history of the work and describes its style as "a bewildering but exhilarating mixture of musical sophistication, philosophical seriousness and naivete, the whole lump leavened by a kind of undergraduate wildness."

705. Holland, Bernard. "Grit and Hard Winters in Rediscovered Ives." *New York Times*, 6 October 1998, section E, 1.

Review of the premiere of the *"Emerson" Concerto* by Alan Feinberg and the Cleveland Orchestra recounts the work's history and reconstruction by David Porter. Holland laments that "the saga of discovery may be more interesting than the music itself," and criticizes the work as "blunt and graceless."

706. Holland, Bernard. "One Way To Control The Chaos In Ives." *New York Times*, 9 November 1996.

Review of a performance of the *Holidays Symphony* by Michael Tilson Thomas and the San Francisco Symphony that considers the appearance of confusion and disorderliness in the work.

707. Holland, Bernard. "Ives and Kindred Spirits." *New York Times*, 28 May 1994, 12.

Review of a performance of *Three Places in New England* by the New York Philharmonic, under Kurt Masur. Describes the work as one of Ives's most successful, particularly "The Housatonic at Stockbridge."

708. Holland, Bernard. "Transience Attending a Sense of Place." *New York Times*, 10 April 1992, section C, 5.

Review of a performance of the Fourth Symphony by Seiji Ozawa and the Boston Symphony describes the work as "bits of memory becalmed on seas of confusion."

709. "How Peculiar?" *Village Voice* 39/24 (14 June 1994): 84.

Report on a New York Philharmonic festival entitled "American Eccentrics" that included works by Ives. Considers attitudes toward experimental music both historically and contemporaneously.

710. Hughes, Allen. "Music: Schonberg, Ives Challenge." *New York Times*, 21 January 1974, 34.

Reviews a concert by the Gregg Smith Singers that included Ives's Psalms 67, 54, and 24, as well as the songs "Like a Sick Eagle," "Charlie Rutledge," "Tom Sails Away," and "General William Booth." Praises the "attractive choral sound and textual expressivity" of the psalms in particular.

711. Hughes, Robert J. "Futures & Options: Labors of Love." *Wall Street Journal*, 1 September 2000, section W, 2.

Notice of a performance of *The Unanswered Question* with brief mention of his musical innovations and career in insurance.

712. "Ives' 4th to Get Premiere: Written Half A Century Ago." *Danbury News-Times*, 13 April 1965, 2.

Reports on a press conference describing the challenges of premiering the Fourth Symphony. Describes Ives's adaptation of hymn tunesuotes, and Stokowski as saying, "Ives saw into the future."

713. Johnson, Harriett. "An Ives Premiere After 50 Years." *New York Post*, 27 April 1965, 20.

Reviews the premiere of the Fourth Symphony. Comments on "America's most audacious, clairvoyant composer" who was, according to Johnson, a "musical primitive." Also mentions his early training and use of quotations.

714. Kastendieck, Miles. "Ives Premiere—After 49 Years." *New York Journal American*, 27 April 1965, from Ives archives.

Review of the premiere of the Fourth Symphony by Stokowski and the American Symphony Orchestra, with attention to Stokowski's efforts to vindicate Ives after decades of neglect.

715. Kastendieck, Miles. "The Pioneering Ives." *New York Journal American*, 25 April 1965, 31.

     Preconcert notice discusses the difficulties in preparing the premiere of the Fourth Symphony. States that the work "forshadows everything that has occurred in the last half-century."

716. Kastendieck, Miles. "Collegiate Chorale Proves Worthy." *New York Journal American*, 4 March 1948, 14.

     Review of the premiere of the *Three Harvest Home Chorales* includes comparison with works by Hindemith and commentary on the work's "granitic" quality.

717. Kennicott, Philip. "NSO, Up To the Challenge Of Ives's Genius." *Washington Post*, 27 April 2001, section C, 1.

     In a review of a performance of the Fourth Symphony by the National Symphony Orchestra, Kennicott describes the outcome of the chronology controversy. Also outlines the experimental aspects of the Fourth Symphony.

718. Kennicott, Philip. "Schuller's Return Blends 'New' Ives, 'Old' Masters." *St. Louis Post-Dispatch*, 2 March 1998, section B, 2.

     Reviews a performance *Yale-Princeton Football Game* and *The General Slocum* by Gunther Schuller and the St. Louis Symphony Orchestra. With brief comments on the works.

719. Kerr, Harrison. "Contemporary Music in New York. I—The Pan-Americans." *Trend* 2/3 (May–June 1934): 145.

     Review of the premiere of "New River" and "December," as well as a performance of "In the Night." Kerr criticizes the choral works but praises "In the Night" as "music of merit."

720. Koch, Gerhard R.. "Das Pardies liegt hinter Danbury." *Frankfurter Allgemeine Zeitung für Deutschland*, 19 February 1975, 23.

     Review of the European premiere of *Celestial Country* examines the inconsistency of the work in comparison with Ives's more experimental compositions.

721. Kolodin, Irving. "Pianist Plays Work by Ives." *New York Sun*, 21 January 1939, from Ives archives; reprinted in *Charles Ives and His World* (item 36), 321–22.

Review of Kirkpatrick's first performance of the *Concord Sonata* criticizes Ives's "single, most serious deficience . . . a lack of discipline, an inability to distinguish between the gold and the dross that issued from his imagination."

722. Kosman, Joshua. "Symphony Traverses Ives' Emotional Terrain." *San Francisco Chronicle*, 2 October 1999, B1.

Review of a concert entitled "An American Journey With Charles Ives," in which Michael Tilson Thomas and the San Francisco Symphony performed various songs, choruses, and orchestral works. Kosman applauds Tilson Thomas's ability to overcome Ives's "combination of aggressive, coruscating dissonance and unbridled sentimentality [which] induce a sort of emotional whiplash, and his unnerving tendency to simultaneously parody and extol the things he loves—patriotism, band music, philosophy, nostalgia."

723. Kosman, Joshua. "Conductor Thomas Juggles a Dazzling Ives Fourth." *San Francisco Chronicle*, 22 November 1991, C4

Review of a performance of the "mammoth, gut-busting" Fourth Symphony by Michael Tilson Thomas and the San Francisco Symphony. Kosman praises the "sprawling, unwieldy genius" of the composer and comments on the "elements of theater" involved in the work's performance.

724. Kozinn, Allan. "On Ives, the Arguments Continue." *New York Times*, 28 February 1996.

Review of the premiere of Henry Brant's orchestration of the *Concord Sonata* by the American Composers Orchestra at Carnegie Hall on Sunday afternoon. Comments on Brant's orchestration in comparison to the original, concluding that "there was something lost in translation."

725. Kozinn, Allan. "Choral Group And Ives's Radicalism." *New York Times*, 14 November 1990, section C, 25.

Reviews a performance of *Psalm 90* by John Daly Goodwin and the New York Choral Society. Outlines the experimental techniques, dissonance and responsive text setting of the work. Describes Ives as "a Yankee Gesualdo, bending the rules to his own directly expressive purposes."

726. Kozinn, Allan. "The Organ Works Charles Ives Wrote or Played." *New York Times*, 26 October 1989, section C, 18.

Review of a program of Ives's organ music by William Osborne at Central Presbyterian Church that included the *Variations on "America"* and the Fugue in C.

727. Kriegsman, Alan. "Singers Perform with Gusto, Style." *Washington Post*, 25 October 1967, section D, 13.

Review of a performance of Ives's choral works by the Gregg Smith singers at the Smithsonian Institution.

728. Kyle, Marguerite Kelly. "AmerAllegro: Premieres, Recent Performances, New Releases: Charles Ives." *Pan-Pipes* 44/2 (January 1952): 34–35.

Reports on recent performances, publications and recordings of Ives's music including the 1951 Bernstein performances of *Symphony No. 2*.

729. Kyle, Marguerite Kelly. "AmerAllegro: Premieres, Recent Performances, New Releases: Charles Ives." *Pan-Pipes* 43/2 (December 1950): 123.

Reports on performances of the Second String Quartet and the Fourth Violin Sonata in Los Angeles and Hollywood.

730. Lang, Paul Henry. "Hearing Things. Charles Ives." *Saturday Review of Literature* 29/22 (1 June 1946): 43–44; excerpt reprinted in *Charles Ives and His World* (item 36), 342–45.

Review of a concert of Ives's songs, chamber works, and the Third Symphony held on 11 May 1946 at Columbia University, as part of the Second Annual Festival of Contemporary American Music. Lang applauds Ives's individuality and "genuine creative talent," but criticizes his "almost inept handling of the orchestra." Also briefly compares Ives to Whitman.

731. Libbey, Theodore W., Jr. "Brooklyn Philharmonia And Foss Open Season." *New York Times,* 28 October 1981, section C, 22.

Review of an Ives tribute concert by Lukas Foss and the Brooklyn Philharmonia compares Cowell's *Saturday Night at the Firehouse* and Lou Harrison's *At the Tomb of Charles Ives* to Ives's own musical style. Also comments on the "inscrutability and mock profundity" of *Unanswered Question*.

732. "Madrigal Singers Heard in Concert." *New York Times*, 7 May 1937, 28.

Review of a WPA-sponsored concert of American choral music conducted by Lehman Engel. Mentions Ives's "unusual" setting of *Psalm 67*.

733. Mangan, Timothy. "An OK Chorale Season-Opener." *Los Angeles Times*, 1 November 1993, section F, 3.

Describes a performance by the Pacific Chorale of the *Psalm 67th*. Mangan states that "it didn't startle in the slightest. That is because Ives' polytonal style has become the accepted norm of modern choir music."

734. Metcalf, Steve. "From Neely Bruce: A Collision of Sounds." *Hartford Courant*, 16 June 2000, D3.

Preconcert report on Bruce's composition, *Convergence: Some Parades for Charlie's Dad*. The work combined multiple marching bands, choirs, organs, a symphony orchestra, and numerous other groups in a spatial performance through New Haven, Connecticut. The work was inspired by the marching band experiments of Ives's father, George Ives.

735. Morton, Lawrence. "Western Evenings with Ives." *Modern Music* 22/3 (March–April 1945): 186–88.

Describes a 1945 performance of the Third Sonata for Violin and Piano in the Evenings on the Roof series in Los Angeles. Includes a summary of the work's use of quotations, overall form, and style.

736. "A New Cantata." *New York Times*, 20 April 1902, 12; reprinted in *Charles Ives and His World* (item 36), 275–76.

Brief review of the premiere of *The Celestial Country* mentions that it "suffered from the want of the chorus" and criticized the conductor's (i.e., Ives's) handling of the dynamics. Also states, "the composition seems worthy of a more complete hearing."

737. Oestreich, James R. "Varèse's Memorable 'Amériques' vs. Ives's Fourth." *New York Times*, 1 May 2000, section E, 5.

Reviews a performance of the Fourth Symphony by Christoph von Dohnanyi and the Cleveland Orchestra with brief comments on the work.

738. Page, Tim. "America, to the Tunes of Ives and Adams." *Newsday*, 14 November 1994, B09.

Report on the festival "The American Transcendentalists" at the Brooklyn Academy of Music maintains that "most of the Ives output continues to strike me as so unrelievedly amateurish." Page offers harsh criticisms of several Ives works, but admits that *The Unanswered Question* is "Ives' masterpiece."

739. Page, Tim. "Masur Leads A Concert Of 'Originals.'" *Newsday*, 31 May 1994, 7.

Review of a performance of *Three Places in New England* by Kurt Masur and the New York Philharmonic. Pages states, "I continue to find 'St. Ives' a fundamentally inept composer who snapped his works together in the manner of a gifted child with a set of Lego blocks and, when all else failed, threw in a hymn or Civil War tune to provide an easy, abrupt change of atmosphere or some spurious genuflection toward formal structure."

740. Page, Tim. "A Rousing Opener At Miller Theater." *Newsday*, 5 October 1992, 45.

In a review of a concert by the Juilliard String Quartet and Dawn Upshaw, Page states that "the great Charles Ives boom of the 1960s has come and gone but many musicians and listeners still consider him an important composer. I don't." He continues to characterize Ives as a "Sunday dabbler who very occasionally hit upon a good idea" and describes his songs as "pretty feeble."

741. Page, Tim. "Continuum in Tribute to Ives." *New York Times*, 9 February 1987, section C, 13.

Review of a concert by Continuum of chamber works and *Psalm 90*. Page applauds "the grasping reach, the raw energy, the technical innovations, and the philosophical implications" of Ives's works, but criticizes his execution as "sloppy and disjunct."

742. Parmenter, Ross. "Music: Lincoln Program." *New York Times*, 11 February 1960, 38.

Reviews the premiere of "Lincoln" for chorus and orchestra, commenting that "its dissonant harmonies made it sound contemporary still, and the sledge-hammer force of its projection was stunning." Also comments on Ives's alteration of the original text.

743. Perkins, Francis D. "Lincoln Day Is Theme at Carnegie Hall." *New York Herald Tribune*, 11 February 1960, 18.

Reviews the premiere of "Lincoln" by Richard Korn and the Dorian chorale, commenting that the work "gave an impression of direction and emotional force . . . yet did not seem to be among his more memorable compositions."

744. Perkins, Francis D. "Pan-American Composers Give Spring Program." *New York Herald Tribune*, 16 April 1934, 12.

Brief review of the premieres of "New River" and "December," described as "roughhewn."

745. Petit, Raymond. "Concerts de musique Américaine." *La Revue Musicale* July–August 1931: 245–46.

In French. Review of Slonimsky's performances in Paris praises the "impressionisme" of *Three Places in New England* and remarks that the work is not without finesse.

746. Prunières, Henry. "American Compositions in Paris." *New York Times*, 12 July 1931, section 8, 6; excerpt reprinted in *Charles Ives and His World* (item 36), 304.

Review of the Pan-American concerts in Paris led by Nicolas Slonimsky that performed *Three Places in New England*. This and other reviews sparked a heated response from Ives that grew into the *Memos* (item 20, pp. 13–16 and 26–29), because of the statement that Ives "knows his Schoenberg, yet gives the impression that he has not always assimilated the lessons of the Viennese master as well as he might have." However, Prunières describes the work variously as "picturesque" and "pretty," and clearly states that Ives "is manifestly a musician."

747. Raynor, Henry. "Miscellany." *Music Review* 27/4 (1966): 331.

Derisive review of performances of the "Fourth of July" criticizes that "Ives's way out of a technical difficulty is to blast it down with brass." Includes comparisons to Arnold and Mahler, concluding that "Ives does not just disdain finesse; he doesn't know it, and his ambitions outrun his technique."

748. Rockwell, John. "A Pianist Juxtaposes Charles Ives and Art Tatum." *New York Times*, 26 March 1990, C12.

Reviews a performance of *Concord Sonata* by Steven Mayer at Alice Tully Hall. With a brief comparison of Ives and Art Tatum, particularly their experimentation with conventional forms and the reception of their music.

749. Rockwell, John. "Ives With a Bit of Help." *New York Times*, 20 November 1988, 67.

Reviews a performance of several chamber works by Leonard Bernstein and the New York Philharmonic. In introducing *"Tone Roads" No. 1*, Bernstein apparently turned to the audience and stated, "You'll hate this one."

750. Rosenfeld, Paul. "Ives' *Concord Sonata*." *Modern Music* 16/2 (January–February 1939): 109–112; reprinted in *Charles Ives and His World* (item 36), 314–316.

This report of Kirkpatrick's performance of *Concord Sonata* at Cos Cob on 28 November 1938 focuses more on the composition itself. With a description of the work's more prominent quotations, mood, style and experimentation, and commentary based on the *Essays*.

751. Ross, Alex. "In Bells and Microtones, A Legend Comes to Life." *New York Times*, 8 June 1996, 13.

Reviews the premiere of Johnny Reinhard's reconstruction of the *Universe Symphony* by the American Festival of Microtonal Music Orchestra. Includes comparisons with Larry Austin's edition, particularly in the pacing and performance of the percussion section.

752. Ross, Alex. "Ives and Mahler, Through the Same Lens." *New York Times*, 20 February 1996, section C, 14.

Review of a concert devoted to both composers by Michael Tilson Thomas and the New York Philharmonic. Compares *From the Steeples and the Mountains* and "Decoration Day" to Mahler's Fifth Symphony. Ross recounts the famous story concerning Mahler's encounter with the score of Ives's Third Symphony, but warns that "the problem with the tale is that it comes from Ives himself, a notorious fabulist and purveyor of unverifiable anecdotes."

753. Ross, Alex. "Tribute to Ives After 30-Year Effort." *New York Times*, 23 February 1996, section C, 1.

Extended discussion of Henry Brant's orchestration of the *Concord Sonata*, entitled *A Concord Symphony*, with attention to its specific techniques and overall effect. Discusses Ives's influence on Brant's spatial compositions, career path, and general aesthetic perspective. Provides an overview of the reception of the *Concord Sonata*. For a review of the premiere, see item 698.

754. Ross, Alex. "The Eccentrics Who Declared Independence for America." *New York Times*, 22 May 1994, section H, 33.

Discussion of a New York Philharmonic series showcasing Ives's works alongside those of Ruggles, Brant, and Riegger. Includes a brief discussion of the chronology controversy as well as comparisons between the four composers.

755. Rothstein, Edward "Nearly 12 Hours of Tribute to Ives." *New York Times*, 19 March 1984, section C, 12.

Description of the Ives Marathon at Symphony Space, which presented twelve hours of music, lectures, and recollections of Ives's grandson, nephew, and son-in-law. Extensive consideration of the *Concord Sonata* as a commentary on the "indulgent" Western tradition, as well as Ives's musical style and reception.

756. Schloezer, Boris de. "La vie musicale à Paris." *Les Beaux-Arts*, 26 June 1931, 1; excerpt reprinted in *Charles Ives and His World* (item 36), 303–4.

Review of the Pro Musica concerts conducted by Slonimsky applauds Ives's audacious talent and emphasizes his independent experimentation and isolation from European musical styles and contemporaries, particularly Stravinsky.

757. Schmitt, Florent. "Les Concerts." *Le Temps*, 20 June, 1931, from copy in the Ives archives; excerpt reprinted in *Charles Ives and His World* (item 36), 302–3.

Review of the Pro Musica concerts conducted by Slonimsky describes the technical innovations (polyrhythms, polytonality) and Transcendental background of Ives's work.

758. Schonberg, Harold. "Music: American Symphony Returns." *New York Times*, 17 October 1967, section L, 54.

Reviews a concert by Stokowski and the American Symphony Orchestra performing the songs "They Are There!," "An Election," "The Masses" and "Lincoln the Great Commoner." Mentions the significance of Ives's political views in these songs.

759. Schonberg, Harold. "Music: Stokowski Conducts Ives's Fourth Symphony in World Premiere After 50 Years." *New York Times*, 27 April 1965, 29.

Review of the premiere of the Fourth Symphony by Stokowski and the American Symphony Orchestra. General comments on the style of the work and audience reaction to it. With photo.

760. Schonberg, Harold. "A Complex Score Is Ives' No. 4." *New York Times*, 25 April 1965, section 2, 13.

Article discusses the forthcoming premiere of the Fourth Symphony. Focuses on the obstacles facing the performers and conductor, the condition of the manuscript sources, importance of quotations, and the "thoroughly American" nature of the music.

761. Schonberg, Harold C. "Ives Score, Composed in Last Century, Bows." *New York Times*, 25 April 1957, 35.

Review of the premiere of the First String Quartet by the Kohon String Quartet. Notes the "unmistakably American" style of the work and states that "despite some awkward writing, this is a work of pronounced individuality and, in many sections, real beauty."

762. "Selected Reviews 1888–1951." Compiled by Geoffrey Block and edited by J. Peter Burkholder. In *Charles Ives and His World* (item 36), 273–360.

Substantial compilation of reviews that appeared during Ives's lifetime. Extensive coverage through the 1920s and '30s, particularly the publication and first complete performances of the *Concord Sonata*, somewhat less inclusive of reviews from the 1940s. Includes reprints of the following, along with numerous others: items 115, 150, 299, 539, 604, 675, 681, 682, 692, 699, 700, 721, 730, 736, 746, 756, 757, 763, and 771.

763. Somervel, Stephen. "Music: Chamber Orchestra of Boston." *Boston Herald*, 26 January 1931, 12; excerpt reprinted in *Charles Ives and His World* (item 36), 299.

Review of a performance by Slonimsky and the Chamber Orchestra of Boston of *Three Places in New England*. Mentions the "extaordinary contrapuntal freedom" of the work and states that its "cacophony . . . does not seem meaningless."

764. Stern, Max. "Portrait of an Original." *Jerusalem Post*, 6 June 1989, 15.

Review of a lecture-recital of songs and choral music by Andre Hajdu, the Brigham Young University Singers, and others in Jerusalem. Includes a brief profile that emphasizes his use of popular music and experimental approaches that predate similar techniques by European contemporaries. Stern observes that Ives's "New World treatments of Old World psalm texts" are "undoubtedly of interest to Jewish audiences."

765. Stone, Peter Eliot. "Charles Ives Wall-to-Wall." *High Fidelity/Musical America* 34/8 (August 1984): MA 25–26.

Account of the 12-hour marathon performance of Ives's music (songs, *Trio*, choral works, orchestral works, and piano sonatas) by the Symphony Space with brief descriptions of the pieces and performance quality. Stone concludes with questions of Ives's use of borrowing and his current standing among composers.

766. Stone, Kurt. "Ives's Fourth Symphony: A Review." *Musical Quarterly* 52/1 (January 1966): 1–16.

    Review of the first recording by Stokowski and the American Symphony Orchestra for Columbia. Extensive discussion of the work outlines its themes, structure, quotations, and program with numerous excerpts. Includes a consideration of the symphony's place in Ives's output as well as its compositional history and sources.

767. Strongin, Theodore. "Symphony by Ives to Get Premiere." *New York Times*, 13 April 1965. From the Ives archives.

    Recounts a press conference concerning the premiere of the Fourth Symphony in which challenges of the manuscript sources and performance difficulties were discussed.

768. Swed, Mark. "Nagano Infuses All-American Concert with a European Flair." *Los Angeles Times*, 30 November 1998, section F, 3.

    Review of a performance of the Fourth Symphony by Kent Nagano and the Los Angeles Philharmonic. Swed reviews the history of the work and labels it "the best candidate for Great American Symphony" and "an ambitious portrait of an enterprising America at an optimistic time in its history."

769. Taruskin, Richard. "Corralling a Herd of Musical Mavericks." *New York Times*, 23 July 2000, section B,1.

    Comments on a San Francisco Symphony's concert series that featured the Second and Fourth Symphonies. Taruskin reflects on the changing reputation of American modernists and addresses Ives's use of engendered language and possible revisionism.

770. Taubman, Howard. "New Music Given by Pan-Americans." *New York Times*, 16 April 1934, 21.

    Reviews the Pan American Association concert, describing the choral premieres of "The New River" and "December" as "acrid and unappealing," while "In the Night" "created and sustained a mood."

771. Thomson, Virgil. "Music—Crude but Careful." *New York Herald Tribune*, 4 March 1948, 17; excerpt reprinted in *Charles Ives and His World* (item 36), 346.

Reviews a performance of *Psalm 67* and the *Three Harvest Home Chorales* by Robert Shaw and the Collegiate Chorale. Praises the chorales as "supreme examples of Yankee ingenuity," while the psalm is dismissed as "a dissonant diatonic piece that never quite comes off."

772. Tommasini, Anthony. "Revisiting A Homage to American Composers." *New York Times*, 23 January 2001.

Reviews a concert by the American Composers Orchestra under Dennis Russell Davies commemorating Slonimsky's European concerts of 1931–32, and including Ives's *Three Places in New England*. Concludes that the performance confirms Ives's position "as the father of us all when it comes to American composers."

773. Tommasini, Anthony. "Ives Upon a Breeze, Unplugged." *New York Times*, 2 August 1996, section C, 27.

Review of a free concert in Central Park by the Naumburg Wind Symphony. Comments on their performance of *The Circus Band* without amplification, and the resonance of this action to Ives's turn-of-the-century work.

774. "The Transcendentalist." *Newsweek* 65 (10 May 1965): 101–2.

Reports the premiere of the Fourth Symphony along with a biographical summary that emphasizes the influence of his father and the Transcendentalists, as well as his insurance career.

775. Trimble, Lester. "Review of Robert Browning Overture, by Charles E. Ives." *Musical Quarterly* 43/1 (January 1957): 90–93.

Review of the premiere by Stokowski and the Symphony of the Air. Discusses Ives's orchestration choices in the work, as well as its polyrhythms and melodic density. Trimble complements "the sureness of ear with which he combines his harmonies" and pronounces the work "monumental . . . and built to wear."

776. Tryon, Winthrop P. "Of Ives and Others." *Christian Science Monitor*, 3 February 1927, 6.

Review of the Pro Musica premiere of parts of the Fourth Symphony under Goossens. Identifies the use of hymn tunes as unusual and states that Ives "stands for an absolutely new style."

777. Tryon, Winthrop P. "New Yorker Writing Music for Quarter-Tone Piano." *Christian Science Monitor*, 13 January 1925, 10.

Announces the upcoming premiere of *Three Quarter-Tone Pieces* and states that, with this innovative work, Ives has placed Varèse as "drum-major of the modernist phalanx." Compares the third chorale to Thoreau's idea of the telegraph harp.

778. Ward, Charles. "Sound Thinking. Da Camera Explores Musical 'Land-scapes.' " *Houston Chronicle*, 1 March 2001, section D, 1.

   Criticizes a performance of the Fourth Violin Sonata by Curtis Macomber and Sarah Rothenberg for their treatment of the quotations.

779. Ward, Charles. "Two Composers Set Themselves Apart in 'American Orig-inals.' " *Houston Chronicle*, 23 January 2001, 7.

   Reviews a concert by the chamber group Context that included the *Trio* and several songs. Describes Ives as "the great original" of American music and as a predecessor of Bernstein through his blending of musical styles and sources.

780. Ward, Charles. "Symphony, Lin Find Baltic Tone, Deliver Moving Sibelius Concerto." *Houston Chronicle*, 18 September 2000, 4.

   Discussion of musical nationalism as expressed by Ives and Sibelius in a review of a Houston Symphony performance of *The Unanswered Question*. Ward mentions that the Ives work "was a novelty for the audience."

RECORDINGS

781. Clarke, Henry Leland, and Kurt Stone. "Reviews of Records." *Musical Quarterly* 50/1 (January 1964): 114–118.

   Includes reviews of recent recordings of the *Concord Sonata*, "Washington's Birthday," *Hallowe'en*, *The Pond*, and *Central Park in the Dark*. Stone's review of the orchestral and chamber works is particularly questioning of Ives's compositional ability through analysis of the works' organization and styles.

782. Clements, Andrew. "Music: Keynotes." *Guardian*, 28 July 2000, 20.

   Reviews several recordings of the Fourth Symphony stating a preference for Stokowski's original.

783. Cohn, Arthur. "Ten Records—Keeping Up with Charles Ives." *American Record Guide* 34/5 (January 1968): 376–81, 437.

Reviews several recent recordings of the string quartets (revised from item 787), First Piano Sonata, *Holidays Symphony*, *Three Places in New England,* and *Robert Browning Overture.* Includes a discussion of the sources and styles of the First Piano Sonata, and comparisons of the structure and motifs of the *Holidays Symphony* movements.

784. Cohn, Arthur. "From RCA Victor: After 68 Years, the First Symphony of Chas. E. Ives." *American Record Guide* 32/11 (July 1966): 1032–33.

Extremely positive review of the First Symphony, as well as *The Unanswered Question* and *Variations on "America"* performed by the Chicago Symphony Orchestra under Morton Gould. Compares the First Symphony to Dvorak, Schubert, Vaughan Williams, and Mahler, concluding that the work "is rich, first-rate imitation done with virtuosity."

785. Cohn, Arthur. "A Divine Document—The Ives Fourth." *American Record Guide* 32/3 (November 1965): 220–22.

Review of Stokowski's recording of the Fourth Symphony with the American Symphony Orchestra. Includes somewhat detailed commentary on the score (a copy of which Harmony Ives sent to Cohn in 1942) and its challenges to performers and conductors. Also describes each movement's overall style and structure.

786. Cohn, Arthur. "On Five Labels Simultaneously, More Music by Charles Ives." *American Record Guide* 31/10 (June 1965): 958–61.

Reviews of several recordings of the *Holidays Symphony*, *Three Places in New England,* and shorter works for piano, with comments on the styles of the works.

787. Cohn, Arthur B. "Cambridge, CRI, and Vox, that Supremely Individual Creative Genius Chas. E. Ives." *American Record Guide* 30/9 (May 1964): 760–64; 768–69.

Reviews several chamber works (mostly performed by The Boston Chamber Ensemble under Harold Farberman) as well as recordings of individual movements of the *Holidays Symphony* on various discs. Includes descriptions of quotations and programs of the works. The second segment reviews a recording by the Kohon String Quartet of the two string quartets with commentary on the works' origins and style: this portion is reprinted with alterations in item 783.

788. Cooper, Frank. "The Ives Revelation: Columbia's Contribution to the Ives Centennial." *Music/AGO-RCCO Magazine* 8/10 (October 1974): 30, 43.

Review of the five-disc Columbia set with commentary on the works themselves and the performances. Cooper considers the recordings of Ives playing his own music to be "the most important piece of documentation in the history of American music."

789. Courtney, Marian. "Pianist with Many Talents and a Mission." *New York Times*, 14 May 1989, section XII, 10.

Interview with Nina Deutsch, a frequent performer of Ives's piano music, includes a discussion of her recordings for Vox and numerous comments on the reception of Ives's music domestically and abroad.

790. Cowell, Henry. "Symphony No. 3." *Musical Quarterly* 42/1 (January 1956): 122–23.

Brief review of the first commercial recording by the Baltimore Little Symphony under Reginald Stewart. Comments on the "expert playing" on this "outstandingly desirable disc."

791. Cowell, Henry. "Violin Sonatas Nos. 1 and 3." *Musical Quarterly* 39/4 (April 1953): 323–25.

Review of the Lyrichord recording by Joan Field and Leopold Mittman. Program-note style comments on the works' style, quotations and overall form, with minimal commentary on the recording itself.

792. Davis, Peter. "The Ives Boom on Disk: Every Sketch, Scrap and Masterpiece." *New York Times*, 20 October 1974, section D, 26.

Reviews the five-disc Columbia set and surveys earlier recordings of the symphonies, *Three Places in New England*, songs, and chamber music.

793. Dickinson, Peter. "Review of recordings: Crumb and Ives." *American Music* 4/2 (Summer 1986): 233–35.

Review of Jan DeGaetani and Gilbert Kalish performing the songs "Tom Sails Away," "The White Gulls," "West London," "Down East," "The Side Show," and "Afterglow." With general comments on the works' musical structure and quotations.

794. Dwinell, Paul. "The Resurrection of Charles Edward Ives." *Listen* 5 (September–October 1964): 15–16.

Overview of recordings from the 1940s to present. Dwinell predicts that the growing interest in Ives may make the 1960s the "Decade of Ives."

795. Frankenstein, Alfred. "New Ivesian Discoveries." *High Fidelity/Musical America* 20/3 (March 1970): 92.

   Brief review of the Gregg Smith Singers' recording of previously unavailable choral and solo songs, including *Let There Be Light* and *Psalms 14, 54, 25,* and *135.*

796. Frankenstein, Alfred. "The Complete Piano Works—Old Friends and Fresh Discoveries." *High Fidelity/Musical America* 18/6 (June 1968): 81.

   Review of Mandel's recording of the "complete" works for piano. Addresses both the quality, quantity, and content of the piano studies. Mandel's playing of the *Concord* is particularly praised, stating that the work is "all handled superbly."

797. Frankenstein, Alfred. "Ives: Music for Chorus." *High Fidelity/Musical America* 17/1 (January 1967): from Ives archives.

   Brief review of the Columbia release "Ives: Music for Chorus" by the Gregg Smith Singers. Focuses on "General William Booth," *Three Harvest Home Chorales* and *Psalm 90.*

798. Freed, Richard. "A Superb New Set of Charles Ives's Violin/Piano Sonatas from Authoritative Performers of His Music." *Stereo Review* 47/11 (November 1982): 70–71.

   Brief review of the Musicmasters recording of the complete violin sonatas by John Kirkpatrick and Daniel Stepner includes comparisons with an earlier Nonesuch recording by Paul Zukofsky and Gilbert Kalish.

799. Gann, Kyle. "That Grumpy Old Pianist Is Ives." *New York Times,* 20 February 2000, section B, 34.

   Reviews the CD "Ives Plays Ives" that collects forty-two piano recordings made by Ives in 1933, 1938, and 1943. Gann considers Ives's choice of repertoire, such as the studies and "Emerson" Transcriptions. Also compares Ives's performances compared to published editions, especially the "Alcotts" movement of the *Concord Sonata.*

800. Glass, Herbert. "On the Record: An American Triple Play." *Los Angeles Times,* 16 May 1993, 51.

   Reviews a recording by Ensemble Modern of "Like a Sick Eagle," "The Rainbow," and "Calcium Light Night." Glass states that Ives built his most characteristic music on his own, rather than European, models.

801. Glass, Herbert. "Ives: Mt. Rushmore of American Music." *Los Angeles Times*, 7 February 1993, 52.

    Overview and evaluation of several recordings of *Three Places in New England* with brief commentary on the work's history and reception.

802. Glass, Herbert. "Ives—Will He Have Staying Power This Time?" *Los Angeles Times*, 14 April 1991, section CAL, 49.

    Within this review of recent recordings, Glass considers the variable reception of Ives's works particularly through the 1960s and 1970s.

803. Glass, Herbert. "On the Record: More Early Americana on CDs." *Los Angeles Times*, 8 October 1989, 62.

    Review of recordings of the *Holidays Symphony* by Michael Tilson Thomas and the Chicago Symphony, and the *Trio* by the Toledo Trio. Recounts the reception of Ives's music over the last two decades, beginning with the "Ivesmania of the 1960s." Based on these recordings, Glass recommends that "a second rediscovery is in order."

804. Glass, Herbert. "On the Record: Mainstream Americana." *Los Angeles Times*, 18 January 1987, 60.

    Reviews a recording of the Second Symphony by Zubin Mehta and the Los Angeles Philharmonic. Discusses the work's style, structure and quotations, and comments on its uneven reception following the centennial.

805. Greenfield, Edward. "Ives from England." *High Fidelity/Musical America* 22/4 (April 1972): 20.

    Account of Bernard Herrmann's recording of the Second Symphony based on the score sent by Ives to Walter Damrosch and presumed lost. Includes a description of Herrmann's efforts to find the score, aided by Damrosch himself.

806. Hall, David. "The Choral Music of Charles Ives." *HiFi/Stereo Review* 18/1 (January 1967): 73–74.

    Review of the Columbia release "Ives: Music for Chorus" by the Gregg Smith Singers with attention to *Three Harvest Home Chorales* and the psalms.

807. Henahan, Donal. "On Listening to Mahler, Ravel and Ives Play Their Own Music." *New York Times*, 14 July 1974, section 2, 13.

170 *Charles Ives: A Guide to Research*

Reviews the five-disc Columbia set with comments on the "surprisingly conventional" cantata *The Celestial Country*. Extensive description of Ives's own recordings of his music as "mystical, excitingly brash and disconcertingly messy [which] accurately reflects his personality, his music and his bifurcated life."

808. "Ives in Sound and Print." *Music Educator's Journal* 61/2 (October 1974): 71, 103–11.

Alphabetical listing by label of eighty-three significant recordings of Ives's music, including performers and titles except for songs. Followed by a basic bibliography.

809. Jack, Adrian. "Charles Ives, *The Celestial Country*." *Records and Recording* 18/6 (March 1975): 62.

Brief review of the recording by Harold Farberman and the London Symphony Orchestra identifies the most interesting aspect of the work as the experimental interludes between movements. Jack concludes that the work is "no great discovery . . . but fun as a novelty."

810. Jack, Adrian. "Ives Recordings." *Records and Recording* 18/2 (November 1974): 81.

Two reviews of recent recordings: *Sonatas for Violin and Piano* by Paul Zukofsky and Gilbert Kalish, and *Piano Sonata No. 1* by Noel Lee. With brief comments on experimental writing and quotations. Also addresses the four violin sonatas as a group, stating that "as a set the Sonatas are a better key to his personality than the Four Symphonies."

811. Jack, Adrian. "Ives, Symphonies." Records *and Recording* 18/1 (October 1974): 47–48.

Review of the First Symphony by the Philadelphia Orchestra with Eugene Ormandy, and *Symphony No. 4* by the London Philharmonic Orchestra with José Serebrier. Comparison of the overall style of the first and fourth symphonies, with added commentary on *Three Places in New England*. Jack dismisses the Third Symphony as "a depressing nonstarter" with "dreary movements clothed in the most drab and meagre orchestration."

812. Konold, Wulf. "Charles Ives—eine Nachlese." *Musica* 26/4 (July–August 1972): 410–11.

Review of five recent Columbia releases including symphonic, chamber, choral, and vocal music. See also item 813.

813. Konold, Wulf. "Schallplatten: Werke von Charles Ives." *Musica* 26/3 (May–June 1972): 296–301.

Survey of fifteen significant single recordings and collections of orchestral, chamber, keyboard, vocal and choral music. See also item 812.

814. Kozinn, Allan. "American Music's Coming of Age." *New York Times*, 10 October 1999, section 2, 29.

Review of the 10-CD collection "An American Celebration" by the New York Philharmonic which includes a recording of *Three Places in New En gland*. Also discusses the position of Ives within American music history.

815. Lyons, James. "A Prophet Passes." *American Record Guide* 20/10 (June 1954): 313–15, 343.

General survey of contemporary recordings including chamber works, songs, the Second and Third Symphonies and *Three Places in New En gland*. Most notable for a rare photograph of Ives ca. 1915–20, apparently provided by the G. Schirmer company.

816. Miller, Philip L. Review of *Robert Browning Overture* by Charles Ives (sound recording). *American Record Guide* 34/5 (January 1968): 437.

General review of a recording of *Robert Browning Overture* by the Royal Philharmonic Orchestra with Harold Farberman. Comments on the work and its performance, along with *The Circus Band March, Set for Theatre Orchestra,* and *The Unanswered Question.*

817. Miller, Philip L. "Music for Chorus." *American Record Guide* 33/5 (January 1967): 410, 412.

Review of the first choral release by the Gregg Smith Singers discusses the innovations of the *Three Harvest Home Chorales* as well as the "haunting and infinitely peaceful setting" of *Psalm 90.* Also briefly mentions the history of choral works on disc.

818. Morgan, Robert. "Let's Hear It for Charlie Ives!" *High Fidelity/Musical America* 24/10 (October 1974): 79–81.

Primarily a review of the Columbia box set and other recordings—*Symphony No. 2* by the Philadelphia Orchestra; *Symphony No. 4* by the London Philharmonic Orchestra; and works for violin and piano by Zukofsky and Kalish. With special emphasis and analyses of Ives's own performances (disc four of the Columbia set, entitled "Ives plays Ives"). Morgan interprets these performances as indicative of the importance of improvisation, rhythmic freedom to Ives.

819. Nicholls, David. Review of "Ives Plays Ives" (sound recording). *American Music* 18 (Fall 2000): 331–33.

Discusses the CRI release of Ives's own recordings. Nicholls asserts that the recordings are strong evidence of Rathert's concept of the potentiality of Ives's music (see item 262). Concludes that "Ives's recordings lead us once again to question the value of self-interpretation."

820. Pincus, Andrew. "Nationalism in Music Recognizes No Boundaries." *New York Times*, 20 October 1985, section 2, 23.

Reviews a recording of *Symphony No. 3* and *Orchestral Set No. 2* by Michael Tilson Thomas and the Concertgebouw Orchestra. Laments Ives's lack of recognition in America, and briefly outlines the history and program of the Third Symphony.

821. Rich, Alan. "The Ives Canon." *Saturday Review* 51/17 (27 April 1968): 75, 80.

Review of Desto's four-disc set (Desto 6458/61) and Vanguard's collection of the four symphonies (Vanguard Cardinal 10032/4) singles out *The Celestial Railroad* as "at least one piece of inescapable evidence of the seriousness and insight of Ives's approach to composition."

822. Salzman, Eric. "Charles Ives: A Centennial Keepsake Album from Columbia." *Stereo Review* 33/3 (September 1974): 122–23.

Review of the five-disc Columbia set discusses Ives's invocation of the past and its appeal to contemporary listeners.

823. Salzman, Eric. "Charles Ives: Music Big as Life." *HiFi/Stereo Review* 19/2 (August 1967): 65–67.

Reviews recordings of the *Orchestral Set No. 2*, *Robert Browning Overture* and "Putnam's Camp" by Morton Gould and the Chicago Symphony Orchestra; and *Three Places in New England*, *Robert Browning Overture* and "Washington's Birthday" by a variety of ensembles and conductors. With commentary on the works and their American inspirations.

824. Salzman, Eric. "Two 'Concords' at Once." *New York Times*, 27 May 1962, section 2, 18.

Review of two recordings of the *Concord Sonata* by Aloys Kontarsky and George Pappastavrou with comments on changing attitudes towards the work and its composer. Salzman maintains that "the closest parallels to the *Concord Sonata* can be found in certain music of Liszt," and criticizes the Kontarsky recording for its lack of understanding of the quotations in the work.

825. Salzman, Eric. "Records: Ives. His Symphony No. 2 Is Really Sophisticated." *New York Times*, 25 September 1960, section 2, 21.

Maintains that the Second Symphony reflects Ives's "musical sophistication," in this review of the first Bernstein recording. Briefly discusses quotations and humor, and challenges prevalent views that Ives produced his works in a cultural vacuum.

826. Schonberg, Harold C. "Records: Ives. The Four Violin Sonatas Played by Drurian." *New York Times*, 15 July 1956, section 2, 8.

Reviews the Mercury issues with comments on the performance as well as "the strange, unorthodox music." Schonberg maintains that "Ives threw too many hurdles into his writing, and a good amount of it is actually unplayable."

827. Shirley, Wayne. "The Challenge of Ives Brings a New Round of Challengers." *High Fidelity/Musical America* 18/6 (June 1968): 80–81.

Subtitled "The Complete Symphonies—The Problems of Performance Practice," this article reviews recent recordings of the four symphonies, with particular attention to recordings of the second and fourth symphonies. Also comments on the structural, textural, and stylistic similarities between the works.

828. Shirley, Wayne. "Ives's 'Holidays': A Glorious 'Fourth,' and No Anticlimax." *High Fidelity/Musical America* 17/9 (September 1967): 79–80.

Review of a recording of the *Holidays Symphony* by the Dallas Symphony Orchestra (Turnabout TV 34146S). Shirley comments on the structure, themes and programs of the individual movements as well, describing the work's style as "mid-Fourth Symphony."

829. Strongin, Theodore. "Ives: Holidays and Places." *New York Times*, 23 July 1967, 19.

Reviews recordings of the *Orchestral Set No. 2*, *Robert Browning Overture* and "Putnam's Camp" by Morton Gould and the Chicago Symphony Orchestra; and *Three Places in New England*, *Robert Browning Overture*, and "Washington's Birthday" by a variety of ensembles and conductors.

Comments on the style of each work with attention to the third movement of the Second Orchestral Set.

830. Strongin, Theodore. "When Charles Ives Was at Yale." *New York Times*, 5 June 1966, section 2, 19.

Review of the first recording of the First Symphony, *The Unanswered Question,* and William Schuman's orchestration of the *Variations on "America"* by the Chicago Symphony under Morton Gould. Extensive commentary on the conservative style of the symphony with comparisons to Brahms and Tchaikovsky, and reflections on its origins in Horatio Parker's classroom.

831. Swafford, Jan. "Answering the Unanswered Question." *Gramophone* 68 (1991): 1494–95.

Reviews the Sony recording of the First and Fourth Symphonies by Michael Tilson Thomas and the Chicago Symphony Orchestra. Integrates discussion of the Fourth's quotations, program, and significance for Ives with details of the recording's approaches and Thomas's own comments.

832. von Rhein, John. "The Whole Range of Charles Ives." *Chicago Tribune*, 4 August 1991, 132.

Reviews recent recordings of orchestral and chamber works by the Chicago Symphony Orchestra and Chorus, Gregory Fulkerson, Robert Shannon, and the Lydian String Quartet.

833. Ward, Charles. "Recordings." *Houston Chronicle*, 29 October 2000, 14.

Reviews a recording of the Second Symphony and *Robert Browning Overture* by Kenneth Schermerhorn and the Nashville Symphony Orchestra. Describes Ives as "a great musical iconoclast" who in these two works "shows his skill and penchant for surprises . . . through unthreatening tonality."

834. Ward, Charles. "Recordings." *Houston Chronicle*, 28 November 1999, 14.

Review of the recording "Ives Plays Ives" recounts the history behind the project and concludes that, although Ives was not a singer "there's something very touching about hearing Ives declaim his innocent democratic ideals during the middle of World War II."

835. Yellin, Victor Fell. Review of *The Celestial Country. Musical Quarterly* 60/3 (July 1974): 500–508.

Significant reconsideration of the cantata in light of its similarities to Horatio Parker's *Hora Novissima.* Yellin refutes Ives's denial of influence by presenting specific parallels between the two works, and reviews scholarly discounting of Parker's influence on Ives's compositional development.

9

Significant Festivals, Conferences, and Concert Series, and Selected Published Reviews

836. Archabal, Nina. "Ives Festivals at Minnesota, Spring 1971 and 1972." *Current Musicology* 18 (1974): 43–45.

   Outlines the overall content of two festivals, "Ives at Minnesota 1971" and "Ives at Minnesota 1972," including participation by Lou Harrison and Alan Mandel.

837. Bolcom, William. "The Old Curmudgeon's Corner." *Musical Newsletter* 4/4 (1976): 20–21.

   Commentary on criticisms of Ives in the wake of the Centennial celebrations, in response to Rich (item 861) and Porter (item 860). Includes Bolcom's own criticisms of Ives's orchestration, overuse of quotation, and his "childish" creation of dissonance countered with praise for this "great and moving composer."

838. Boody, Charles G., and Margaret Snell. "The Charles Ives Festival, Spring 1970: Reflections." *Current Musicology* 11 (May 1971): 57–58.

   Overview of the first "Ives at Minnesota" festival in 1970, with mention of concerts, lectures, and courses, as well as a preliminary evaluation of the impact of the festival on the campus participants.

839. Boulez, Pierre. "Mini-Festival Around Ives." *Stagebill* 2/2 (October 1974): 31.

   Description of the festival considers the bizarre chronology of Ives's works. Compares Ives to European contemporaries and American modernists.

840. "Charles Ives." Bard Festival, Annandale-On-Hudson and New York, NY, August and November 1996.

In keeping with the Bard Festival format, this festival presented concerts and lectures in Manhattan and on the campus of Bard College in upstate New York. Hosted by Bard College at Annandale-on-Hudson during August 1996, and at Lincoln Center, New York, during November 1996. For the published volume, see *Charles Ives and His World* (item 36).

841. "Charles Ives Centennial Festival-Conference." New York and New Haven, CT, 17–21 October 1974.

Sponsored by the Institute for Studies in American Music, Brooklyn College, City University of New York, and the School of Music, Yale University. The festival-conference included six conference sessions and seven concerts, outlined in the program booklet (item 847). A thorough collection of papers, transcriptions of panels, and compositions was published in 1975 in *An Ives Celebration: Papers and Panels of the Charles Ives Centennial Festival-Conference* (item 50).

842. "Charles Ives und die amerikanische Musiktradition bis zur Gegenwart." Westdeutschen Rundfunk, University of Cologne and the city of Duisburg, Germany, 1987–88.

Concert series and symposium. Papers published in *Bericht über das Internationale Symposion 'Charles Ives und die amerikanische Musiktradition bis zur Gegenwart' Köln 1988* (items 76, 99, 267, 505, and 618).

843. Dickinson, Peter. "New York, New Haven." *Musical Times* 115 (December 1974): 1067–69.

Report on the Charles Ives Centennial Festival-Conference includes a summary of the concerts, lectures, and panel discussions. Concludes with observations on the importance of his early music and context.

844. Fleming, Shirley. "Of Ives, Elephants, and Polish Independence: A Five Day Festival Covers It All." *High Fidelity/Musical America* 25/2 (February 1975): MA 26–29.

Reports on the Ives Centennial Festival-Conference, based on the statement: "If an elephant is whatever you want to make of him, Charles Ives seems no less so." Fleming recognizes the trend toward cultural studies, foreign aspects of Ives's appeal and theoretical discussions of the music. She concludes that the Festival represented a "clear battle line "between the first generation of scholars and "the bright young academicians" eager to find new approaches.

845. Griffiths, Paul. "Burnishing Ives's Reputation Yet Again." *New York Times*, 5 November 1996, section C, 13.

    Reviews performances as part of the Bard Music Festival. Includes discussions of the *Robert Browning Overture*, *Trio* and the Second String Quartet, as well as comparison with works by John J. Becker and Henry Cowell.

846. Helms, Hans G. "Charles Edward Ives—Ideal American or Social Critic?" *Current Musicology* 19 (1975): 37–44.

    Critique of the Charles Ives Festival-Conference in which Helms raises the issue of Ives's sociopolitical views. Helms maintains that such occasions idolize Ives "as an All-American hero instead of finally recognizing his universal importance as one of the earliest protagonists of a music which is truly for the people," which Helms compares to the theories of Lenin, Lévi-Strauss, and Fuller. Also assesses Ives's views in light of Watergate. For a response to Helms, see item 310. A German version of this article appears under the title "Charles Edward Ives—idealer Amerikaner oder Sozialkritiker?: Zum Ives-Jahr," *Beitrage zur Musikwissenschaft* 20/1 (1978): 16–22.

847. Hitchcock, H. Wiley, ed. *Charles Ives Centennial Festival-Conference*. New York: G. Schirmer and Associated Music Publishers, 1974.

    Program booklet for the 1974 event (item 841) that includes complete concert programs and conference session listings with notes and biographies, plus several published statements by participants.

848. "Ives and Copland." University of Northern Colorado, Greeley, October 1993.

    Concerts and lectures on both composers, organized by Kenneth Singleton and James Sinclair.

849. "Ives at Bard: The 7th Music Festival, featuring compositions of Charles Ives and his contemporaries." *Piano & Keyboard* 182 (September–October 1996): 13.

    Brief report on the Bard Festival mentions performances of Ives's keyboard music.

850. "Ives at Yale." Yale University and the Charles Ives Society, New Haven, CT, April 1998.

    Concerts, panels, and lectures celebrating the centennial of Ives's graduation from Yale.

851. "Ives the Commuter." Bloomfield Presbyterian Church, Bloomfield, NJ, February 1999.

Series of concerts, panel discussions, and lectures on the centennial of Ives's career as organist at Bloomfield Presbyterian Church.

852. "Ives the Innovator." *Time* 104/19 (4 November 1974): 85, 87, 89–90.

Overview of centennial events including the Miami festival, the festival-conference, and the Mini-Festival Around Ives. Discussion of the recent publication of item 62 and the five-disc Columbia set. Mentions the symphonies and *Three Places in New England* within a somewhat extended biographical summary.

853. Kerr, Hugh H. "Report from Miami: Ives Centennial Festival, 1974–75." *Current Musicology* 18 (1974): 41–42.

Announcement of the South Florida Ives festival with details regarding world premieres, other concerts, and lectures.

854. Kirkpatrick, John. "Thoughts on the Ives Year." *Student Musicologists at Minnesota* 6 (1975–76): 218–23.

Reflections on numerous concerts between 1973 and 1975, as well as the festival-conference. Concludes with a consideration of the "spiritual transcendence" of Ives's music.

855. Kupferberg, Herbert. "Ives Centennial Hits Crescendo." *National Observer*, 26 October 1974, 26.

Overview of centennial celebrations mentions concert series throughout the country and examines his "fiercely independent style."

856. "Mini-Festival Around Ives." New York Philharmonic, New York. October 1974.

Series of concerts celebrating Ives and his contemporaries, organized by Pierre Boulez. For related articles see items 463, 839, 852, 857, 864, 867, and 868.

857. Morgan, Robert P. "Charles Ives." *Stagebill* 2/2 (October 1974): 6–11.

Article accompanying the Mini-Festival Around Ives discusses the emerging interest in American music generally and Ives in particular. Describes Ives's isolation and the "anti-establishment" perspective of his lifestyle and compositions.

858. O'Reilly, F. Warren. *South Florida's Historic Festival 1974–1976*. Coral Gables, FL: University of Miami, 1976.

Collection of essays from papers presented at the festival. With photos and calendar of performances. See items 163, 203, 243, 250, 291, 293, 295, 333, 337, 379, 406, and 603.

859. Palisca, Claude V. "Report on the Musicological Year 1974 in the United States." *Acta Musicologica* 47/2 (July–December 1975): 283–89.

Includes a summary of the concerts, panels and papers of the Centennial Festival-Conference (pp. 285–86). Quotes liberally from Hitchcock's preliminary report in the *ISAM Newsletter* 4/1 (November 1974): 1.

860. Porter, Andrew. "Songs His Father Taught Him." *New Yorker* 50/37 (4 November 1974): 187–90.

Negative review of the centennial celebrations. Denounces Ives's overuse of quotations, and draws on Rossiter's dissertation (item 276) in criticizing the distortions of the Ives legend.

861. Rich, Alan. "Must We Now Praise Famous Men?" *New York* 7/43 (28 October 1974): 95–96.

Scathing criticism of Ives's musical innovations as "trickery." Rich maintains that the reputation gained during his centennial is undeserved, and relegates him to the role of "accidental" innovator.

862. Ross, Alex. "Vindicating Ives on Dates and Music." *New York Times*, 20 August 1996, section C, 13.

Report on the Bard Festival summarizes concerts and lectures, and comments on the controversy over the chronology of Ives's works.

863. Ross, Alex. "How Ever Did You Do It, Mr. Ives?" *New York Times*, 15 November 1994, section C, 20.

Reports on the festival "American Transcendentalists" at the Brooklyn Academy of Music, which included concerts and lectures addressing Ives's relationship to Transcendentalism.

864. Saal, Hubert. "Connecticut Yankee." *Newsweek* 84 (4 November 1974): 71.

Summarizes numerous centennial events including the Centennial Festival and the New York Philharmonic's Mini-Festival. Profiles the *Concord Sonata* and mentions Ives's insurance career and Yale education.

865. Scherer, Barrymore Laurence. "Charles Ives: In Concert and Context." *Wall Street Journal*, 15 August 1996, section A, 8.

Report on the Bard Festival with background on Ives's innovative musical style. Claims that his quotations are much more memorable than his original melodies.

866. Schiff, David. "The Many Faces of Ives." *Atlantic Monthly* 279/1 (January 1997): 84–87.

Review of the Bard Festival on Ives with perceptive commentary on the changing approaches to and reception of Ives's biography and works. Also includes comparison to Frank Zappa and Charles Mingus. Available online at www.theatlantic.com/issues/97jan/ives/ives.htm (accessed 14 May 2001).

867. Sherman, Robert. "Charles Ives in Bard Spotlight." *New York Times*, 4 August 1996.

Report on the Bard Festival's summer performances and panels devoted to Ives, entitled "Rediscoveries." Includes a brief biographical sketch highlighting the Fourth Symphony, and commentary on Ives's conservative contemporaries.

868. Sherman, Robert. "Music Fair to Open Site of Ives Center." *New York Times*, 23 September 1984, section 11CN, 19.

Description of "Music Fair America '84" at the Charles Ives Center for the Arts, which was inaugurated to celebrate all types of American music. In honor of Ives, the festival included several bands, classical ensembles, fiddle groups, and a jazz ensemble.

869. Schonberg, Harold C. "Innovation—So What Else is New?" *New York Times*, 20 October 1974, section D, 21.

Discusses the New York Philharmonic Mini-Festival Around Charles Ives and the impetus of the festival according to its music director, Pierre Boulez.

870. Schonberg, Harold. "The Pulse of America Beats in the Music of Ives." *New York Times*, 6 October 1974, from Ives archives.

Report on the Mini-Festival Around Ives by the New York Philharmonic includes comments from the director, Pierre Boulez, on the choice of works. Outlines reception since Ives's death.

871. Tuvelle, Howard. "Festival in Ives Country—Year-Long, Complete Festival in Miami." *Clavier* 13/7 (1974): 12–13.

     Reports on the Ives Centennial celebrations in Danbury, Connecticut, including the performances on July 4 at the Danbury State Fairgrounds. Profiles the concerts of the Ives festival in Miami.

872. Wallach, Laurence. "The Ives Conference: A Word from the Floor." *Current Musicology* 19 (1975): 32–36.

     A summary of the events of the Charles Ives Festival-Conference including a description of contemporary trends in Ives scholarship, and of reactions to the performances.

873. Yellin, Victor Fell. "Current Chronicle: Charles Ives Festival-Conference." *Musical Quarterly* 61/2 (1975): 295–99.

     Review of the conference with informed commentary on the mood of the conference and overall procedings, plus frank evaluations of individual papers and concerts.

10

Theatre, Dance, Poetry, Film, and Fiction

874. Addiego, J. "Charles Ives." *Epoch* 31/2 (1982): 127.

Poetic tribute to Ives. (Source not available for consultation.)

875. Anderson, Jack. "Balanchine and Ives: Marriage of Mysteries." *New York Times*, 15 June 1999, section E, 5.

Reviews a performance of Balanchine's "Ivesiana" by the New York City Ballet using the scores of *Central Park in the Dark*, *The Unanswered Question*, "In the Inn," and "In the Night." Anderson describes the work as a combination of "Classical steps with distorted Expressionist movements" that establish "a sense of nocturnal mystery."

876. Anderson, Jack. "A Dutch Tribute to Ives's Life and Music." *New York Times*, 14 October 1993, section C, 18.

Review of "Ives" as performed by the Dansers Studio in New York and choreographed by the Dutch dancer Beppie Blankert. With some description of the staging and conclusion, which used "Serenity."

877. Anderson, Jack. "Small-Town America." *New York Times*, 14 February 1989, section C, 16.

Review of a New York City Ballet performance of Jerome Robbins's "Ives' Songs." Compares it to Thornton Wilder's "Our Town," and describes the choreography in some detail.

878. Balanchine, George, and Francis Mason. "Ivesiana." In *Balanchine's Complete Stories of the Great Ballets*. 2nd ed. Garden City, NY: Doubleday, 1977. ISBN 0385113811. MT 95 .B3 1977.

Story for Balanchine's "Ivesiana," a ballet choreographed to *Central Park in the Dark*, *Unanswered Question*, "In the Inn," "In the Night," and, variably, *Hallowe'en*, *Over the Pavements*, "Arguments," and "Barn Dance." Balanchine observes that "The choreographer has little music than can twist him out of his habitual methods of design, but I found in Ives's work the shock necessary for a new point of view. . . . The music I find hard *not* to work with."

879. Beck, Jill. "Principles and Techniques of Choreography: A Study of Five Choreographies from 1983." Ph.D. dissertation, City University of New York, 1985.

Among others, discusses and analyzes a 1983 choreography by Anna Sokolow entitled *Scenes from the Music of Charles Ives* using Labanotation score reading and video documentation.

880. Copland, Aaron. "Night Thoughts (Homage to Ives)." *Parnassus: Poetry in Review* 3/2 (Spring/Summer 1975): 295–299.

Piano piece dedicated to Ives and published as part of the journal's centennial tribute "A Garland for Charles Ives."

881. Cowell, Henry. "Ivesiana." *Musical Quarterly* 41/1 (January 1955): 85–89.

Review of Ballanchine's ballet "Ivesiana" (item 878). Cowell comments that "the ballet is original and somewhat daring, even if not always very closely related to the music or to Ives's philosophies." With somewhat detailed analysis of *Hallowe'en* and "In the Inn."

882. Dunning, Jennifer. "Care to Try the Special? It's Beefcake." *New York Times*, 29 March 2001, section E, 9.

Review of a premiere of "Journey" by the junior ensemble of the Alvin Ailey company, Ailey II. The work was choreographed by Joyce Trisler and restaged by Regina Larkin to unidentified music by Ives.

883. Dunning, Jennifer. "A Serving of American, Garnished with Russian." *New York Times*, 4 February 2000, section E, 17.

Reviews a performance of the dance "The Unanswered Question" choreographed by David Feld, with commentary on the staging and props.

884. Dunning, Jennifer. "Venturing out to the Limits of Partnering." *New York Times*, 13 June 1998, section B, 7.

Reviews a performance of the 1977 ballet "Calcium Light Night" choreo-graphed by Peter Martins to the Ives piece.

885. Goodman, Hal. "Home Video; Music." *New York Times*, 1 November 1987, section 2, 38.

Review of the video release of "Charles Ives: A Good Dissonance" states that the film "is at its best when showing the places and events that Ives tried to capture, while his music fills the soundtrack . . . .The film is at its worst in overdone, predictable scenes purporting to show the reactions of tradition-bound people who didn't understand what the composer was trying to do."

886. Henry, Derrick. "Atlanta Ballet Performing 'Carmina Burana' and 'Prisma.'" *Atlanta Constitution*, 8 May 1997, section G, 2.

Describes the premiere of the ballet "Prisma," which uses parts of Ives's *Trio* and *A Set of Three Short Pieces*. Choreographed by John McFall.

887. Henry, Derrick. "Baritone's Dramatic Portrayal Brings Music of Composer Charles Ives to Life." *Atlanta Constitution*, 2 October 1989, section B, 3.

Describes a dramatic performance by singer David Majoros using songs and soliloquies to portray the life and music of Ives.

888. Johnson, Ronald. "Charles Ives: Two Eyes, Two Ears." *Parnassus: Poetry in Review* 3/2 (Spring/Summer 1975): 345–349.

A literary collage combining original writings with excerpts from Ives, Thoreau, and others. Published as part of the journal's centennial tribute "A Garland for Charles Ives."

889. Kisselgoff, Anna. "On Pulling Teeth, and 'Degenerate Art' Brought to Life." *New York Times*, 8 January 2000, section B, 17.

Review of a dance performance by the Grenke Company that included a performance of "Chasing His Tail: Volume II" choreographed by David Grenke to music by Ives and Arvo Pärt.

890. Kisselgoff, Anna. "The Stage Turned into a Circus, with Tricycle." *New York Times,* 19 June 1999, section B, 15.

Reviews a revival of Eliot Feld's 1988 ballet "The Unanswered Question" by the New York City Ballet. The score uses both the Ives work of the same name and portions of "In the Barn." The work, according to Kisselgoff, "suggests a surreal allegory about music" within a circuslike atmosphere.

891. Kisselgoff, Anna. "The Divergent Progeny of Granddaddy Ives." *New York Times*, 18 June 1999, section E, 28.

Reviews a performance of Jerome Robbins's ballet entitled "Ives, Songs" by the New York City Ballet, along with works set to music by Charles Wuorinen and Philip Glass. Kisselgoff maintains that Ives is "the granddaddy of American music's 20th-century experimentalists" including Wuorinen and Glass.

892. Larson, Thomas. "Unanswering the Question." *Perspectives of New Music* 20/1–2 (1981–82): 363–405.

Creative poem/essay explores the connections between Ives and poet Charles Olson using Larson's original writings and quotations from both Ives and Olson. Includes descriptions of Ives's education, aesthetics, and views on art and experience.

893. Lopate, Phillip. "Above the Battle, Musing on the Profundities." *New York Times*, 17 January 1999, section 2, 11.

Review of the film "The Thin Red Line" comments on the apt use of Ives's *The Unanswered Question* during a pivotal scene, stating "by its title alone, there could not be a better reference for this movie."

894. Lynds, D. "Charles Ives and the President of the United States." *South Dakota Review* 27/4 (Winter 1989): 156–61.

Fictional story; source not available for consultation.

895. Mackrell, Judith. "Witching Hour: Black Magic and Slapstick Are an Unlikely Mix for a Night of American-Themed Ballet." *Guardian*, 15 April 2000, 5.

Review of William Tuckett's new ballet "The Crucible," loosely based on the Arthur Miller play and set to unidentified music by Ives.

896. Phillips, A. "Blankert: 'Charles Ives.' " *Dance Theatre Journal* 11/1 (Winter 1993): 37.

Reviews a performance of a work choreographed by Dutch dancer Beppie Blankert and set to Ives's music.

897. Price, Jonathan. "The Rough Way up the Mountain." *Yale Alumni Magazine* (April 1968): 28–37; reprinted in *Music Educator's Journal* 55/2 (October 1968): 38–45.

General biographical summary emphasizes experimentalism and the role of George Ives. Accompanied by an extended "typographical tribute" of creative dialogue and personal reactions which the author describes as "an attempt to disorient and reorient the reader just as Ives does."

898. Redmond, Michael. "Filmers Give Bloomfield Church a Second "Look' at Charles Ives." *Star-Ledger (New Jersey)*, 21 October 1975, 29.

Report on the filming of "A Good Dissonance Like a Man" (item 904) interviews participants, director Timreck, and the composer's grandson Charles Ives Tyler.

899. Rickey, Carrie. "Fashion/Style/Custom: Alan Cote and David Diao." *Artforum* 17 (October 1978): 30–34.

Includes a description of a color illustration by Alan Cote entitled *Red Song for Charles Ives*. The illustration appears in an earlier issue, *Artforum* 17 (Summer 1979): 69–70.

900. Ridgway, Rick. *Three Squirt Dog.* New York: St. Martin's Press, 1994. ISBN 0312110790.

In this coming-of-age novel the main character, Bud Carew, listens to Ives recordings in suburban Cleveland in 1983. (Annotation from published abstract; source not available.)

901. Rodgers, Harold A. "Lenox Arts Center: 'Ives.' " *High Fidelity/Musical America* 25/12 (December 1975): MA 26–27.

Report on the theater piece "Meeting Mr. Ives," a production by Richard Dufallo and Brendan Gill that was performed at the Lenox Arts Center, 20–24 August 1975. The show included musical scenes alternating with dialogue and portrayals of both Ives and his father George. Most music appears to have been drawn from the songs, as well as from *The Unanswered Question*.

902. Schlocker, Georges. "Christoph Marthaler: Memory Resurrected." *Art Press* 232 (February 1998): 54–56.

Examines the work of German theater director Christoph Marthaler including a production entitled "The Unanswered Question," which uses the Ives piece.

903. Thomson, David. *Silver Light.* New York: Alfred A. Knopf, 1990.

Fictional novel that concludes with an allegorical concert of Ives's music, here used as a metaphor for the engrossing myth of American history. (Annotation from published abstract; source not available.)

904. Timreck, Theodor W., director and producer. "A Good Dissonance Like a Man." Made-for-television movie. Under the supervision of Vivian Perlis, 1977.

Unique video profiles Ives's life using original locations and extensive musical excerpts. Reenacts scenes recounted in *Memos* and elsewhere using professional actors.

Reviews: David Hajdu, *Video Review* 8/12 (February 1988): 84–85; Robert Levine, *San Francisco Chronicle*, 28 January 1990, section rev., 13.

905. Williams, Jonathan. "A Celestial Centennial Reverie for Charles E. Ives (the Man Who Found Our Music in the Ground)." *Parnassus: Poetry in Review* 3/2 (Spring/Summer 1975): 350–373.

A creative essay and extended poem inspired by the *Essays*. Published as part of the journal's centennial tribute "A Garland for Charles Ives."

11

Web Sites

906. Baron, Carol K. "New Sources for Ives Studies: An Annotated Catalogue." [http://depthome.brooklyn.cuny.edu/isam/ivescat.html]. Accessed 19 May 2001.

    Annotated listing of sources found in the Ives house at Redding under the following categories: Music-Related Material; Politically Related Material; Music; and Librettos in English Translations. For an overview of this material, see item 907.

907. Baron, Carol K. "New Ives Sources." *Institute for Studies in American Music Newsletter* 29/2 (Spring 2000). [http://depthome.brooklyn.cuny.edu/isam/baron.html]. Accessed 19 May 2001.

    Description of the materials indexed in item 906.

908. Boynick, Matt. "Classical Music Pages: Charles Ives (1874–1954)." [w3.rz-berlin.mpg.de/cmp/ives.html]. Accessed 14 May 2001.

    Includes biography excerpted from *New Grove*, first edition (item 662), links to item 913, and photo gallery of several pictures of Ives and Harmony.

909. "Charles Edward Ives." [www.thirteen.org/ihas/composer/ives.html]. Accessed 14 May 2001.

    Site related to the PBS special "Thomas Hampson: I Hear America Singing," contains a brief biography of Ives and sound samples from "The Houstatonic at Stockbridge" and "Circus Band."

910. "The Charles Ives Society, Inc." [www.charlesives.org/]. Accessed 14 May 2001.

Excellent site with a calendar of significant dates in Ives's life; programming suggestions; an extended biographical essay by Jan Swafford from the Peer Music site (item 918); list of works including audio clips; information on the society itself; and links to related sites.

911. "Composers: Charles Ives." [www.msu.edu/user/sullivan/CompoComposers Ives.html]. Accessed 14 May 2001.

Links to several other Ives sites, brief bibliography, and select quotations.

912. "Danbury Museum & Historical Society." [www.danburyhistorical.org]. Accessed 14 May 2001.

Home page for the Danbury Museum and Historical Society with information on the Ives museum such as hours, phone number, and directions. Also includes many photos of the museum, Ives, and his family; biographical summary; and links.

913. Garber, J. Ryan. "The Influence of George Ives on His Son Charles." *Classical Music Pages Quarterly*, added June 1996. [w3.rz-berlin.mpg.de/cmp/ives_fathers_influence.html]. Accessed 14 May 2001.

Somewhat elementary study draws heavily on earlier sources by Wallach, Feder, and Cowell (items 326, 37, and 42) in determining George's ideological and musical influences, including the use of polytonality, quarter-tones, and twelve-tone composition.

914. "Ives, Charles (1874–1954)." [www.hnh.com/composer/ives.htm]. Accessed 14 May 2001.

General biography and summary of output by genre with brief commentary. Aimed at K–12 audience. With caricature.

915. Monkman, Martin H. "Charles Ives (1874–1954)." [www.coastnet.com/~monkman/ives/ceives.htm]. Accessed 14 May 2001.

Program notes and personal evaluations of recordings for the symphonies and other orchestral works. Valuable links to numerous sites including those that describe or represent each of the *Three Places in New England*.

916. Schuster, Claus-Christian. "Charles Edward Ives: *Trio*." [www.altenberg. co.at/txt/ive11_e.htm]. Accessed 15 May 2001.

Excellent program notes for the *Trio* in German. Describes each movement according to overall structure, programs, and quotations. With specific measure numbers and quotation title for the second movement, and numerous excerpts from Ives's manuscript memos and other writings.

917. Sudik, Nancy F. "Charles Ives—Danbury's Most Famous Composer." [www.housatonic.org/ives.html]. Accessed 14 May 2001.

General biographical introduction with specific information and links to locations associated with Ives, including the Ives homestead (now a museum), Putnam Park, downtown Danbury, and the Charles Ives Center for the Arts.

918. Swafford, Jan. "Charles Ives." [www.peermusic.com/classical/Ivesessay.htm]. Accessed 14 May 2001.

Biographical essay summarizes George's influence, early experimentation, Yale education, choice of career, relationship with Harmony, mature musical style, and belated recognition.

Appendix

List of Ives's Works with Appropriate Dates of Composition

This list is adapted from the worklist for the Ives entry for the second edition of *New Grove* (item 645) by Burkholder, Sherwood and Sinclair which contains a concise list of complete and nearly complete works with publication information and dates. This index adopts standard titles from Sinclair 1999 (item 7) with cross-references to commonly used titles. This list does not include miscellaneous fragments, exercises, arrangements, rejected or lost movements. Dates in square brackets are Ives's own and represent pieces or stages of composition for which no manuscripts survive.

I. ORCHESTRAL WORKS

Symphonies

Holidays Symphony: see *A Symphony: New England Holidays*
New England Holidays: see *A Symphony: New England Holidays*
New England Symphony: see *Orchestral Set No. 1: Three Places in New England*

Symphony No. 1	c1898-c1901, c1907–8
i. Allegro	c1898-c1901, c1908
ii. Adagio molto	c1898–9, c1907–8
iii. Scherzo	c1898–9, c1907–8
iv. Allegro molto	[1898], c1907–8
Symphony No. 2	[1899–1902], c1907–9
i. Andante moderato	c1907–8
ii. Allegro	c1908–9
iii. Adagio cantabile	c1908–9
iv. Lento	c1908
v. Allegro molto vivace	c1907–9, new ending c1950

Symphony No. 3	[1904], c1908–11
i. Old Folks Gatherin'	c1909–10
ii. Children's Day	c1908–10
iii. Communion	c1909–11
Symphony No. 4	c1912–18, c1921–5
i. Prelude	c1916–17, c1923–4
ii. Allegretto	c1916–18, c1923–5
iii. Fugue	c1912–13, c1923–4
iv. Largo	c1915–16, c1921–4
A Symphony: New England Holidays	assembled ?c1917–19
i. Washington's Birthday	[1909–13], c1915–17
ii. Decoration Day	[1912–13], c1915–20, rev. c1923–4
iii. The Fourth of July	[1912], c1914–18, rev. c1930–31
iv. Thanksgiving and Forefathers' Day	c1911–16, rev. 1933

Three Places in New England: see *Orchestral Set No. 1: Three Places in New England*

Universe Symphony	1915–28
i. Prelude No. 1	c1923
ii. Prelude No. 2	c1923
iii. Section A	1915–28
iv. Section B	1923–8
v. Section C	1923–8

Orchestral Sets

Orchestral Set No. 1: Three Places in New England	c1912–17, c1919–21
i. The "St. Gaudens" in Boston Common	c1916–17
ii. Putnam's Camp, Redding, Connecticut	c1914–15, c1919–20
iii. The Housatonic at Stockbridge	c1912–17, rev. c1921
Orchestral Set No. 2	assembled c1919
i. An Elegy to Our Forefathers	c1915–19, c1924–5
ii. The Rockstrewn Hills Join in the People's Outdoor Meeting	c1915–16, c1920–22
iii. From Hanover Square North	1915-c1916, c1918–19, c1926, c1929
Orchestral Set No. 3	assembled c1921
i. [no title]	c1921–2, c1925–6
ii. An Afternoon or During Camp Meetin' Week	c1912–14, c1921–2
iii. [no title]	c1921

Sets for Chamber Orchestra

Set No. 1	assembled c1915–16
i. Scherzo: The See'r	[1913], c1915–16
ii. A Lecture	[1909], c1915–16
iii. The Ruined River	[1912], c1915–16
iv. Like a Sick Eagle	[1909], c1915–16
v. Calcium Light Night	[1907], c1915–16
vi. Allegretto sombreoso	c1915–16
Set no. 2	assembled c1916–17
i. Largo: The Indians	[1912], c1916–17
ii. Gyp the Blood- or Hearst!?	
Which is Worst?!	?1912, c1916–17
iii. Andante: The Last Reader	[1911], c1916–17
Set no. 3	assembled c1919
i. Adagio sostenuto: At Sea	c1918–19
ii. Luck and Work	c1919
iii. Premonitions	c1918–19
Set no. 4: Three Poets and Human Nature	?c1925–30
i. Robert Browning	
ii. Walt Whitman	
iii. Matthew Arnold	
Set no. 5: The Other Side of Pioneering	?after c1925
i. The New River	
ii. The Indians	
iii. Charlie Rutlage	
iv. Ann Street	
Set no. 6: From the Side Hill	?c1925–30
i. Mists	
ii. The Rainbow	
iii. Afterglow	
iv. Evening	
Set no. 7: Water Colors	?c1925–30
i. At Sea	
ii. Swimmers	
iii. The Pond	
iv. Full Fathom Five	
Set no. 8: Songs without Voices	?c1930
i. The New River	
ii. The Indians	
iii. Ann Street	

Set no. 9 of Three Pieces assembled   ?1934
i. Andante con moto: The Last Reader
ii. Scherzo: The See'r
iii. Largo to Presto: The Unanswered Question

Set no. 10 of Three Pieces   assembled ?1934
i. Largo molto: Like a Sick Eagle
ii. Allegro-Andante: Luck and Work
iii. Adagio: The Indians

Set for Theatre Orchestra   assembled c1915, rev. c1929–30
i. In the Cage
ii. In the Inn
iii. In the Night

Overtures

Emerson Overture	c1910–14, rev. c1920–21
Overture and March "1776"	[1903–4]; c1909–10
Overture in G Minor	c1899
Robert Browning Overture	c1912–14, rev. c1936–42

Marches

Holiday Quickstep	1887
March no.2, with "Son of a Gambolier"	1892, c1895
March no.3, with "My Old Kentucky Home"	c1895
March: The Circus Band	c1898–9, arr. c1932–3

Other Orchestral

Central Park in the Dark	[1906], c1909, rev. c1936
Chromâtimelôdtune	c1923
"Country Band" March	[1905], c1910–11, c1914
The General Slocum	[1904], c1909–10
The Gong on the Hook and Ladder	arr. c1934
The Pond	[1906], c1912–13
Postlude in F	c1898–9
Four Ragtime Dances	[1902–11], c1915–16, c1920–21
The Rainbow	1914
Skit for Danbury Fair	[1902], c1909
Take-Off no. 7: Mike Donlin - Johnny Evers	1907
Take-Off no. 8: Willy Keeler at Bat	c1907

Tone Roads et al.
i. Tone Roads no.   c1913–14
ii. Tone Roads no.   lost
iii. Tone Roads no.   c1911, c1913–14
The Unanswered Question   1908, rev. version c1930–35
Yale-Princeton Football Game   [1899], c1910–11

II. BAND WORKS

Fantasia on "Jerusalem the Golden"   [1888]
March in F and C, with "Omega Lambda Chi"   1895–6
March "Intercollegiate," with "Annie Lisle"   c1895
March "Omega Lambda Chi": see *March in F and C, with "Omega Lambda Chi"*
Runaway Horse on Main Street   c1907–8

III. CHAMBER WORKS

String Quartet no. 1:
   From the Salvation Army   c1897-c1900, c1909
i. Chorale   c1897–8
ii. Prelude   c1900, c1909
iii. Offertory   c1897–8, c1909
iv. Postlude   c1900, c1909

String Quartet no. 2
i. Discussions   [1911], c1913–14
ii. Arguments   [1907], c1913–14
iii. The Call of the Mountains   [1911–13], c1914–15

Pre-First Sonata for Violin and Piano   [1901–3], c1908–13
i. Allegretto moderato   [1902–3], c1909–10, rev. c1911–12
ii. Largo   [1902, 1908], c1911–12
iii. Largo—Allegro   [1908–10], c1911–13

Sonata no. 1 for Violin and Piano   assembled c1914 or c1917
i. Andante—Allegro vivace   [1906], c1910–12, c1914, rev c1917
ii. Largo cantabile   c1914, rev. c1917
iii. Allegro   [1909], c1911–12, rev. c1917–18, c1924–5

Sonata no. 2 for Violin and Piano   assembled c1914–17
i. Autumn   c1914, rev. c1920–21
ii. In the Barn   c1914, rev. c1920–21
iii. The Revival   c1915–17, rev. c1920–21

Sonata no. 3 for Violin and Piano	1914
i. Adagio	
ii. Allegro	
iii. Adagio cantabile	
Sonata no. 4 for Violin and Piano:	
Children's Day at the Camp	
Meeting assembled	c1914–16
i. Allegro	c1911–12
ii. Largo—Allegro (conslugarocko)—	
Andante con spirito—Adagio cantabile—	
Largo cantabile	c1914–15
iii. Allegro	c1916

Other Chamber

Adagio cantabile: The Innate: see *A Set of Three Short Pieces*, iii	
Decoration Day for Violin and Piano	arr. c1919
From the Steeples and the Mountains	[1901], c1905–6
Fugue in Four Keys on "The Shining Shore"	c1903
The Gong on the Hook and Ladder/	
Firemen's Parade on Main Street	c1912
Hallowe'en	[1911], c1914
In Re Con Moto et al.	[1913], c1915–16, rev. c1923–4
Largo for Violin, Clarinet and Piano	arr. ?1934
Largo cantabile: Hymn: see *A Set of Three Short Pieces*, i	
Largo risoluto no.1	c1908–9
Largo risoluto no.2	c1909–10
An Old Song Deranged	arr. c1903
Polonaise	c1887–9
Practice for String Quartet in Holding	
Your Own!	1903
Prelude on "Eventide"	[by 1902], c1907–8
Scherzo: All the Way Around and Back	c1907–8
Scherzo: Over the Pavements	c1910, rev. c1926–7
Scherzo for String Quartet	1904
A Set of Three Short Pieces	assembled ?c1935
i. Largo cantabile: Hymn	[1904], c1907–8
ii. Scherzo: Holding Your Own!	assembled c1935
iii. Adagio cantabile: The Innate	c1908–9
Take-Off no.3: All the Way Around and Back: see *Scherzo: All the Way Around and Back*	
Take-Off no. 3: Rube Trying to Walk 2 to 3!!	c1909
Trio for Violin, Violoncello and Piano	c1909–10, rev. c1914–15

i. Moderato	c1909–10
ii. Presto ("TSIAJ" or Medley on the Fence on the Campus!)	c1909–10
iii. Moderato con moto	c1909–10, rev. c1914–15

IV. PIANO WORKS

Sonatas

Sonata no. 1 for Piano	assembled c1915–16, c1921
i. Adagio con moto—Allegro con moto— Allegro risoluto—Adagio cantabile	c1909–10, c1915–16, rev. c1921, c1926–7
iia. Allegro moderato—Andante	c1915–16, c1920–21
iib. Allegro—Meno mosso con moto (In the Inn)	c1915–16, c1920–22
iii. Largo—Allegro—Largo	c1915–16, rev. c1921–2
iva. [no title]	c1921
ivb. Allegro—Presto—Slow	c1921
v. Andante maestoso—Adagio cantabile— Allegro—Andante	c1920–22, rev. c1926–7
Sonata no. 2 for Piano: Concord, Mass., 1840—60	c1916–19; rev. 1920s-40s
i. Emerson	c1916–19
ii. Hawthorne	c1916–17
iii. The Alcotts	c1916–17
iv. Thoreau	c1918–19
Three-Page Sonata	[1905], c1910–11, rev. c1925–6

Piano Studies

Study no. 1: Allegro	c1910–11
Study no. 2: Andante moderato— Allegro molto	c1910–11, rev. c1925
Study no. 5: Moderato con anima	c1912–13
Study no. 6: Andante	c1912–13
Study no. 7: Andante cantabile	c1912–13
Study no. 8: Trio (Allegro moderato—Presto)	c1912–13
Study no. 9: The Anti-Abolitionist Riots in the 1830's and 1840's	c1912–13
Study no. 11: Andante	c1915–16
Study no. 15: Allegro moderato	c1917–18

Study no. 16: Andante cantabile	c1917–18
Study no. 19: Andante cantabile	c1914
Study no. 20: March (Slow—Allegro or	
Fast Andante)	c1917–19
Study no. 21: Some Southpaw Pitching	c1918–19
Study no. 22: Andante maestoso—	
Allegro vivace	c1918–19, c1922–3
Study no. 23: Allegro	c1920–22

Marches for Piano

March no. 1 for Piano, with	
"Year of Jubilee"	[1890], c1894–5
March no. 2 for Piano,with	
"Son of a Gambolier"	1895
March no. 3 for Piano, with	
"Omega Lambda Chi"	c1895–6
March no. 5 for Piano, with "Annie Lisle"	c1895
March no. 6 for Piano, with	
"Here's to Good Old Yale"	c1895–6
March in G and C for Piano, with	
"See the Conquering Hero Comes"	c1896–7
March for Piano: The Circus Band	c1898–9
The Celestial Railroad	c1922–5
Three Improvisations	1938
i. Improvisation I	
ii. Improvisation II	
iii. Improvisation	
Invention in D	c1898
Minuetto, op.4	1886
New Year's Dance	1887
Three Protests: see *Varied Air and Variations*	
Set of Five Take-Offs	c1909
i. The Seen and Unseen?	
ii. Rough and Ready et al.	
iii. Song without (good) Words/The Good & the Bad (new & old)	
iv. Scene Episode	
v. Bad Resolutions and Good WAN!	
Four Transcriptions from "Emerson"	c1923–4, c1926–7
i. Slowly	c1923–4, c1926–7
ii. Moderato	c1926–7
iii. Largo	c1926–7

iv. Allegro agitato—Broadly	c1926–7
Varied Air and Variations	c1920–22
Waltz-Rondo	1911

Two Piano Pieces

Three Quarter-Tone Pieces	1923–24
i. Largo	
ii. Allegro	
iii. Chorale	

V. ORGAN WORKS

"Adeste Fideles" in an Organ Prelude	[1898], c1903
Canzonetta in F	c1893–4
Fugue in C Minor	c1898
Fugue in E-flat	c1898
Interludes for Hymns	c1898–1901
Variations on "America"	1891–2, additions c1909–10, rev. c1949

VI. CHORAL WORKS

Sacred Works – Multi-Movement:

The Celestial Country	1898–1902, additions c1912–13
Introduction before no. 1	added c1912–13
i. Prelude, Trio, and Chorus	
Prelude before no. 2	added c1912–13
ii. Aria for Baritone	
iii. Quartet	
Interlude before no. 4	added c1912–13
Intermezzo for String Quartet	
Interlude after no. 4	added c1912–13
v. Double Quartet, a cappella	
vi. Aria for Tenor	
Introduction to no. 7	added c1912–13
vii. Chorale and Finale	
Communion Service	c1894
i. Kyrie	
ii. Gratias agimus	
iii. Gloria tibi	
iv. Sursum corda	
v. Credo	

vi. Sanctus
vii. Benedictus
viii. Agnus Dei

Three Harvest Home Chorales	c1902, c1912–15
i. Harvest Home	c1902, c1915
ii. Lord of the Harvest	c1915
iii. Harvest Home	c1912–15

Psalms

Psalm 14	c1902, rev. c1912–13
Psalm 24	c1901, rev. c1912–13
Psalm 25	c1901, rev. c1912–13
Psalm 42	c1891–2
Psalm 54	c1902
Psalm 67	c1898–9
Psalm 90	1923–4
Psalm 100	c1902
Psalm 135	c1902, rev. c1912–13
Psalm 150	c1898–9

Other Sacred

All-Forgiving, look on me	c1898–9
Benedictus in E	c1894
Bread of the World	c1896–7
Crossing the Bar	c1894
Easter Anthem	c1890–91
Easter Carol	c1896, rev. c1901
Gloria in Excelsis	c1893–4
I Come to Thee	c1896–7
I Think of Thee, My God	c1895–6
The Light That Is Felt	c1898
Lord God, Thy Sea Is Mighty	c1900–01
Processional: Let There Be Light	c1902–3, rev. c1912–13, late 1930s
Turn Ye, Turn Ye	c1896

Secular Works for Chorus and Ensemble

December	c1914, rev. 1934
An Election	[1920], c1923
General William Booth Enters Into Heaven	arr. 1934

He Is There!	c1918–21
Johnny Poe	c1927–9
Lincoln, the Great Commoner	c1922–3
The Masses (Majority)	c1916, rev. c1920–21
The New River	c1915
Sneak Thief	1914
They Are There! (A War Song March)	adapted 1942
Two Slants (Christian and Pagan)	c1912–14, c1916–17
i. Duty	
ii. Vita	
Walt Whitman	c1914–15, rev. c1920–21

Secular Partsongs

The Bells of Yale	c1897, rev. c1900–01
The Boys in Blue	c1895–6
For You and Me!	?1895–6
My Sweet Jeanette	c1900
O Maiden Fair	c1900
Serenade	c1895–6
A Song of Mory's	c1896
The Year's at the Spring	c1892

VII. SONGS

Abide with me	c1890–91, rev. c1921
Aeschylus and Sophocles	1922-c1924
Afterglow	1919
Allegro	adapted after c1902–3
The All-Enduring	c1898-c1900
Amphion	adapted after c1896–7
Ann Street	1921
At Parting	c1897-c1900
At Sea	arr. 1921
At the River	arr. [1916]
August	1920
Autumn	c1907–8
Because of You	1898
Because Thou Art	c1901–2
Berceuse	adapted c1920
The Cage	[1906]
The Camp Meeting	arr. [1912]

Canon [I]	[1893], c1895–6
Canon [II]	adapted after c1895–6
Chanson de Florian	c1898
Charlie Rutlage	1920/21
The Children's Hour	c1912–13
A Christmas Carol	before 1898
The Circus Band	adapted ?c1899 or ?c1920–21
The Collection	1920
Country Celestial	c1895–8
Cradle Song	1919
December	c1913–14
Disclosure	1921
Down East	1919
Dreams	[1897]
Du alte Mutter	[1900], c1902
Du bist wie eine Blume	c1896–7
Duty: see Two Slants	
Ein Ton	c1900
An Election: see Nov. 2, 1920	
Elégie	c1901–2
The Ending Year	1902
Evening	1921
Evidence	adapted [1910]
Far from my heav'nly home	c1893–4
Far in the wood	c1900
A Farewell to Land	c1909–10
La Fede	1920
Feldeinsamkeit	c1897–8
Flag Song	[1898], c1900
Forward into Light	1902
Friendship	c1898–9
Frühlingslied	c1898
General William Booth Enters into Heaven	1914, rev. c1933
God Bless and Keep Thee	c1898, c1901–2
Grace	c1900–03
Grantchester	1920
The Greatest Man	1921
Gruss	c1898–9, c1902–3
Harpalus	adapted [1902] or c1920
He Is There!	1917
Hear My Prayer, O Lord: see A Song – For Anything	

Her Eyes	c1898
Her gown was of vermilion silk	1897
His Exaltation	arr. [1913]
The Housatonic at Stockbridge	arr. 1921
Hymn	arr. 1921
Hymn of Trust	adapted c1899-c1900
I hear a tone: see Ein Ton	
I knew and loved a maid	c1898–9, c1901–2
I travelled among unknown men	adapted [1901]
Ich Grolle Nicht	c1898–9, rev. c1900–01
Ilmenau	c1903
Immortality	1921
In April-tide	c1896–7
In Autumn	c1896
In Flanders Fields	1917, rev. 1919
In My Beloved's Eyes	c1899
In Summer Fields: see Feldeinsamkeit	
In the Alley	[1896]
The "Incantation"	arr. 1921
The Indians	arr. 1921
The Innate	arr. [1916]
Kären	c1900, c1905–6
The Last Reader	arr. 1921
The Light That Is Felt	adapted c1899–1900, [1903–4], c1919–20
Like a Sick Eagle	arr. 1920
Lincoln, the Great Commoner	c1919–20
Die Lotosblume	c1897–8, rev. c1900–01 and c1908–9
The Love Song of Har Dyal	c1899-c1900, c1902–3
Luck and Work	c1919–20
Majority	arr. 1921
Maple Leaves	1920
Marie	[1896], c1901–2, second version c1903–4
Memories: a. Very Pleasant, b. Rather Sad	[1897]
Minnelied	c1901
Mirage	adapted [1902]
Mists [I]	1910, c1912–13
Mists [II]	c1912–13, rev. c1920
My Lou Jennine	c1894
My Native Land [I]	c1897-c1900
My Native Land [II]	c1900–01
Nature's Way	adapted [1908], c1909–10

Naught that country needeth	c1898–9, rev. 1902
The New River	1914–15, ?rev. 1921
Night of Frost in May	adapted [1899] or c1920
A Night Song	adapted ?c1920
A Night Thought	adapted c1916
No More	1897
Nov. 2, 1920 (An Election)	c1921
An Old Flame	c1898, c1901
Old Home Day	c1920
The Old Mother	?1898, c1902
Omens and Oracles	[1899], c1902
On Judges' Walk	c1901–2
On the Antipodes	c1922–3
On the Counter	1920
"1, 2, 3"	1921
The One Way	c1922–3
The Only Son	c1898–9
Over all the treetops: see Ilmenau	
Paracelsus	1921
Peaks	c1923–4
A Perfect Day	1902
Pictures	1906
Premonitions	arr. 1921
Qu'il m'irait bien	c1897–9
The Rainbow (So May It Be!)	arr. 1921
Religion	arr. c1910–11
Remembrance	arr. 1921
Requiem	1911
Resolution	1921
Rock of Ages	c1892
Romanzo (di Central Park)	[1900], c1911
Rosamunde	c1898–9, c1901–2
Rosenzweige	c1902–3
Rough Wind	adapted [1902]
A Scotch Lullaby	1896
A Sea Dirge	1925
The Sea of Sleep	1903
The See'r	c1914–15, arr. 1920
Sehnsucht	c1902–3
September	c1919–20
Serenity	arr. [1919]

The Side Show	adapted 1921
Slow March	c1887, rev. 1921
Slugging a Vampire	adapted [1902] or c1920
So May It Be!: see The Rainbow	
Soliloquy	c1916–17
A Son of a Gambolier	arr. c1919–21
Song	c1897
A Song – For Anything	c1921
a. When the waves softly sigh	[1892]
b. Yale, Farewell!	c1898–9
c. Hear My Prayer, O Lord	c1889–90
Song for Harvest Season	1894, rev. c1932–3
The Song of the Dead	?1898
Songs my mother taught me	[1895], c1899-c1901
The South Wind	adapted 1908
Spring Song	1907
Sunrise	1926
Swimmers	[1915], ?rev. 1921
Tarrant Moss	c1902–3
There is a certain garden	[1893], c1896–8
There is a lane	adapted [1902] or c1920
They Are There!	adapted 1942
The Things Our Fathers Loved	1917
Thoreau	arr. c1920
Those Evening Bells	adapted [1907]
Through Night and Day	adapted c1897–8
To Edith	1919
Tolerance	arr. 1921
Tom Sails Away	1917
Two Little Flowers	1921
Two Slants (Christian and Pagan)	
a. Duty	arr. 1921
b. Vita	arr. 1921
Vote for Names! Names! Names!	1912
The Waiting Soul	adapted [1908]
Walking	c1912
Walt Whitman	c1920–21
Waltz	c1894–5, rev. 1921
Watchman!	adapted [1913]
Weil auf' mir	[1902]
West London	1921

When stars are in the quiet skies	adapted c1899–c1900
Where the eagle cannot see	adapted c1906
The White Gulls	c1920–21
Widmung	?1898
Wie Melodien zieht es mir	c1898–1900
Wiegenlied (Des Knaben Wunderhorn)	c1906
William Will	1896
The World's Highway	1906–7
The World's Wanderers	adapted after c1898–9
Yale, Farewell!: see A Song – For Anything	
Yellow Leaves	1923

Index of Non-English Sources

Articles, books, and their published translations are listed by item number. List does not include reviews listed within annotations.

Periodical Index

This list does not include unannotated reviews or other sources listed below the main annotation. Numbers refer to item numbers.

Spectator 190
Sports Illustrated 162
St. Louis Post-Dispatch 718
Stagebill 839
Star-Ledger (New Jersey) 898
Stereo Review 798, 822
Student Musicologists at Minnesota 143,
    181, 220, 256, 280, 408, 420, 430, 448,
    454, 559, 568, 578, 600, 854
Studies in Music 443
Sunday Republican Magazine 330

Tempo 281, 437, 537
Theory and Practice 500
Time 470, 685, 852
Times Literary Supplement 57
Tomorrow 155
Trend 185, 719
20th Century Literature 435

USA Today 573

*Verundzwanzigsteljahrsschrift der Interna-
    tionalen Maultrommelvirtuosen-
    genossenschaft* 485, 501
View 432
Village Voice 226, 696–698, 709
Vogue 206

Wall Street Journal 711, 865
Washington Post 717, 727

Yale Alumni Magazine 897
Yale Review 285
*Yearbook for Inter-American Musical
    Research*: see *Anuario interamericano
    de investigacion musical*

Zeszyty naukowe 534

Index of Authors and Editors

Please note: Only authors and editors from the main bibliographic listing have been included. This index does not include authors of reviews or translators listed in the annotation.

Groh, Jack C. 586
Gruhn, Wilfried 429
Grunfeld, Frederic 176
Gurwitt, Alan 144, 160

Hall, David 14, 177, 806
Hamm, Charles 630, 654
Hansen, Chadwick 430
Hansen, Peter S. 655
Harley, Maria Anna 431
Harrison, Lou 178, 380, 432, 636
Harvey, Mark Sumner 179, 180
Helms, Hans G. 181, 182, 846
Henahan, Donal 183, 398, 704, 807
Henck, Herbert 3, 631, 632
Henderson, Clayton W. 47, 381–383
Henry, Derrick 886, 887
Hentoff, Nat 48
Hepokoski, James 384
Herchet, Jörg 184
Herrmann, Bernard 185, 489
Hertz, David Michael 433, 555
Hilliard, John Stanley 490
Hinson, Maurice 556
Hitchcock, H. Wiley 49, 50, 186–188, 527,
    528, 587, 611–614, 633, 634, 656, 662,
    847
Holland, Bernard 189, 705–708
Holloway, Robin 190
Hommel, Friedrich 191
Houtchens, Alan 192, 615
Howard, John Tasker 193, 657
Hughes, Allen 710
Hughes, Robert J. 711
Hunnicutt, Ellen 361
Hüsken, Renata 491
Hutchinson, Mary Ann 194
Hutton, Edna Rait 195, 196

Isham, Howard 197
Ivashkin, Aleksandr 51, 198
Ives, Charles E. 20–25

Jack, Adrian 809–811
Jacobson, Bernard 434
Johnson, Harriett 713
Johnson, Ronald 88
Johnson, Russell I. 200
Johnson, Timothy A. 385
Johnston, Walter 435
Jolas, Betsy 529
Josephson, Nors S. 492, 493

Kakinuma, Toshie 436
Kämper, Dietrich 38, 201, 616
Karmel, Richard 158, 159
Karolyi, Otto 660
Kastendieck, Miles 714–715
Kay, Norman 437
Kelly, Kevin 617
Kennicott, Philip 717, 718
Kerman, Joseph 375
Kerr, Harrison. 719
Kerr, Hugh H. 853
Khittl, Christoph 202
Kingman, Daniel 661
Kirkpatrick, John 5, 20, 52, 53, 203, 636,
    662, 854
Kisselgoff, Anna 889–891
Klemm, Eberhardt 204
Knight, John Wesley 494
Koch, Gerhard R. 205, 720
Kolleritsch, Otto 265
Kolodin, Irving 206, 721
Kolosick, J. Timothy 557
Kolter, Horst 207
Konold, Wulf 208, 438, 812, 813
Kopetz, Barry E. 495
Koppenhaver, Allen J. 439
Kosman, Joshua 722, 723
Kostelanetz, Richard 24, 440, 441
Kozinn, Allan 209, 210, 724–726,
    814
Kramer, Jonathan D. 496
Kramer, Lawrence 211, 212

Keyword Index

This index is a detailed guide (by item number) to works, names, authors, and editors for all chapters. Additionally, chapters 1–6 are thoroughly indexed according to topic. The remaining chapters (textbooks, performance and recording reviews, etc.) are indexed by work and performers only. Scholars who are particularly interested in the content of these listings are advised to read through them.

For specific compositions, check under the title (e.g., "Putnam's Camp") and the genre listing (e.g., orchestral works). Only works that are specifically listed in the annotations are included in this index. For a list of complete and nearly complete works, see the Appendix (pp. 193-208); for a list of all compositions and fragments, see Sinclair's catalogue (item 7).

Abdul, Raoul 674
"Abide with me" 602
Adams, Henry 220
Addams, Jane 419
Addiego, J. 874
Adirondacks 322, 468
Adler, Paula 74
aesthetics 51, 56, 64, 65, 75, 135, 182,
    197, 292, 327, 334, 342, 351, 361, 365,
    368, 370, 418, 422, 443, 450, 455, 456,
    463, 469, 472, 473, 504, 505, 534, 575
aggregates 217, 219, 530, 538
Ahlstrom, David 474
Albert, Thomas Russel 347
"The Alcotts" (third movement of *Sonata
    No. 2 for Piano/Concord Sonata*) 304,
    395, 651
Aldrich, Thomas Bailey 607
aleatoric procedures 266

Alexander, Michael J. 29, 537
Alexander, Shaina 75
All the Way Around and Back: see *Scherzo:
    All the Way Around and Back*
Alvin Ailey American Dance Theatre 882
Alwes, Chester L. 581
amateur, Ives's representation of 80, 629
amateur, Ives described as 138, 154, 466,
    738–740
American Composers Orchestra 698, 701,
    724, 772
American music, Ives and: see also indi-
    vidual composers and traditions, 94,
    103, 112, 141, 143, 271, 309, 389, 437,
    440, 555, 595
American Symphony Orchestra 688, 695,
    758, 759, 785
American Transcendentalists (festival)
    738, 863

Mason, Daniel Gregory 241, 460
Mason, Francis 878
Masselos, William 548
"The Masses (Majority)" (choral song) 758
Masur, Kurt 707, 739
Mauceri, John 230
Mauk, David C. 362
Mayer, Steven 748
Mays, Kenneth Robert 388
McCalla, James W. 450
McCandless, William Edgar 531
McClure, John 231
McCrae, Elizabeth 560
McCue, George 386
McDonald, Charlene Harb 561
McFall, John 886
Mead, Rita H. 232–235
Medieval 287
Mehta, Zubin 804
Mellers, Wilfrid 57, 236, 363, 664
Mellquist, Jerome 112
melody 37, 56, 66, 379
Melville, Herman 337, 344
"Memories: a. Very Pleasant, b. Rather
    Sad" 303
memory 189
Memos 20, 27, 37, 124, 125, 346, 656
Mendel, Arthur 193
Metcalf, Steve 58, 734
Metz, Gunther 447
Metzer, David 237
Meyer, Felix 59
Miami Ives Festival: see South Florida's
    Historic Ives Festival
microtones 130, 186, 458, 566, 567
Middle Ages: see Medieval
Mihura, Brian L. 501
Milhaud 154, 185
military 47
Miller, Philip L. 817
Milligan, Terry G. 238, 239, 532
Mini-Festival around Ives 463, 839, 852,

856, 857, 864, 867, 868
misogyny: see gender, sexuality
"Mists" 616
Mittman, Leopold 791
Mize, J. T. H. 658
Modern Music 221
modernism 117, 141, 146, 167, 185, 213,
    225, 255, 302, 314, 413, 465, 471
Monkman, Martin H. 915
Monteverdi 417
Moody, William Vaughn 484
Moomaw, Charles J. 512
Moor, Paul 240
Moore, MacDonald Smith 241
Morgan, Robert P. 15, 242, 389, 451, 452,
    618, 665, 818, 857
Moross, Jerome 95, 243
Mortenson, Gary C. 244
Morton, Lawrence 735
motivic analysis 32, 171, 172
Mozart, Wolfgang Amadeus 417
multimedia 188, 280, 438
multiplicity: see also eclecticism, hetero-
    geneity, simultaneity, spatial, etc. 220,
    491
Mumelter, Martin 245
Mumma, Gordon 188
Mumper, Dwight Robert 562
"Music and its Future" 24, 31
Music Fair America '84 870
Musil, Robert 202
Mutual Life Insurance 406
Myers, Betty Dustin 503
Myers, Kurtz 16
Myrick, Julian 205, 407, 408

Nagano, Kent 768
naïve 342
Nashville Symphony Orchestra 833
National Symphony Orchestra 717
nationalism: see also Americanism and
    patriotism 99, 103, 252, 273, 320, 426